RELATIONSHIP
AND
FELLOWSHIP

David R. Anderson, Ph.D.

President and Professor of Biblical Languages and
Systematic Theology at Grace School of Theology

GRACE
THEOLOGY PRESS

Relationship and Fellowship

© 2022 David R. Anderson

Published by Grace Theology Press

eISBN: 978-1-957202-00-6
ISBN: 978-1-957202-01-3

Printed in the United States of America

First Edition 2022

CONTENTS

FOREWORD

The concept of Relationship/Fellowship is so fundamental to the basics of living the Christian life that a book on it almost seems gratuitous. That is, if you are oriented to the concept. Alas, after pastoring and preaching and teaching for over forty years I find that most of the Christians I run into have never even heard the difference between our Relationship with God and our Fellowship with God. I'll never forget a three-hour conversation with Robert Shank, who wrote *Elect in the Son*. He was a Church of Christ scholar (Ph.D. in Sociology). We went round and round on the meaning of 1 John. In his view, known sin caused loss of salvation. Confession reinstated the lost person into God's good graces. He actually believed one could lose and regain his eternal salvation multiple times in a day.

I suggested another way of looking at it. Could it be that faith in Jesus brings the sinner into a new family in which God is our Father and we are His children? Being born into such a family would be a forever proposition. After all, how can someone who is born be unborn? Some things, like adding water to cement, are irreversible. The Relationship (Father-Child) is forever. So simple, as with our own children. Once my son is born into our family, he can never get out. Our Relationship is eternal: father-son. Even if one of us were to go to heaven and the other, God forbid, should go to hell, the Relationship is still intact: father-son.

Relationship and Fellowship

But simply because my son and I have a forever Relationship does not mean we are enjoying the Relationship. If he were to become a serial killer and be imprisoned for life, we still have a Relationship: father-son. But we probably are not enjoying our Relationship. Enjoying the Relationship is what we call Fellowship. Could it be that when one of God's children knowingly sins, his guilt through conviction by the Holy Spirit keeps him from enjoying his Relationship with his heavenly Father? Could it be that he loses his Fellowship with his Father but not his Relationship?

When I suggested this approach to 1 John to Dr. Shank, especially since the word "fellowship" occurs in the first chapter three times and this fellowship is to generate joy (v. 4), his eyes got wide and he admitted he had never even thought in terms of Relationship and Fellowship. He was humble enough to say he would consider this approach. That was over forty years ago. Since that time, I cannot number the people who have told me that understanding these two categories and discerning which verses or passages belong in which category has done more for their understanding of the Christian life than any other single concept. Yet I have also been amazed to learn how few people have ever even heard these concepts. So, although this book may seem simplistic to many, I trust it will also be helpful to equally as many or more.

My approach will be unique among my writings. I will present the material in two parts. The first part will explain Relationship/Fellowship in the Old and New Testaments, respectively. I will then present the scholarship behind these concepts. This second part is designed for those with seminary training, the first part is designed for those without. If you have not had seminary training, I wouldn't even bother to look at the second part of this book. But hopefully you will find the first part elucidating and edifying. For the scholars willing to humble themselves to consider these ideas, I hope you will find the scholarship behind the Relationship/Fellowship dichotomy solid and thorough enough to at least give this approach to the Christian life consideration. I learned long ago that we humans do not make most of our decisions based on the facts (see Scott Adam's book *Win Bigly: Persuasion in a World Where Facts Don't Matter*[1]), but rather on our emotions, biases, and prejudices. Therefore, I do not hold out hope that the facts I present here will sway those with prior emotional commitments. However, for those who have found the Christian life more of a riddle than a revelation, perhaps what we present here will help them make sense of it all.

---

[1]   Scott Adams, *Win Bigly: Persuasion in a World Where Facts Don't Matter* (New York: Portfolio/Penguin, 2017).

A COUPLE OF
NEW TESTAMENT EXAMPLES

It might be helpful to start off with a couple of simple examples from the New Testament. One is from Luke 17:3-4. Luke writes: "Take heed to yourselves. If your brother sins against you, rebuke him; and if he repents, forgive him. And if he sins against you seven times in a day, and seven times in a day returns to you, saying, 'I repent,' you shall forgive him." We can all understand the concept of forgiving someone who has sinned against us once, especially if it's our brother. But to continue forgiving him time after time after time, perhaps even for the same sin, goes beyond all reason. Of course, that's why Luke has included this teaching from Jesus; it is so counterintuitive. Who but a fool would keep on forgiving someone who sins against them over and over and over? So, we have to ask ourselves just what is at play here? Is there some basis for forgiveness ad infinitum? Of course, there is. The basis for forgiveness over and over and over is because of the family relationship the two brothers have: brothers. It is possible Luke is talking about two Israelites from different families, but more likely he's talking about two brothers in the same family. But it really doesn't matter. If they're brothers as Israelites, then they are from the same family, just a larger one (children of Abraham).

1

But why would Jesus tell them to forgive one another just because they're in the same family? Well, that's pretty obvious, isn't it? It's because of their relationship: brothers. That relationship can never change; they're born into the same family. That's the relationship. And because they have a relationship that can never be broken, Jesus argues that forgiveness should be offered when sought by the repentant brother until one of them should die. Now it goes without saying the offended brother is not enjoying his relationship with the brother who sinned against him. Why should he? The offense is a stumbling block to their fellowship, which we have already defined as "enjoying the relationship." Now once forgiveness is granted to the sinning brother, a new relationship between the two does not start again; the relationship is already there. It wasn't lost and doesn't need to be reestablished. What has been lost by the sin of one brother against another? It's their fellowship, the enjoyment of their relationship.

In the epistles, we find the same distinction between what we might call Relationship forgiveness and Fellowship forgiveness. We find Relationship forgiveness in Ephesians 1:7 where Paul states "In Him we have redemption through His blood, the forgiveness of sins, according to the riches of His grace." In his introduction to Ephesians Paul lists the heavenly blessings his readers have "in Christ." Over and over, he mentions "in Christ," "in the Beloved," "in Him," "in Himself" 11 times. It's an overview of the many wonderful blessings we have right now in heavenly places via our new position "in Christ." While we may be sinful in our condition on earth, we are seen as perfectly holy and forgiven as we sit at the right hand of God the Father "in Christ." In Romans 4:2-5, Paul uses the word "to justify" (*dikaioō*), which the Reformers (Melanchthon, Calvin, and Luther) understood to mean not a change in their condition on earth, but rather a change in their position or standing before God in heaven.[2] God declared them righteous. In this declaration of

---

[2]   See my book *Position and Condition* (Houston: Grace Theology Press, 2017).

righteousness, no future sins could separate them from the love of God in Christ Jesus (Rom 8:38-39, "things to come"). In other words, they had advanced forgiveness for any sins they might commit after they believed in Christ: future forgiveness. They have been born into a new family, the family of God. As such they were His children and would be forever.

Most married couples are overjoyed with the news that they are expecting a child. If someone were to ask them, "Do you think your child is going to commit sins after he's born?" I'm certain they would agree that their child would commit a sin after their birth, as soon as they were capable of making a moral decision. If the inquisitor were to continue and ask, "So you know this child is going to sin, but you're still willing to bring him into this world?" Again, I'm sure the couple would say, "Yes we are willing." The questioner goes on to ask, "On what basis?" The couple might say, "Based on 'family forgiveness.' Any child that comes into our family will enjoy unconditional love and acceptance no matter what they do. Acceptance is not the same as approval. We will offer that child our unconditional love. That assumes their future forgiveness from the time they are born until we or he dies."

God extends the same kind of forgiveness to all children in His family. He knew who they would be before the foundation of the world. He also knew that unless they were aborted or were a case of infant mortality, they would sin. The fact that His love is unconditional speaks of the kind of forgiveness we read about in Ephesians 1:7. This blessing not only provides for forgiveness of any sins we committed before we became Christians, but also for our future sins, since they would be committed after we become Christians. We will call this Relationship Forgiveness. Because of our relationship with God, as His child, nothing we do in the future will put us out of the family. Hence, we have future forgiveness based on our relationship with God.

Nevertheless, a persistent question crops up now and then in the Christian circles I have experienced: "If I have already been forgiven of my future sins, why do I have to ask forgiveness for them

(1 Jn 1:9)?" Or in our previous example, if the sinning brother has future forgiveness for all his sins against his brother, why does he have to ask forgiveness each time he knowingly sins against him? Answer: there is one forgiveness for a Relationship and another forgiveness for Fellowship. Remember, we are suggesting that fellowship is to enjoy the relationship. How many siblings have you met in your lifetime who are at such odds with one another, they refuse to go to reunions and refuse to communicate? Is their relationship intact? Of course, it is because they're born in the same family. They cannot change that. Are they enjoying the relationship? Obviously not. They're not even talking with one another. They may even harbor bitterness or resentment over past wrongs. For them to enjoy their permanent relationship, there would have to be a reconciliation, and that invariably involves forgiveness.

Another way to understand the two different types of forgiveness is this: Relationship Forgiveness is judicial and occurs in the court-room of heaven; Fellowship Forgiveness is personal and occurs when the offender asks forgiveness from the offended. We're saying that the forgiveness in Ephesians 1:7 deals with our Relationship with God, while the forgiveness in 1 John 1:9 deals with our Fellowship with God. Relationship and Fellowship, twin truths that are inter-related but distinct. We hope these two illustrations are enough to show how simple these principles are, but also how paramount they are for us to understand the Christian life.

RELATIONSHIP AND FELLOWSHIP IN THE OLD TESTAMENT

To understand the principles of Relationship and Fellowship in the Old Testament (hereafter "OT"), we need a basic understanding of the covenants of God with Israel and/or her representatives (Abraham, Moses, David). We also need to understand the parallelism between Israel and the individual believer in the New Testament (hereafter "NT"). The parallel with Israel in the NT is not the Church; it is the individual. The covenants with Israel apply to the nation as a whole, but not necessarily to all the individuals in the nation. But the same principles God uses in dealing with Israel are those He uses with individuals during the NT era. That is why the OT is profitable for doctrine, for reproof, for correction, and for instruction in righteousness (2 Tim 3:16) because we may glean lessons for ourselves as individual believers from observing God's dealings with the nation of Israel.

Though there are many types of covenants in the OT, most of them fall into one of two categories: motivation for future obedience and reward for past obedience. The first category is what scholars call a Suzerain (Lord)/Vassal (servant) covenant or treaty. A treaty like this was drawn up by a conquering king to help govern his newly conquered vassals. He would like them to pretty much govern them-selves. So, he would lay out what he expected of them (stipulations) and motivate them by laying out his blessings to them should they decide to become faithful servants. That's on the positive side. He would also explain certain curses he would impose on these servants should they choose to be unfaithful. The purpose of this kind of cov-enant was to motivate them to future obedience.

The second category of covenants that play a significant role in our understanding of God's relationship with Israel in the OT is the reward covenants, known in the scholarly world as covenants of grant. As its name implies, these covenants outline rewards for past obedience. In particular, we want to look at the Abrahamic and Davidic Covenants. In each case, we shall see that the covenants to Abraham and to David were given as rewards for their past obedience. Let's look at the Abraham Covenant first.

When we mention the Abrahamic Covenant, those not familiar with the covenant forms usually look to Genesis 12:1-3. Those from the Reformed tradition like to explain that God sovereignly stooped down from heaven and plucked Abraham from his polytheistic cul-ture and made a Jewish patriarch of him, like it or not. However, there're two problems with this approach. First, Genesis 12:1-3 is quite short and lacks the components found in either the Lord/Serv-ant or the Reward covenants. Hence, we surmise that these three verses give us a summary of God's promises to Abraham. But make no mistake: these promises are motivations to future obedience. And, there is a stipulation: go. Abraham had to leave his home in Ur of the Chaldeans and go to the land chosen by God or he would not get what was promised. Since these verses are motivation for future obe-dience, we suggest that they form a summary of the suzerain/vassal (Lord/Servant) relationship between God and Abraham before he ever left Ur.

In Acts 7, Luke quotes Stephen: "The God of glory appeared to our father Abraham when he was in Mesopotamia, before he dwelt in Haran,[3] and said to him, *'Get out of your country and from your relatives, and come to a land that I will show you.'* This informs us that Abraham and the God of glory had a personal relationship before he ever left Ur. We must remember that Abraham lived in a culture of many gods. But the true and Almighty God showed up and revealed Himself to Abraham. No doubt He explained Himself to Abraham as the Creator of heaven and earth. At some point, Abraham believed in this Supreme Being. Most interpreters would say that Abraham passed from death into life when he believed God in Genesis 15:6, for there his "faith was reckoned unto him for righteousness" (Rom 4:3). However, it's hard to imagine that Abraham did not believe in this Almighty God back in Ur. Why else would he pack up his belongings and leave his homeland for who knows where? He must have put his faith in this new God and His promises. And as soon as he arrived in the land of the Canaanites, he began to build altars as a witness to the true God in the midst of another polytheistic culture (Gen 12:8 and 13:4). Why did He build this altar between Bethel and Ai and call on the name of the Lord if he did not believe in Him?

May I suggest that Abraham believed in the only true God before he ever left Ur. God established a Suzerain/Vassal treaty with Abraham in order to motivate him to leave his homeland and family. That required some pretty stout motivation, and I think we can agree that the three promises listed in Genesis 12:1–3 are significant motivation indeed: land, seed, and blessing. So, Abraham sets out, "not knowing where he was going" (Heb 11:8). It says Abraham obeyed "by faith" when he went out from Ur. This is clear biblical proof that he believed before he ever left. What we see in Abraham from Genesis 12-22 is a pilgrim's progress. He had his moments when his faith faltered, but it kept increasing until he was ready to make the ultimate sacrifice of the son through whom the promises were to be fulfilled.

When Abraham got to the Promised Land, he built his altars and worshipped God. His faith slipped when the famine hit the land and he equivocated with Pharaoh. But after God delivered him from that predicament, he went back to the altar he had built between Bethel and Ai and recommitted himself by calling on the name of the Lord. After separating from Lot, the Lord reaffirmed His promise to Abraham concerning the land. Abraham must have believed the Lord's promise for he went down to Hebron and made another altar to the Lord.

Abraham's faith was growing. After rescuing Lot from Chedorlaomer, he paid tithes to Melchizedek, who was a priest of God Most High, showing his belief that He was the One who gave Abraham success in battle and also riches. The King of Sodom made one last attempt to seduce him to the dark side, but Abraham's faith triumphed. As a result of Abraham's faithful obedience, the Lord decided to reward him. Genesis 15:1 is best translated, "I am your shield; your reward will be very great" (ESV; NASB; NRSV: וְגֶמ יְכֹנָא דְאָמ הְבְרַהְ דְּרַכְשׁ הָל) Now God was going to give Abraham a Reward Covenant. Keep in mind that Abraham has been in the land at least fourteen years by the time he met Melchizedek (Gen 14:5). It was because of his past faithfulness that God was going to give him this reward. It is **because** Abraham served his Suzerain (Lord) faithfully that he was rewarded with a land grant:

> By Myself I have sworn, says the Lord, <u>because</u> you have done this thing, and have not withheld your son, your only *son*—blessing I will bless you, and multiplying I will multiply your descendants as the stars of the heaven and as the sand which *is* on the seashore; and your descendants shall possess the gate of their enemies. In your seed all the nations of the earth shall be blessed, <u>because</u> you have obeyed My voice" (Gen 22:16-18).

And again:

> Then the Lord appeared to him [Isaac] and said: "Do not go down to Egypt; live in the land of which I shall tell you. [3] Dwell in this land, and I will be with you and bless you; for to you and your descendants I give all these lands, and I will perform the oath which I swore to Abraham your father. [4]

And I will make your descendants multiply as the stars of heaven; I will give to your descendants all these lands; and in your seed all the nations of the earth shall be blessed; [5] <u>because</u> Abraham obeyed My voice and kept My charge, My commandments, My statutes, and My laws" (Gen 26:5).

We see, then, a cause/effect relationship between Abraham's obedience and the rewards for said obedience. An interesting feature of these reward covenants are the benefits accrued to the progeny of the one who received the reward. Once given, the reward would never be taken away. We see this in God's dealing with Jacob:

And behold, the Lord stood above it and said: "I *am* the Lord God of Abraham your father and the God of Isaac; the land on which you lie I will give to you and your descendants. [14] Also your descendants shall be as the dust of the earth; you shall spread abroad to the west and the east, to the north and the south; and in you and in your seed all the families of the earth shall be blessed. [15] Behold, I *am* with you and will keep you wherever you go, and will bring you back to this land; for I will not leave you until I have done what I have spoken to you" (Gen 28:13-15).

Here we see the commitment of God to the progeny of Abraham. God will fulfill His promises to Abraham regardless of how long it takes or how many generations pass. Of course, with regard to the land promise, and to enjoy the promise, they had to be in the land. When they left their land (in Egypt), things did not go well for them (slavery). To enjoy the promise of the land, they had to get back to the land.

However, before we allow Moses to enter the story, let's summarize the importance of the Abrahamic Covenant. We have seen that it was conditioned on the obedience of Abraham for its reception. In other words, it was a reward. However, once given, it could not be taken away or annulled (Gal 4) by anything Abraham did. That was the significance of putting Abraham to sleep when God ratified the covenant by walking up and down between the animals and birds. In other words, it was a unilateral covenant that depended only on the faithfulness of God for its fulfillment. It was not a bilateral covenant that depended on the faithfulness of both parties. It belonged to Abraham and his progeny in perpetuity, even if he/they were disobedient. This is precisely where the difference between Relationship and Fellowship kicks in. With the establishment of the Abrahamic Covenant, God and Israel have an eternal relationship, just as a human father and his human child have an eternal relationship: father/child. Nothing the child ever does can change that relationship.

But just because an eternal relationship exists does not mean the covenant parties are enjoying the relationship, which is what we call fellowship. If Israel were disobedient, she would not enjoy the relationship because as a loving father would discipline his child, God would discipline Israel. That means she would not enjoy the relationship. Initially, God did not spell out for Israel exactly how they could please Him other than to remain in the land. But when Moses led the people out of Egypt, God decided to spell out His conditions for fellowship. That was Mt. Sinai and the Mosaic Covenant. The Mosaic Covenant was not given as a guidepost to receive the gift of eternal life. We are operating under the conviction that the nation as a whole already had an eternal relationship with God. As for the individuals in the nation, they received the free gift of eternal life just as Abraham did: by faith. We propose that every individual who expressed faith in God by putting the blood of a lamb over his door and celebrated the Passover also received eternal life if he did not already have it. In other words, those who followed Moses out of Egypt were redeemed. Their faith may have waned when faced with reports of "giants in the land," but their forty years of wandering was God's discipline, not His rejection.

Though the basics of the Mosaic Law were laid out in the Ten Commandments (Ex. 20), a full expression of what pleased God was written by Moses during the forty years of wandering (the Torah: Genesis through Deuteronomy). The fifth book, Deuteronomy, has been shown by scholars to follow the precise form of the Suzerain-Vassal (Lord-Servant) treaties or covenant: Titles; Historical Introduction; Stipulations; Blessings and Curses. But let's remember: this type of covenant was a motivation to future obedience. We think God and Abraham had just such an agreement. If he would leave Ur and go to a land the Lord would show him, then he would be rewarded. The agreement was a motivation to future obedience.

Just so, the Mosaic Law was a motivation to future obedience. If the people kept the Law, then it would go well for them. They would enjoy a long life in the land. But rebel against the Law and God promised to put them out of the land. If they repented as a nation, He would bring them back into the land. (Again, I am writing this so a twelve-year-old could understand; the scholarship behind all this is in the second part of the book.) Deuteronomy 4 lays out the motivation for future obedience as well as any section of this Lord/Servant covenant:

> Now, O Israel, listen to the statutes and the judgments which I teach you to observe, that you may live, and go in and possess the land which the Lord God of your fathers is giving you. You shall not add to the word which I command you, nor take from it, that you may keep the commandments of the Lord your God which I command you (4:1-2).

And a few verses later:

> So He declared to you His covenant which He commanded you to perform, the Ten Commandments; and He wrote them on two tablets of stone. And the Lord commanded me at that time to teach you statutes and judgments, that you might observe them in the land which you cross over to possess (4:13-14).

11

So, if the people kept the commandments and statutes, it would go well for them in the land; their days will be prolonged. On the other hand, if they become rebellious and idolatrous:

> I call heaven and earth to witness against you this day, that you will soon utterly perish from the land which you cross over the Jordan to possess; you will not prolong *your* days in it, but will be utterly destroyed. [27] And the Lord will scatter you among the peoples, and you will be left few in number among the nations where the Lord will drive you (4:26-27).

God destroyed some of them and drove the rest of them out of the land. He scattered them among the nations. Nevertheless, should Israel see the error of her ways and repent:

> But from there you will seek the Lord your God, and you will find *Him* if you seek Him with all your heart and with all your soul. When you are in distress, and all these things come upon you in the latter days, when you turn to the Lord your God and obey His voice (for the Lord your God *is* a merciful God), He will not forsake you nor destroy you, nor forget the covenant of your fathers which He swore to them (4:29-31).

God will restore Israel and bring her back to the land to possess it once again. Does this not sound like the way He deals with individual believers in the NT era? Of course, it does, because the issue with Israel in Deuteronomy is Fellowship, not Relationship. Because of their eternal relationship (via the Abrahamic Covenant), God does not permanently cut Israel off or completely destroy her when she is disobedient. He puts her out of the land but does not forget the covenant of their "fathers which He swore to them." What covenant? The Abrahamic Covenant was cut in Genesis 15 and confirmed to Abraham (Gen 17), to Isaac (Gen 26), and to Jacob (Gen 28). This is the covenant sworn to the "fathers" which God would not forsake.

That covenant was for Relationship. But to enjoy the relationship, He provided another covenant, the Mosaic Covenant, which was their means to Fellowship with their Maker.

Deuteronomy certainly had its lists of do's and don'ts (stipulations) along with its rewards and punishments (blessings and curses). But, Leviticus details the various ceremonies that would enable the people to maintain their fellowship with God. The problem, of course, is that believers still have a sinful nature. God can't fellowship with sin itself, so what is He going to do with a nation or individuals who lapse into sin? The big day of the year was Passover, the feast day celebrating when the angel of death spared those Israelites in Egypt who put the blood of an unblemished lamb over the entrance to their homes. Once a year, on this day, the High Priest entered the Holy of Holies in the tabernacle to sprinkle the blood of an unblemished lamb over the mercy seat. Was this to win entrance to heaven for the Israelites? No, it was to seek forgiveness of sins for the whole nation for one year. In other words, it was for Fellowship, not Relationship. This forgiveness was on a national level.

Another example of forgiveness on a national level is found in Numbers 15:22-26:

If you sin unintentionally, and do not observe all these commandments which the Lord has spoken to Moses—all that the Lord has commanded you by the hand of Moses, from the day the Lord gave commandment and onward throughout your generations—then it will be, if it is unintentionally committed, without the knowledge of the congregation, that the whole congregation shall offer one young bull as a burnt offering, as a sweet aroma to the Lord, with its grain offering and its drink offering, according to the ordinance, and one kid of the goats as a sin offering. So the priest shall make atonement for the whole congregation of the children of Israel, and it shall be forgiven them, for it was unintentional; they shall bring their offering, an offering made by fire to the Lord, and their sin offering before the Lord, for their unintended sin. It shall be forgiven the whole congregation of the children of Israel and the stranger who dwells among them, because all the people *did it* unintentionally.

So much for the "whole congregation." But what about individuals who sinned? Numbers 15:27-29 continues:

And if a person sins unintentionally, then he shall bring a female goat in its first year as a sin offering. So the priest shall make atonement for the person who sins unintentionally, when he sins unintentionally before the Lord, to make atonement for him; and it shall be forgiven him. You shall have one law for him who sins unintentionally, *for* him who is native-born among the children of Israel and for the stranger who dwells among them.

There is one sacrifice for unintentional sin, as seen above. But there were different instructions for the intentional sin (Num 15:30-31):

But the person who does *anything* presumptuously, *whether he is* native-born or a stranger, that one brings reproach on the Lord, and he shall be cut off from among his people. Because he has despised the word of the Lord, and has broken His commandment, that person shall be completely cut off; his guilt *shall be* upon him.

If we did not have other biblical passages to consider, it might appear as though the presumptuous brother has lost his salvation. However, we believe the NT teaches the eternal security of the believer (Relationship) (John 10, Rom 8, Eph 1). That would apply to OT believers as well or the God of the OT would contradict the God of the NT. So, the "presumptuous" brother must be teaching us something about fellowship, not relationship. We might find the answer in the original Hebrew that is translated as "presumptuous."

There are two Hebrew words translated "presumptuous": "raised" (רָמָה) and "with hand" (בְּיָד). The presumptuous sin is one committed "with the hand raised." Some of us remember the medal-winning Olympic sprinters (Tommie Smith and John Carlos) in the 1968 Mexico Olympics, who raised their fists and looked at their feet during the playing of the United States national anthem. It was their sign of rebellion or protest against the treatment of African Americans in America and minority groups around the world. Apparently, the raised hand or fist has been a sign of rebellion in some cultures for centuries. The high priest was not instructed to make an offering of atonement for the person committing this kind of sin of rebellion. They were to be put outside the camp; their guilt was upon them. Was this a permanent banishment? The text does not tell us, but it is probably fair to assume as long as the hand is raised against God, there would be no fellowship with Him. We learn in Deuteronomy 4:29-31 and 30:1-6 that an idolatrous Israel can be restored if she turns back to God and seeks Him with her whole heart, "for the Lord your God is a merciful God."

In fact, it is interesting to note that God promises to restore the repentant nation to even greater blessings after her repentance than she enjoyed before her turning from the Lord (Deut 30:4-5):

> If *any* of you are driven out to the farthest *parts* under heaven, from there the Lord your God will gather you, and from there He will bring you. Then the Lord your God will bring you to the land which your fathers possessed, and you shall possess it. He will prosper you and multiply you more than your fathers.

In both cases, unintentional and intentional, offerings for the sins of the guilty individuals remove the personal offense of the sins against the Lord so fellowship can be reestablished. The nation does not nullify the Abrahamic Covenant (Relationship) by its sin; nor does the individual "lose his salvation" because of his personal sins. In both cases, the Law provides for forgiveness so fellowship (enjoyment of the relationship) can be restored.

It is interesting to note that all references to a covenant in Deuteronomy 29-30 point either to Sinai after coming out of Egypt (the Ten Commandments) or to that which is written forty years later in Deuteronomy itself: "These *are* the words of the covenant which the Lord commanded Moses to make with the children of Israel in the land of Moab [just east of the Dead Sea], besides the covenant which He made with them in Horeb [Mt. Sinai]" (Deut 29:1) Regarding this covenant (Deuteronomy) God says, "Therefore keep the words of this covenant, and do them, that you may prosper in all that you do." Do you see it? This covenant is a motivation for future blessings. It is the Mosaic Covenant teaching the people how to prosper through good fellowship with their Lord (their Suzerain).

The remainder of the OT chronicles Israel's fellowship or lack thereof depending on her faithfulness to the Mosaic Covenant. Joshua describes Israel's entrance and partial occupation (possession) of the land. She enjoys God's blessing from the dating of Joshua through most of Solomon's life (1250-900 BC). But Solomon introduces idolatry into Judaism as he marries foreign wives and adopts some of their gods with their demonic practices. Therefore, God judges through the Assyrians, and the ten northern tribes are destroyed. Fellowship is restored for about one hundred years, but then the monarchy became utterly corrupt, to the point of temple prostitution (both male and female). This time God judges through the Babylonians and seventy years of captivity.

Finally, there is no more record of idolatry in the land. She enjoys fellowship with the Lord for a time after the Babylonian Captivity is finished (538 BC). Although foreign powers continue to occupy Israel (Medo-Persians, Greeks, Romans), she is still able to continue her temple sacrifices and fellowship with the Lord, excepting the brief period with Antiochus Epiphanes (from 167 BC until the Maccabees reinstituted the cult). Nevertheless, corruption ate its way through the nation via a corrupted priesthood. It became so bad that God decided to judge once again through the Romans. John the Baptist and Jesus gave Israel forty years to repent of their evil ways to avoid coming judgment. Alas, she did not repent, so judgment came in the form of Titus and his Roman army. According to Josephus, the Roman army killed 1,100,000 Jews and took 90,000 captives back to Rome.[3] The temple was destroyed; fellowship was broken. After the Bar Kokhba Revolt (AD 132-36), the Jews were almost completely scattered from the land of Israel into other nations.

Fellowship between Israel and her God has been completely destroyed at this point, but not her Relationship. As noted previously in Deuteronomy 30:1-5 (a book about fellowship, not relationship) regarding Israel:

> Now it shall come to pass, when all these things come upon you, the blessing and the curse which I have set before you, and you call *them* to mind among all the nations where the Lord your God drives you, and you return to the Lord your God and obey His voice, according to all that I command you today, you and your children, with all your heart and with all your soul, that the Lord your God will bring you back from captivity, and have compassion on you, and gather you again from all the nations where the Lord your God has scattered you. If *any* of you are driven out to the farthest *parts* under heaven, from there the Lord your God will gather you, and from there He will bring you. Then the Lord your God will bring you to the land which your fathers possessed, and you shall possess it. He will prosper you and multiply you more than your fathers.

We see the curse carried out: Israel was scattered among all the nations. But if she will turn back to the Lord with all her heart, God

---

[3] Josephus Flavius, *War Against the Jews*, Book VI, Chapter 9, Section 3, www.bible.ca/pre-flavius-josephus-70AD-Mt24-fulfilled htm. Accessed January 10, 2018.

will have compassion and gather her from the nations. He will bring the Jews to the land their fathers possessed, and they will possess it. The beginning of this return occurred at the end of the 19th Century with Theodore Herzl and the Zionists. They sought a homeland where they could live safely far away from the Russian pogroms and other countries of persecution. Lord Rothchild helped them start buying up land in Israel. The Jews began to trickle in, but this was not the return mentioned in Deuteronomy 30 because it was a secular movement without religious motivation at all. When I began taking tourists to Israel in 1993, the population of Jews was 90% secular. However, the religious Jews have been declaring their Aliya (their ascent), meaning their return to Israel and their beloved Jerusalem. Currently about 25% of the Jewish population is "religious." Some of these may well be among the future remnant of Jews that will say, "Blessed is He who comes in the name of the Lord" (Matt 23:39).

Israel will not fully possess the land until their Messiah, Jesus Christ, returns and takes over the land after the Battle of Armageddon. At that time the Jewish nation will hail Jesus as their Messiah and beg for His return. That is when full fellowship of the Jewish nation is restored. But let us not forget, all through these centuries of dispersion throughout the world, God's relationship with Israel has been intact. We refer to the nation, not individuals within the nation, who came to God through faith, just as Abraham did (Gen 15:6; Heb 11:8). It is the nation that had an "eternal covenant" with God (Gen 17:7). In fact, it is one of the proofs that God exists. The king of Prussia once asked one of his spiritual advisors how he could prove the existence of God. The advisor's answer? "The Jew, your majesty. The Jew." No ethnic group has ever been dispersed and maintained its ethnicity except the Jews. It is a sociological anomaly.

The Abrahamic Covenant is still to be fulfilled. Part of it has already been fulfilled. Abraham's seed has become more than the stars Abraham could see in the night sky (about 4,000 on a clear night). And his Seed (Jesus—Gal 3:16) has become a blessing to the entire world. Only the possession of the land remains unfulfilled. God's Relationship with Israel has never changed. But Fellowship has been on again and off again ever since the relationship with Abraham and his progeny was established. Her fellowship was measured by her obedience to the Mosaic Covenant until the ultimate break with the destruction of Herod's temple in CE 70. Nevertheless, Israel will return to fellowship with God and they will worship Him in a millennial temple for a thousand years (Ezek 40-48; Rev 20).

Thus, what we have established from the OT is God's system of Acceptance and Approval. When He gave the Abrahamic Covenant, Abraham and his offspring (Israel) were granted total Acceptance. Nothing they could do would annul that Acceptance or improve on it. Their Acceptance was one hundred percent and everlasting. But Approval was another matter. Israel could do something to win God's Approval: keep the Law of Moses. Of course, God knew that the nation would make mistakes, and individuals within the nation would fail from time to time. So, He made provisions within the Law of Moses for them to find forgiveness: the sacrificial system. When a sacrifice was made, the nation or the individual was confessing their sin. They were seeking forgiveness and restoration to fellowship.

We are suggesting that God's *modus operandi* in the NT has not changed. The big difference is that since the destruction of the temple (AD 70), God does not deal with the nation again except in discipline. Now He is concerned with individual believers. Israel has served as a type of the individual believer and is used often in the NT as an illustration of how God deals with individuals. He has the same system of Acceptance and Approval, of Relationship and Fellowship, which we will attempt to show book by book.

RELATIONSHIP AND FELLOWSHIP IN THE NEW TESTAMENT

With the principles of Relationship and Fellowship established in the OT through the Abrahamic and Mosaic Covenants, we now turn to see how this Relationship/Fellowship theology continues in the NT. Let's recall that how God deals with the nation of Israel is a picture of how He deals with us as NT believers. I will illustrate the Relationship/Fellowship principles from select NT passages I have preached through the years. We will consider some illustrations from the synoptics (Matthew, Mark and Luke).

"THE COST OF RELATIONSHIP VS. FELLOWSHIP"

LUKE 14:16-33

INTRODUCTION

Afailure to recognize the stark difference between Relationship truth and Fellowship truth can mean the difference between heaven and hell. When we turn the requirements for intimate Fellowship with God into the requirements for an eternal Relationship with God, we consign the sensitive Christian to a life of defeat, morbidity, and even depression. Even great minds appear confused on this distinction. Consider Dietrich Bonhoeffer, for example. In one place he writes: "Salvation is free, but discipleship will cost you your life."[4] Yet, in another place he says: "Faith without works is not faith at all, but a simple lack of obedience to God."[5] Or, "Cheap grace is the deadly enemy of our church. We are fighting today for costly grace."[6] Or, "The only man who has the right to say

---

[4] https://quotefancy.com/dietrich-bonhoeffer-quotes

[5] Ibid.

[6] Dietrich Bonhoeffer, *The Cost of Discipleship* (New York: Macmillan Publishing Co., 1976), 45.

that he is justified by grace alone is the man who has left all to follow Christ."[7] In our first quote it would appear that Bonhoeffer makes a distinction between salvation, which is free, and discipleship, which "will" cost you your life. But then he goes on to promote costly grace as opposed to what he calls "cheap" grace.[8]

Now let me state clearly that I love the life and genius of Dietrich Bonhoeffer. He certainly understood the cost of discipleship. However, what he thinks is required to open the gates of heaven is not quite as clear. Is it free . . . or is it costly? He appears either contradictory or confused. We propose that understanding contrasting but complementary categories of truth in Scripture is essential to dispel this kind of confusion. I call it "A" truth and "B" truth:

"A" TRUTH	"B" TRUTH
RELATIONSHIP	FELLOWSHIP
POSITION	CONDITION
JUSTIFICATION	SANCTIFICATION
SALVATION	DISCIPLESHIP
INDWELT BY THE SPIRIT	LED BY THE SPIRIT
ETERNAL	TEMPORARY
SEALED BY THE SPIRIT	FRUIT OF THE SPIRIT
SUB. DEATH OF CHRIST	SUB. LIFE OF CHRIST
GIFT	PRIZE
ACCEPTANCE	APPROVAL

---

[7] Ibid., 55.

[8] Dietrich Bonhoeffer, *The Cost of Discipleship* (New York: Macmillan Publishing Co., 1976), 45-60.

We are suggesting that a failure to keep these categories distinct casts Christianity right back into the Galatian problem of trying to be justified by the law (Gal 5:4). Such theologians would claim:

- If I am not in fellowship with Christ, I don't have a relationship with Christ.
- If I am not walking by the Spirit, I don't have the Spirit.
- If I am not being sanctified, I was never justified.
- If I have not given everything to Christ, I have never received Christ.
- If I am not led by the Spirit, I am not indwelt by the Spirit.
- If I am not enjoying the fruit of the Spirit, I don't have the Spirit.
- If I don't have His approval, I don't have His acceptance.

In simple terms, we might say they have put the cart before the horse. But God never intended this kind of confusion. There are times Jesus clarified these categories of truth by means of contrast. Luke 14:16-33 is just such a passage. Although the contrast is more between salvation and discipleship than relationship and fellowship, it is a helpful lesson in learning to spot these contrasting categories listed above, a list that is not exhaustive by any means.

If we have attended a Bible-believing church for any length of time, most of us have heard many messages on discipleship. Often, they are laden with guilt: "He gave His all for you; the least you can do is to give your all for Him." Perhaps an altar call is given, and the preacher practically begs the people to come forward to give their all to the Savior. Sometimes they are told if they are not willing to yield everything, including their own lives, to Jesus, they have never been "saved." All too often the young person reluctantly trudges down the aisle to join God's army, afraid if he doesn't, the pit of hell awaits him with open jaws.

I propose a gross failure here on the part of the preacher. Not only has he not understood the difference between "A" truth and "B" truth, he apparently has completely overlooked the little word "desires" that Jesus uses as a qualifier in so many of His discipleship passages (Matt 16:24; Mark 8:34; and Luke 9:23). "Whosoever <u>desires</u> to come after me, let him deny himself and take up his cross and follow me." It is the Greek word *thelō* and includes the idea of wishing and wanting. There is no hint of coercion or force or pressure by guilt. We don't get the impression that God has a draft board conscripting people into His army. It appears to be completely voluntary. However, joining His army comes with a price. In order to underscore the price, Jesus tells the crowd a parable before He unfolds the cost of discipleship. Bonhoeffer doesn't say much about this parable or its position in the text. It is the Parable of the Great Supper (Luke 14:16-24).

I. THE COST OF SALVATION   LUKE 14:16-24

[16] Then He said to him, "A certain man gave a great supper and invited many, [17] and sent his servant at supper time to say to those who were invited, 'Come, for all things are now ready.' [18] But they all with one *accord* began to make excuses. The first said to him, 'I have bought a piece of ground, and I must go and see it. I ask you to have me excused.' [19] And another said, 'I have bought five yoke of oxen, and I am going to test them. I ask you to have me excused.' [20] Still another said, 'I have married a wife, and therefore I cannot come.' [21] So that servant came and reported these things to his master. Then the master of the house, being angry, said to his servant, 'Go out quickly into the streets and lanes of the city, and bring in here *the* poor and *the* maimed and *the* lame and *the* blind.' [22] And the servant said, 'Master, it is done as you commanded, and still there is room.' [23] Then the master said to the servant, 'Go out into the highways and hedges, and compel *them* to come in, that my house may be filled. [24] For I say to you that none of those men who were invited shall taste my supper.'"

Let's make a few observations from the text:

Who paid the price for the supper? Obviously, "a certain man."

What, then, did the guests pay for their meal? Obviously, nothing. It was free.

Who did not partake of the free meal? Obviously, those who rejected the invitation.

Who did partake of the free meal? Obviously, "the poor and the maimed and the lame and the blind"—in other words, those without any personal qualifications of merit.

What was the desire of this "certain man"? Obviously, he wanted his house full.

The "lord" of the house is so desirous of having a full house that he tells his servants to "compel" people to become his guests at the free meal. That might sound like force, but this verb *anankazō* also means "to invite (urgently) or urge (strongly)" (BDAG). God does not force people into His kingdom, nor does He force them to become disciples. In fact, Jesus discourages His followers from becoming disciples almost as much as He encourages them. The rest of Luke 14 tells us how He did it.

II. THE COST OF DISCIPLESHIP   14:25-33

25 Now great multitudes went with Him. And He turned and said to them, 26 "If anyone comes to Me and does not hate his father and mother, wife and children, brothers and sisters, yes, and his own life also, he cannot be My disciple. 27 And whoever does not bear his cross and come after Me cannot be My disciple. 28 For which of you, intending to build a tower, does not sit down first and count the cost, whether he has enough to finish it—29 lest, after he has laid the foundation, and is not able to finish, all who see it begin to mock him, 30 saying, 'This man began to build and was not able to finish.' 31 Or what king, going to make war against another king, does not sit down first and consider whether he is able with ten thousand to meet him who comes against him with twenty

thousand? [32] Or else, while the other is still a great way off, he sends a delegation and asks conditions of peace. [33] So likewise, whoever of you does not forsake all that he has cannot be My disciple.

A. The Caution

SALVATION	DISCIPLESHIP
Maimed; unfit	Fit
Free; offered to the poor	Costly—v. 33
Strong Persuasion	Caution
No Qualifications	Many Qualifications

Notice first of all in the Parable of the Great Supper the invitation is extended to those who are unfit and unqualified to participate. It is the poor and the maimed and the lame and the blind who fill up that banquet house. But quite the opposite is true of our Lord's terms for discipleship. Here, it is not the unfit. Our Lord lays down the most stringent and strict requirements by which discipleship must be entered.

Perhaps the most glaring contrast is between the price charged for the participants at the Great Supper as opposed to those called to discipleship. The supper was free of charge. As a matter of fact, those who accepted the invitation had nothing they could pay. By way of contrast, the way of discipleship our Lord presents is something very costly indeed. In Luke 14:33 He says, "whoever of you does not forsake all that he has cannot be my disciple." Herein lie some important contrasts between salvation truth and discipleship truth, or "A" truth and "B" truth. For salvation is extended to those who are utterly unqualified to receive it. But discipleship belongs only to those who are qualified by a willingness to walk the path of self-sacrifice. Salvation is absolutely free, but discipleship is extravagantly costly.

Today many popular Bible teachers are trying to join together what God has put asunder. And there is a great deal of confusion between the terms of salvation and the terms of discipleship. Sometimes these are so blended and amalgamated, the result is more than mere confusion; it is rank heresy. Regardless of the prestige or the influence of those who present such a gospel, the result is another gospel than that of our Lord. At the end of our Bibles, He reminds us of the glorious message of the Great Supper: "And the Spirit and the bride say, 'Come!' And let him who hears say, 'Come!' And let him who thirsts come. Whoever desires, let him take the water of life freely" (Rev 22:17). There's that little word "desires" (*thelō*) again. This is the message of the Holy Spirit to a world that desperately needs it. "Whosoever will"—if you just want it, take it without strings and without conditions, freely.

Is this what Bonhoeffer calls cheap grace? No, it is not cheap at all. It's free—free grace—for us. But remember in the Parable of the Great Supper someone did pay for the supper. It just wasn't the guests. The Lord of the house paid the price. Our Father sent His only begotten Son to pay the price—the ultimate price. Salvation couldn't get more costly—for Him. But free for us. Not so with discipleship.

There is yet another contrast between these two portions of Scripture. It's just this. In the Parable of the Great Supper, urgent methods are used to strongly persuade the guests to come in. You'll notice He says, "Go outside and urgently invite (we have already explained why this doesn't mean "compel") them to come in." But after that parable there is no language that would suggest any strong urging, let alone any hint of compulsion. As a matter of fact, exactly the opposite is the tone with which our Lord presents these words. These words on discipleship are nothing at all if they're not a caution to hasty, reckless discipleship to the Savior.

I'd like you to notice that what the Lord is actually saying here is this. Unless you measure up to these qualifications, unless you hate your mother, father, wife, children, sister, brother, yes even your own life . . . you cannot make it. You're not able to be my disciple. Unless you bear the cross, you cannot make it. You're not able to be my disciple. Unless you sit down and calculate very carefully the resources required to build your tower, you'll never make it. Unless you calculate the resources necessary to enter into the battle, you'll never make it. And if you find you do not have the resources, the Lord implies, the best thing to do is to make peace while you're still a long way off from the battle. Now is the time to get out. Get out now while the getting out is good.

When you get out into the battlefield, the spiritual landscape is dotted with towers, which servants of the Lord were able to build but never able to finish. You'll find the spiritual terrain around you covered with corpses of soldiers in the king's army who went out to battle without adequate resources and experienced a crushing and disastrous defeat. The battle out there is very intense and very severe, and casualties are very high. I think what our Lord Jesus is trying to do in this passage is to cut the losses.

Jesus is doing very much what Gideon did when he acquired his army. He got rid of the fearful, the unprepared. As our Lord addressed this audience, it is exactly these He is trying to discourage. And He is saying, if you're unprepared, don't even begin. It would be well for us to sit down and calculate what the pathway of discipleship to our Savior could mean. What inner spiritual resources are we prepared to throw into this battle? And if we come to the conclusion that to launch out would be to risk calamitous failure, then it is better not to launch out at all. Why should we risk a defeat that is not only shameful to ourselves, but a reproach to the cause and the name of Christ?

I can only imagine a young man who aspires to be a Navy Seal must go through the same searching of his soul before he tries to make the grade. Probably most of us men have watched documentaries on what it takes to make it as a Navy Seal. If I remember correctly, no more than 10% who enter Seal school actually graduate. But more than that, I imagine there's something else besides the trials of Seal school that goes through the mind of a would-be Navy Seal. It's just this. Becoming a Navy Seal could cost that Seal his life. They don't train those guys for backyard wargames. They don't all return from some of those missions. Becoming a Navy

Seal is a life and death matter. It is to risk one's life. I just bet that risk goes through the mind of every person who tries to become a Seal. "Am I willing to die for the cause?" And if they cannot say yes to that question, best for them not to sign up. Jesus is calling for that kind of commitment. He knew His time on earth was short. Without a commando group with the commitment of Navy Seals, His movement would be a failure to launch. Of course, we know He got that kind of commitment from at least the twelve (assuming the substitution of Matthias for Judas) plus Paul. They all willingly died as martyrs for the cause.

Yes, Jesus surely issues a caution to those who would become His disciples, but underlying this caution is also a challenge. It's wrapped up in His two illustrations.

B. The Challenge

1. Construction

When faced with the stringent requirements of a task, some people shrink back and quit. This is precisely the type of person our Lord is trying to warn from the path of discipleship. But there're others who, when faced with a task that requires everything they have, are challenged to meet the task head-on and to be victorious in it. And I think our Lord is also speaking to these kinds of people in His illustration of the tower.

With the tower, He is suggesting that the life of a disciple is a life of construction. It was a life in which something is built. As a matter of fact, in ancient times one of the chief functions of a tower was defensive. And I think our Lord is also suggesting that the disciple is one who is building a tower, a refuge, something in which he can withdraw from the vicissitudes, the difficulties, and the hardships of human life and experience. He has a resource on which to fall back, and more than this, he has an outlook from a vantage point to survey the landscape of human experience, a vantage point not possible to those who know nothing of the path of discipleship. In this, there is a challenge.

2. Conflict

With His next illustration, the Lord shows us the life of discipleship is not only defensive, it is also offensive. He speaks of a king, and the king is going forth to make war. He is not waiting for the attack to come to him; he's going forth to engage the enemy who is coming against him. And so, He speaks of an aggressive activity of discipleship. More than this, discipleship is not only a life of construction, it is also a life of conflict. He points out to those who are willing to see that the disciple is a kingly person. He is like a king, royal, who is marshaling his forces and getting ready to lead them into the fray.

Jesus also points out by way of warning, and I think by way of a challenge, that the forces arrayed against the disciple are more numerous than the forces he has at his command. Because of the high cost of discipleship, we can be assured the Commandos for Christ will always be in the minority: "Narrow *is* the gate and difficult *is* the way which leads to life, and there are few who find it" (Matt 7:14). It was Charles Haddon Spurgeon who said that the further one goes in the Christian life, the lonelier it gets. The path of discipleship is straight and narrow indeed. And it is well to be warned, that if we really are going to walk the pathway of discipleship with the Savior, our company will be meager and the forces and the hosts which the prince of this world will array against us will be vast indeed.

You'll notice that the Savior also suggests in the second illustration that if you find yourself unready for battle, you'd better send an embassage and find out what the terms of peace are. In the ancient world when one king submitted to another, the terms of peace more often than not were vassalage, or at the very least, the submitting king had to pay tribute. Lying behind this part of the illustration is the thought that we can make our peace with the hostile king of this world—we can make our peace with him, but there will be conditions; there will be a form of vassalage to the world system which lies around us. There will be a tribute to pay—moral values and spiritual values which must be surrendered in order to avoid the conflict.

So, although the Lord is cautioning us from thoughtless adherence to the pathway of discipleship, He is also challenging us. I'm so grateful Christ has given us a transcendent cause (Matt 6:33) to live for. I can only imagine how pointless life might seem without the Christian worldview. Malvina Reynolds captured this thought in a song entitled "Little Boxes," which she wrote in 1962:

Little boxes on the hillside,
Little boxes made of ticky tacky,
Little boxes on the hillside,
Little boxes all the same.
There's a green one and a pink one
And a blue one and a yellow one,
And they're all made out of ticky tacky
And they all look just the same.

And the people in the houses
All went to the university,
Where they were put in boxes
And they came out all the same,
And there's doctors and lawyers,
And business executives,
And they're all made out of ticky tacky
And they all look just the same.

And they all play on the golf course
And drink their martinis dry,
And they all have pretty children
And the children go to school,
And the children go to summer camp
And then to the university,
Where they are put in boxes
And they come out all the same.

And the boys go into business
And marry and raise a family

In boxes made of ticky tacky
And they all look just the same.
There's a green one and a pink one
And a blue one and a yellow one,
And they're all made out of ticky tacky
And they all look just the same.

Of course, I cannot speak for you, but for me, though I suppose I could live a life like that, I don't think I would be fulfilled and satisfied no matter how peaceful it may seem to be. In every group, there are some who want the challenge of discipleship, who want a life in which they are building something. They don't want a life where they're sitting on the sidelines in the all-important conflict going on in the world today. They want to be in the midst of the battle. I know the forces arrayed against them are overwhelming. I trust they want to be in the train of the One who will overwhelm the overwhelming. And you want to enjoy the victory which will belong ultimately to our Lord Jesus Christ. On that kind of pathway, friends, and it is wonderful to think of it, you are a king serving under the King of kings. This is a supreme challenge—to launch out into such a life as this.

Finally, this passage contains not only a word of Caution and a word of Challenge, but also a word about Commitment.

C. The Commitment

Here I am thinking in particular of verse 33, which I consider to be the climax of the passage. Our Savior says, "Whoever of you does not forsake all that he has cannot be My disciple." The word "forsake" (*apotassō*) can mean "forsake," but everywhere else in the NT and most specifically in Luke it means "to say goodbye." I suggest to you that this meaning makes the most sense here. So, the Savior is saying, "Whosoever among you who does not say farewell to all that he has cannot be my disciple."

Now notice that this entire incident, which begins in verse 25, was prompted by the fact that great multitudes went with our

Lord. Throngs of people followed Him. And suddenly, we might say abruptly, He turns to confront the multitudes; His words are shocking. He says to the crowd, "If anyone comes to Me and does not hate his father and mother, wife and children, brothers and sisters, yes, and his own life also, he cannot be My disciple. And whoever does not bear his cross and come after Me cannot be My disciple." Whatever else we may say about these words, they're certainly not an illustration of the latest technique on how to build a megachurch. I have a feeling the seeker-sensitive disciples at this point might've raised their hands in holy horror and said, "Lord, look at how many people you're drawing. You've just become the most popular preacher in Israel. We have a lot of bills to take care of: air conditioning, nursery workers, TV crew, and our new branch campuses down in Jericho and up at Caesarea Philippi. Please, we beg you, don't rock the boat. You talk to these people like this, and they may leave you. They may find another man who claims to be the Messiah and start a new church. Be careful what you say. Be careful you don't offend them."

But you know, there's always one thing about our Lord in which He proved himself amazingly discerning—He was never fooled by the crowds. He could look on those crowds and knew better than any other man how shallow they were. He knew their fickleness, their looseness, and the superficiality of their attachment to Him and His word. Our Lord knew what sooner or later was likely to happen to this crowd, as doubtless it had happened to other crowds. He knew that sooner or later someone would come to Him and say something like this: "Lord, I've been traveling with you some 3 weeks now and I want you to know it's been quite a ride. But I have a wife and three kids, and although I'd like to spend more time with you, I have to get back to them. So, for now, Lord, farewell. It's been a pleasure, Lord, but for now, goodbye."

A little later someone else will approach Him and say, "Lord, these have been great days. I'll never forget when you fed thousands of us and I got to hear your Sermon on the Mount. You put on quite a good show with those miracles of yours. But mom and dad are back on the farm with only my brother and sister to help them. So, I better get back. But I did want you to know I really appreciate your ministry and all you're trying to accomplish, and I hope someday you will pass through our village again. If only we had more dedicated young men like you, this world would be a better place. In the past few weeks, I almost feel as though I was one of your disciples. But I have to go. So, for now, farewell."

Do you know what I think our Savior is saying as He turns to these people? He's saying this: "I'm not so sure that you said goodbye to everything you should say goodbye to. Likewise, he who has not said goodbye to all that he has, is not able to last as my disciple." Now, friends, this comes to us as a very penetrating question. Do you count yourself as one of His disciples? Then we must ask: "Have we, have you and I, said goodbye to all that we have: persons, pleasures, possessions?" There's a difference between saying goodbye to something and actually forsaking it. I think there are very few of the Lord's servants who will have to forsake everything in order to serve Him. There are some who do, and some who do this by the pathway of martyrdom. But I don't think that's the thought of verse 33. *What our Savior wants is that we be ready to do so.* And in order to be really ready, all our goodbyes have to be said before we start down the discipleship road.

If you haven't done so before, now is a good time to ask yourself, "Can I say goodbye to this? Can I say goodbye to this? Can I say goodbye to this?" And should you come upon something to which you cannot say goodbye, then be assured, that very thing may well become a major stumbling block in your path of discipleship and dedication to the Lord. "So likewise, whoever of you does not forsake all that he has cannot be My disciple."

Now I don't want this message to be misunderstood. This is not a demand the Lord is laying upon His audience. It is not an edict telling what He requires of them. It is a test. In this test, our Lord is plumbing the depths of our commitment, the reality and extent of our dedication to Him. In essence, I think the Lord Jesus wants to say this: are you willing to say farewell to everything but Me? Again, are

36

you willing to say farewell to everything but Me? The question He is asking in these verses is simply this: how much am I really worth to you? How much do you want to follow Me? How much do you want to know Me? How much do you want to be with Me (Fellowship)? What is it worth to you?

If our answer is this: "Lord, you're worth everything that I have," then we're ready to be His disciple. And, friends, happy is the believer and blessed is the Christian who has said all his goodbyes. For in the moment all our farewells have been said, in that moment we have sealed our commitment to the Savior. In that moment we have liberated our souls, for in that moment, in the words of the hymn writer, "we're clinging to nothing, nothing but Christ, the Christ of God."

One of the most famous aerial missions for U.S. pilots in the Pacific theater of World War II was the bombing of Tokyo in a raid led by Jimmy Doolittle in 1942. The Japanese had surprised us at Pearl Harbor, and President Roosevelt wanted to send a message to the Japanese: "You're not impregnable; we can reach you." The bombing of Tokyo sent that message. But the raid was a suicide mission. The men who volunteered knew their chances of coming back were slim. You see, there wasn't enough gasoline in their planes to fly from their carrier to Tokyo and back. Most likely they would have to ditch their planes in the sea or bail out into enemy territory. No one was forced to go. Each pilot could reject this opportunity without embarrassment or setback in his career. They were putting their lives on the line, and most of them did not come back. Doolittle himself had to bail out. Fortunately, he made it into Chinese territory and landed in a dung heap, which saved his already injured ankle from being broken. A Christian missionary protected him until he could return to the States.

Can you imagine Doolittle's speech to his men before they made their decision to join this mission or not? It must've been something like the challenge of Jesus to His followers in Luke 14. I have a feeling Doolittle told them to say their goodbyes because they may never come back alive. How could a man make such a commitment? It's no mystery. They believed in their cause. They thought their cause was more important than their own lives. Their cause was to defend their nation. A great cause; a cause worth dying for. Is our Christian cause worth any less?

CONCLUSION

We began the study by talking about the distinction between "A" truth and "B" truth. We suggested that "A" truth is about Relationship, while "B" truth is about Fellowship; "A" truth is about justification, while "B" truth is about sanctification. We also suggested that great confusion arises when these two categories of truth get mixed up, or when the conditions for sanctification are made to be the conditions for justification, or when the conditions for discipleship are turned into the conditions for salvation. When that happens, we have put the cart before the horse, and the slide down the slippery slope into a works-oriented approach to heaven is inevitable.

Look at these words from a well-known and popular Bible teacher on how to go to heaven:

"Saving faith is no simple thing. It has many dimensions . . . Unless we receive this, the array of conditions for salvation in the New Testament will be utterly perplexing. Consider the following partial list. What must I do to be saved?

- Believe (Acts 16:31)
- Receive (Jn 1:12)
- Repent and turn (Acts 3:19)
- Obey (Heb 5:9)
- Childlikeness (Matt 18:3)
- Self-denial (Mark 8:34-35)
- Love Jesus more than anyone else (Matt 10:37)
- Be free from the love of possessions (Luke 14:33)

These are just some of the conditions that the New Testament says we must meet in order to inherit final salvation. We must believe on Jesus and receive him and turn from our sin and obey him and humble ourselves like little children and love him more than we love our family, our possessions, or our own life. This is what it means to be converted to Christ. This alone is the way of life everlasting."[9]

I hope we are being clear. Jesus obviously taught these things. But we would put them into the category of "B" truth and say they are the conditions for discipleship, not salvation. That was the whole point of His teaching by contrast in the Parable of the Great Supper and the costs of discipleship in Luke 14. But even if we understand these distinctions, we are still left with the question of motivation. Why would anyone want to pay such a stupendous price to become a disciple? We have suggested that part of the reason is to do something eternally meaningful with our lives. But what we have not discussed is how that meaning is measured.

In 1898 over 100,000 hopeful people left their homes and businesses in the "lower forty-eight" to head to the wild frontier of Alaska. It was the Klondike Gold Rush. The trek was arduous. Only thirty to forty thousand made it. Of those, only four thousand found gold, and only a few hundred got rich. Most of these prospectors were not prepared for the harsh realities of Alaska and Canada. Many died of starvation. As a result, the Canadian government imposed stringent requirements before they allowed anyone to enter the Yukon Territory. A person needed to have a year's supply of food. When all the other requirements were added, the would-be prospector had a ton of supplies to get over Chilkoot Pass. Part of this was so steep that animals could not be used. It took an entire day for a man carrying a

---

[9]   John Piper, *Desiring God* (Sisters, OR: Multnomah Publishers, 2003), 68-70.

pack to get up just a thousand feet. The average was thirty round trips and ninety days to get up and through the pass.

So, we have to ask: why would anyone take such risks and endure such hardships to get up to the Klondike? The answer is not difficult: there is gold up there. There is gold up there.

It is not so different for the disciple. One reason he or she is willing to suffer the sacrifices and endure the hardships along the pathway of discipleship is simple: there is gold up there. 1 Corinthians 3:12-15 tells us our Lord will look through our time on earth with all of its hills and valleys, rivers and tributaries to find gold. He will extract from our lives gold, silver, and precious stones at His judgment seat to create crowns. These gems and the crowns they make are a measure of how much of our lives will count forever. Ultimately, we will cast these crowns before His feet, for it is through His supernatural power and the power of the Holy Spirit that we are able to do anything that will last for eternity (Jn 15:5 and Rev 4:8-9). That He could use my life, my time on earth, to bring glory to Himself forever and forever? Now that is motivating!

"WHO IS THE GREATEST?"
John 13:1-17

INTRODUCTION

At the time I thought it was one of the dumbest things I had ever done. I had taken fifty hard-earned dollars and bought a ticket to see a boxing match I probably could have seen better on television. I fought my way through Astrodome traffic so I could sit in the peanut gallery, too far away to tell the difference between the notorious Cleveland Williams and infamous Muhammad Ali. But, then, you only go around once in life, so you might as well see it in person. And if you're going to see a boxing match, who would be more entertaining than Muhammed Ali, the then undisputed heavyweight champion of the world, whose upper lip moved faster than his left jab. That night he promised to introduce his "Ali Shuffle" in which he performed a little dance to announce his intention to come in and hit you before he did exactly that.

My college roommate and I started going up the ramps of the Astrodome, passing by one famous person after another. There's Robert Goulet; there is Doug Sanders, the golfer; there's Frank Sinatra. We settled in our seats and broke out the binoculars. We found ourselves surrounded by a sea of women, who began to chant, "We want the champ. We want the champ." A clang signaling the beginning of the first round rewarded their request and the fight was underway. But it wasn't really a fight; it was a massacre. Cleveland was too old, and Ali was too tough. Five times Cleveland's body went down before the fight was called. One hundred yards away we were oblivious to his pain. The ladies around us had a new chant: "Kill 'im, Cassius; kill 'im, Cassius" (Ali's former name). He almost did. When the referee raised Ali's hand in triumph, the champ began his own boastful cheer: "Who is the greatest? Who is the king? Who is the greatest?" Well, I've never forgotten that question: who is the greatest?

That question was answered for Ali centuries before he asked. Jesus Himself told us who is the greatest in John 13 during the Last Supper. And as we wander through this passage the backdrop of Relationship/Fellowship truth will help unlock the powerful lessons Jesus had for His disciples in the Upper Room and for us today. But before we unpack the details of this text, we need to take a moment to see where we are and where we're going in the Gospel of John. As we have pointed out in another work,[10] we believe John had the temple arrangement in mind when he constructed his gospel. The first twelve chapters deal with where John selects seven miracles or seven signs to prove that Jesus was the Messiah. This is a picture of the outer court of the temple.

Then in John 13-16, we find the upper room discourse in which Jesus gives intimate truths to His disciples. There's nothing about evangelism in these chapters. They're not about relationship, but they most certainly are about fellowship. That's why Judas is sent out of the room. He doesn't even have a relationship with Jesus, that is, he has not trusted in Him as his Messiah. These chapters are parallel to the holy place where we find the bread and the light (the table of shewbread and the candelabra). Then in John 17, we see Jesus functioning as our high priest. Just as the high priest interceded on behalf of the people by going into the holy of holies, so Jesus interceded on behalf of His disciples. Then the high priest would sprinkle the

---

[10] David R. Anderson, *Maximum Joy* (Houston: Grace Theology Press, 2016), 18.

blood of the lamb over the mercy seat above the ark of the covenant. The parallel is in John 18-20 where John provides the eighth sign that Jesus was the Messiah as predicted by Jesus Himself in John 2:18-22, His death and resurrection. He became our mercy seat and, in effect, sprinkled His own blood on our behalf. Then after the resurrection, Jesus commissioned His disciples to go into the world (Jn 21).

It is important for us to capture the disjuncture between John 1-12 and John 13-16. The first section is primarily about how to have a relationship with Christ as one's Messiah; the second is about how to experience fellowship and full joy in the Christian life. In other words, we have fellowship with Christ when we enjoy our relationship with Christ. The Upper Room Discourse itself can be divided into three parts: Preparation (Jn 13:1-30), Preaching (Jn 13:31-16:33) and Prayer (Jn 17), assuming we include chapter 17 as part of the discourse; or Introduction, Instruction, in Intercession.

By way of preparation, two things had to be done. First, the hearts of His disciples had to be prepared for the verbal instruction Jesus was about to give. And secondly, the collective group had to be prepared for Christ's closing message to His own by removing the unbelieving Judas. It would be like trying to teach a small group when one member of the group is antagonistic. A little leaven can leaven the whole lump. Often one oppositional spirit can destroy the harmony of the whole group. So, in the first thirty verses of this discourse, Christ is preparing the hearts of His disciples for His teaching. We are just going to look at 13:1-17. We want to see these verses in their Setting, their Substance, and their Symbolism. This passage exemplifies the importance of distinguishing between Relationship and Fellowship.

First, the Setting in John 13. It is the Feast of the Passover. Jews from all over the known world gather in Jerusalem to celebrate this important Jewish feast. They celebrate the deliverance from Egypt when the Lord passed over the Jewish homes but took the firstborn of the Egyptians. Messianic expectation was unusually high. Many believed the ultimate deliverance from the scourge of Gentile rule was at hand. And so, the Passover was not only about Jewish remembrance of the past, it also looked to the future when their long-awaited King would deliver them from the oppression of Roman dictators and stomp on the nations like so many ugly roaches.

Amidst this festive activity, Jesus sent two of His disciples, Peter and John, into the city to prepare the Passover lamb. It would be bought from the stable of the high priest, inspected by the temple officials for blemishes and defects, and then prepared for the feast. Jesus instructed them to find a man carrying a pitcher of water and follow him to his master's house. We know from other studies this was the house of John Mark. There they requested a room where they could eat the Passover and were told the best room in the entire house was prepared for them. It was even furnished. So, probably not more than one hundred meters from where Jesus would soon be tried for blasphemy, preparations for the Passover were made by Peter and John.

We're told that the room was furnished. It is key to the understanding of our passage to picture the furnishings of this room. Entering the room from an outside stairway, we see the soft lighting from the oil lamps. In the very center of the room we see a long table, perhaps rectangular. It is not a high table as portrayed by Leonardo da Vinci. Rather it is a low, middle Eastern table about one foot high. Around the table in a horseshoe pattern are thirteen cushions such as we might have on our couches. One-third of the table is uncovered. The other two-thirds have a table cloth. On the uncovered end of the table are the dishes, the goblets, and the utensils. On the cloth itself is the wine, a red wine. Here also is the freshly baked matzo, the unleavened bread. Finally, we smell the fragrance of the lamb itself. But one more thing: by the door opening into this upper chamber we see a towel, an empty basin, and a pot of water.

Now for the arrangement of the cushions. The head of the feast, again contrary to Leonardo da Vinci's painting of the Last Supper, was not in the middle of the table. Rather He sat second from the end. This is where Christ would recline since it is a low table. The Jews leaned upon their left forearms with their feet to the wall and ate with their right hands. To the left of the host of the feast sat the guest of honor. This would be Judas. This is how Jesus was able to pass the sop to him first without drawing attention, since this was the customary gesture to the guest of honor. To the right of Jesus was John. At the ends of the table, sitting opposite one other, were Peter and John. They were the servants who prepared the feast and occupied the cushions for the servants. This explains how John, the disciple Jesus loved, could lean on the chest of Jesus. It also explains how Peter could gesture John from across the table. So, starting from the end of the horseshoe, going right to left, it was John, Jesus, and Judas. At the other end of the horseshoe, directly across from John, was Peter.

This arrangement was not coincidental. In Mark 10:39-43, we find an age-old question which plagued the disciples: who would receive the seats of honor in Christ's kingdom? Who would be the greatest? Christ explained to them that the least among them would be the greatest. Christ came not to be served, but to serve. Unfortunately, like you and me, the disciples did not catch on. It was foreign to their thinking—counterintuitive. They misunderstood greatness in terms of power, influence, wealth, prestige, and admiration. And even at the Last Supper in Luke 22:24 His disciples are disputing this same question: who among them was the greatest?

It's interesting that this was a problem among men who seem so unselfish. After all, haven't these very men left all to follow Christ? Have they not given up any hope or ambition for fortune and fame and the comforts of this world to follow Jesus? Foxes have holes and birds have nests, but the Son of Man doesn't have any place to lay His head. Neither did His disciples. "My, what unselfish men," we might say. But this is not the case at all. Christians are sometimes more selfish than non-Christians. The only difference is faith. The Christian believes in a life to come, and gives up any hope for selfish ambitions in this world in trade for selfish ambitions in the world to come. His faith tells him the ambitions of this world will bring him glory which fades away. But the fulfilled ambitions of the next world can bring eternal glory that will never fade away. So reasons the selfish heart of the carnal Christian.

And so even at this last feast, after spending these many months watching the selfless nature of Jesus Christ, after rubbing shoulders with God Himself, these men still seek glory for themselves. They jostle for the seat of honor, but in a stunning rebuke, Christ appoints the seat of honor to Judas and the seats of servants to Peter and John.

So, the setting is complete. It's a beautiful scene: the soft glow from the oil lamps, the fresh smell of the matzo, and the sweet aroma of the Passover lamb. A beautiful setting indeed. With one exception. One detail mars the beauty of this setting: all the disciples had dirty feet. For Christ this was intolerable because, you see, the towel was there, and the water was there, and the basin was there. But so were the dirty feet. And their appointed servants for the feast, Peter and John, would not stoop further. They prepared the wine, the lamb, the cushions, and the tablecloth. They had done the work of women, of servants. Then they reclined on the servants' cushions. But that was as far as they would go. They would not wash the feet of their fellow disciples. That was just going too far. And the existence of the dirty feet and the water and the towel side-by-side in the same room was more than Christ could bear. It showed their hearts were full of pride. Rather than serving the world, they wanted to be served. The dirty feet were proof of this, as was the disease of pride. The dirty feet were an outward sore of an inward cancer. These dirty feet could cause the downfall of His future church. His hour had come. He was about to depart from this earth unto His Father. He was entrusting His entire mission to these men in the Upper Room. In fifteen hours, He would be upon the cross. For three years He tried to show these men the way of God, and yet, here they are, uptight over who is the greatest. They had dirty feet. Dirty feet don't spread the gospel. The church would've died. It's like a man who's too selfish to share his life with another in marriage. He will die without children. So, would a selfish church. It would die without reproducing.

So, our Lord is well aware that He must wash not only dirty feet, but also dirty hearts. He needed to show them how to serve others and not be served. He tried to get this message across with words (Mark 10), but it didn't sink in. That was His last opportunity. He would impress them by actions. And so, after offering a prayer for the wine and passing it around, the head of the feast arises to wash His hands. When Christ arises, no one is surprised. But to the amazement of the disciples, He does not wash His hands. Instead, He removes His outer robe, girds Himself with a towel, picks up the water basin, and begins to wash dirty feet.

Finally, Jesus approaches Peter. Peter immediately reacts, "Lord, what are you doing?" Christ replies, "What I'm doing you don't realize now, but you will hereafter." Obviously there must be symbolism here. Peter knows very well what Christ was doing–He was washing Peter's feet. But Peter didn't understand the significance of the act, that is, what it symbolized. Now I am suggesting a basic twofold symbolism involved here. This act of Christ symbolizes the need to have a clean heart; it also symbolizes true greatness for showing us how to serve one another.

It symbolizes the cleansing of dirty hearts. Everything Christ does here is symbolic. It's a picture of Philippians 2:5-11 where Christ comes out of Heaven to die as a man:

- Rises from supper—leaves His Father in Heaven
- Removes His clothing—leaves His glory in Heaven
- Girds His body—symbolizes the cross
- Bath of water—the blood which cleanses us of sin once and for all: Relationship
- Washing feet—cleansing of the human heart: Fellowship

If we miss the symbolism here, especially of the total bath (Relationship) versus the foot washing (Fellowship), then we become hopelessly confused about what is required to be with Christ in heaven. He makes it very clear that Peter does not need a bath. He had the bath (cleansing of all sin—past, present, and future) when he trusted Christ as his Messiah (no later than Matthew 16). But if all his sins have been washed away, why does he need to have his feet washed? Daily sin. He still gets his feet dirty every day. As Martin Luther said: *simul iustus et peccator* (at the same time just and a sinner). He was just in his Position (Relationship) but still sinful in his Condition (a barrier to Fellowship).

But Peter doesn't understand all this. Can you sense the guilt Peter must have felt as his Lord and Savior bends down to do the work he should have been doing? So, he trivializes the event: "OK, Lord, if you insist, then just give me a sponge bath. Let's do the whole thing." Of course, this is where Jesus tries to point out Peter's need for foot washing instead of an entire bath. Although Peter did not comprehend what Christ was doing at the time, his first epistle gives evidence that he later understood. He addresses his readers in 1 Peter 5:5-7 urging them to "be clothed with humility, for God resists the proud but gives grace to the humble." Jesus tells Peter if his feet are not washed, ". . . you have no part with Me."

The word "part" (*meros*) deserves special attention. Does this mean if Peter doesn't have his feet washed, he will not be part of Christ's kingdom, that is, will not spend eternity with Him? We think not. Several biblical uses point in another direction:

- In Greek language outside the Bible and with the verb "to have" (*echo*, which we have here) it means "allotted portion" or "share." In this case, it could mean Peter would forfeit his place as an apostle and all that would accrue from that position (*TDNT*).

- In Proverbs 17:2 in the Greek translation of the Hebrew Bible called the Septuagint referred to as the LXX, meros is used to translate the Hebrew word נַחֲלָה, meaning "inheritance" in English: "A wise servant will rule over a son who causes shame and will share an inheritance among the brothers." So, this could mean Peter's refusal to have his feet washed would cause him to lose his inheritance or rewards (see Col 3:24) at the Judgment Seat of Christ.

48

- The conclusion of Johannes Schneider in *TDNT*: "In Jn. 13:8 Jesus makes it clear when He washes the feet of Peter that only the purified disciple can have any part in Him (ἔχεις μέρος μετ' ἐμοῦ). Purification (from sin) is an unconditional presupposition for fellowship with Christ Jesus." Note the word "fellowship." The issue in foot washing was not Relationship; it was Fellowship. (However, we should probably note that Schneider goes on to blur the meanings of Relationship and Fellowship.)

- "Part" can be used as a promise or a warning. In Revelation 22:19 we read: "if anyone takes away from the words of the book of this prophecy, God will take away his part in the tree of life . . ." Eating from the tree of life is a symbol for fellowship. This warning sounds somewhat like the warning to Peter.

We conclude that not having his feet washed symbolized a dirty heart that could cause Peter to lose his "part" with Jesus, which could be the loss of his privilege to rule over one of the twelve tribes of Israel (Matt 19:28), the loss of inheritance in the kingdom, and the loss of intimate fellowship with Christ for eternity. Peter must confess his sins of pride, self-seeking, and self-ambition. Only then could Christ really use him. He had dirty feet from walking through this world, and they must be washed.

Therefore, after receiving Christ we don't need another bath (justification), but we need to wash our feet daily (progressive sanctification). We stumble through the dust and filth of this world, and our hearts become dirty in a hurry, perverted by the values of this world system. They need cleansing daily if we are to have "part" with our Savior, that is fellowship. That's one side of the symbolic coin of foot washing.

On the other side of the coin, we see the symbolism of true greatness. Who is the greatest of all? It's not Muhammad Ali, and it's not Ali's Muhammad. The Lord of lords and King of kings, Jesus Christ, answers their question through His actions. Christ performed the duty of the lowest servant or slave. The greatest among you is the servant. But since our twisted hearts can even turn servanthood into something selfish, Jesus teaches them further. He tells them, and us, how to serve one another.

In John 13:4-11 Christ is talking about the need for clean hearts. But in John 13:12-16, He addresses humble service. He is Lord. They call Him teacher and Lord, but He calls himself Lord and teacher. He can't really teach them anything until they see Him as Lord. Then they will follow His teaching. I once had a golfing buddy who had trouble breaking one hundred for 18 holes. But to hear him talk you'd think he could shoot sixty. And every time I hooked one into the rough, he began advising me how to improve my game. Do you think I listened? Of course not. But if Jack Nicklaus, the lord of the links, suggested a way to cure my hook, I'd memorize every word he said. So, Christ reasons with His disciples, "If I, being the Lord, stoop to such humble service, so should you." If the Lord and Master so acts, His servants are morally obligated to do the same. But how? Here are three suggestions from the text:

1. **The Mark of a Servant**—the little things. Let us note the occasion once again. This is Christ's hour of glorification— He is about to provide the means of salvation for all men. You would think at this time He would move a mountain or cause an earthquake. Instead, He did a little thing— He washed dirty feet. Christ always magnified the little things: the widow's mite, a cup of water in His name. It's the little things anyone can do that are recorded for eternity.

2. **The Motive of a Servant**—Love. John 13:1 says, "He loved them." He sought their highest good. In Christ's day it was despicable to be a servant. Today businessmen have capitalized on this principle. The greatest servant makes the most money. Now, we all appreciate good service. I once pastored a man (Greg Brenneman) who

brought Continental Airlines out of bankruptcy. When he took over, I believe Continental's customer service rating was last in the industry. So, Brenneman thought he would make a game of turning that around. If I remember correctly, he said every time their rating went up a notch, he rewarded everyone in the company with one hundred dollars. It worked, and in the process, he took Continental from six to a split-adjusted one hundred and twenty on the New York Stock Exchange. Nothing wrong with that at all. Better service made Continental a better company. But Jesus calls for a different motive for the kind of service that will count for eternity. It's love: seeking God's will for the person you are loving.

3. **The Measure of a Servant**—to the uttermost (v.13:1). The idea of "to the end" is not to the end of His life, although that would be true. It's more the idea of "completely" or "fully" or "to the uttermost." In other words, He did not put a limit on how far He would go to serve His disciples. Peter and John put a limit on their service. Did they serve? Of course. Did they do menial tasks like preparing the room and the meal and the table? Of course. But they would only go so far to serve their peers. They would not stoop to wash dirty feet. I spent much of my career starting churches. In a small, launching church there is always need for help in the nursery. One Sunday morning we were caught short, so I asked one of our deacons if he would be willing to help in the nursery. He said, "Are you kidding me? I've raised my kids; I'm not about to raise someone else's." He was willing to count the money, but he wasn't willing to change a diaper.

So, who is the greatest? He's the servant of all who is willing to do even the smallest task out of love with a clean heart. Simple. Look around you. Do you see any dirty feet—any needs? Do you see a pitcher of water—a way to meet those needs? If you see a need . . . and a way to help meet the need . . . and just sit there, . . . then you have a dirty heart. When we see dirt in close proximity to water, we should put them together, if we can.

Jesus concludes all this (v. 17) by saying if you know these things, happy (blessed = *makarios* = happy) are you if you do them. Notice He doesn't say if you know these things, you're happy. He says if you know these things **and** do these things, then you're happy. Looking for happiness in life? Who isn't? Then find a place to serve others.

"SPIRITUAL HYDROPHOBIA"
Matthew 18:23-35

INTRODUCTION

A woman bitten by a dog was told by her physician to write her last wishes, as she might succumb to hydrophobia (rabies). He handed her a pen and paper, and she proceeded to write. But she spent so long with the pen and paper the doctor finally remarked something about how long the will would be. "Will?" she snorted. "This is not a will. I'm writing a list of the people I'm going to bite."

Many of us have been bitten by an unforgiving spirit and wound up with spiritual hydrophobia. Spiritual hydrophobia is the dreaded disease which manifests symptoms like anger, hatred, revenge, and bitterness. One deep bite from the teeth of a fellow Christian is enough to start the infection, which can leave us foaming at the mouth. Such spiritual hydrophobia can spread from the area of the bite throughout our entire bloodstream until it cripples the heart of our spiritual life. To stop the spread of the disease immediate attention from a physician is necessary and the proper injections of serum administered. If not, the lives of many people as well as our own may be affected. Spiritual hydrophobia can spread faster than COVID-19. The Scripture says, "If you bite and devour each other, beware lest you consume one another" (Gal 5:15). We can see, then, the seriousness of this deadly disease. Let us, therefore, study spiritual hydrophobia: its Cause, its Consequences, and its Cure. As we do so, once again we shall see how important the distinctions between Relationship and Fellowship are for understanding and applying this text.

I. ITS CAUSE

While I was studying back in seminary on spiritual diseases, we were told we needed to understand the cause and nature of a disease before we could recognize its symptoms or begin treatment. Let's, then, follow the Great Physician as He discusses this aspect of spiritual hydrophobia. The Bible is our textbook on spiritual diseases. Spiritual hydrophobia is found in Matthew 18, where we can peer through the observation glass at the Great Physician lecturing to His students.

Wait a minute. One of them has a question. Turn to verse 21: "How many times should I forgive my brother when he sins against me? Till seven times?" Now every class has one who likes to play up to the teacher and show off his progress by parading his knowledge. This is exactly what Peter is doing. At the local "law school" the scribes and Pharisees taught to forgive a man twice. But if very gracious, then forgive three times. In other words, let him hit you on the cheek and then turn the other cheek. To really be gracious, let him also punch you. Anything more than this is beyond reason. But these professors are really quacks. Their university philosophy is humanistic and outdated. So, when the students enrolled in the special lecture series given by the Great Physician, their minds were expanded by His new and modern concepts for healing the soul and spirit. He talked about praying for those who spitefully use you, blessing those who curse you, and loving your enemies. That came in the first lecture, so some of the students caught on quickly. They thought they would try to apply some of these principles.

Peter, for example, really thought he was outdoing himself when he suggested forgiving a brother up to seven times. That was more than twice as many times as the law school professors suggested. Well,

Peter thought he would be the star pupil for the day. He expected the Great Physician to pat him on the back and say, "Very good, Peter. You're beginning to catch on. I see you have been studying your notes." But instead of a pat on the back and an "A" on the daily quiz, Peter was shocked and embarrassed to receive an "F." He flunked. Forgiving the offending brother just seven times was like prescribing aspirin for an appendicitis. An internal organ was about to explode and spread its fatal poison. A mild pain killer would only postpone the deadly consequences. Emergency surgery was needed to provide permanent results. The Great Physician thought this was such a vital lesson He made up a story to illustrate this principle so His students would never forget it.

Now in order to understand parables, we need to keep a couple of principles in mind. First, a parable makes just one main point. An allegory has many points of correspondence; a parable has just one. Secondly, the parable usually answers a question that's hanging in the atmosphere. Jesus would answer that question with a parable. In this case, the obvious question answered by the parable is, "How often do I have to forgive my brother when he sins against me?" For example, in Matthew 18:23-27, Jesus teaches a story of salvation. If that is not seen, much confusion arises. In 18:24-25, the servant becomes aware of the enormous debt he owes the king. Ten thousand talents would be worth about $15 million in today's economy. The debt was insurmountable for the average blue-collar worker. It was too big to pay. Nothing the servant could give up, his possessions or even his family, could repay this huge debt.

At this point, the servant realizes that it is impossible to save himself. He falls before the king to beg for mercy. The mercy he receives is beyond his wildest dreams. The entire debt is forgiven— it's wiped out. Here's a man who had come face-to-face with God Himself. Whenever a man faces God, inevitably he sees his own sinfulness. He sees his sins as so numerous and great he could never repay them. He falls to his knees to worship the King. God has compassion on every man who admits his sinful debt to God and cries out for grace and mercy. So, we see a man who has humbled himself before God as he realizes he cannot save himself. God in His mercy forgives him an insurmountable debt.

But then the same servant who is forgiven so much ran into one of his own servants who only owed him a small debt (around $200 in today's economy). It was a sum that could be repaid. He grabbed him by the throat to try to make him pay. The poor servant pled for mercy but was thrown in prison. When the others reported this to the King, he was very upset. He called out the unmerciful servant and took him to task for his unforgiving spirit. The one forgiven an insurmountable debt would not forgive another man a very small debt. The Lord said he should have forgiven as he had been forgiven. So how much should we forgive our brother? As much as God has forgiven us.

Now that is the basic teaching of the text. But before we see how it explains spiritual hydrophobia, we must answer a few more questions raised by the text lest we be accused of glossing over the difficulties. Let's look at those last two verses again. Keep in mind the first servant has been forgiven his debt. But then when he would not forgive his brother, the king said the first servant would be turned over to the tormentors to repay the insurmountable debt. Likewise, He says we must forgive our brothers or we will not be forgiven by our heavenly father. What does this mean? Must we forgive our brothers to be saved? Or, if once saved and not forgiving our brothers, do we lose our salvation? That's what it looks like on the surface.

We want to get at the very root of spiritual hydrophobia. Why did this unmerciful servant foam at the mouth, rant and rail at the debtor, resort to physical violence like a mad dog, and seek revenge by throwing him in prison? Well, this passage teaches that the problem was caused because this man had an unforgiving spirit. But that's like discovering a malignant tumor which makes a man ornery. What causes the cancer? What's inside the tumor? The answer: selfishness. The unmerciful servant wanted his $200. He was selfish. When the man couldn't repay him, he blew up. When the debtor pleaded for forgiveness, he was cast into prison. What was the root cause of all this rancor and revenge? Selfish greed. Selfishness is the underlying cause for most offenses. When Jacob offended his brother Esau, there was selfish greed in his heart. And what caused the corresponding grudge of hatred and vow to kill on the part of Esau? Selfishness. When he was hungry, he was ready to sell his birthright. When he was full, he wanted it back. Both men were selfish, and this caused conflict. What causes otherwise pleasant and congenial people to react with sudden rage, anger, and vindictiveness? Just plain selfishness. In his book *Spirit-Controlled Temperament*, Tim LaHaye writes, "Although we love to excuse our weaknesses and justify them to ourselves as we nurse our grudges and indulge in angry, vengeful, and bitter feelings, they are all motivated by selfishness. When I am angry, it is because someone has violated my rights, and I am interested in myself. When I am bitter against someone, it is because they have done something against me, and again I come back to selfishness. Vengeance it is always inspired by selfishness."

Judy is a good example. She came to me one night, plotting how she could get back at a member of her family. As she spoke of the despised family member and the offense she suffered, her eyes began to roll, her lips quivered, and her hands shook. Blood began rising up in her neck, and any minute I expected her hair to stand on end. As it turned out, she felt swindled out of a relatively small sum of money. But it wasn't about the money, Judy assured me. It was the principle behind it. Her rights had been violated, and she wouldn't put up with that from anyone. Note: both parties were Christians. Note: selfishness was the cause.

So much then for the cause of this disease. What are the consequences?

II. ITS CONSEQUENCES

We have already mentioned the obvious signs of attitudinal sins such as anger, wrath, malice, bitterness, strife, and so on, which express themselves in snapping, snarling, grudges, and hatred. But there are more symptoms which are subtler and just as serious. Remember the tormentors of verse 34? The servant with an unforgiving spirit was turned over to the tormentors. What are they? The tormentors are the physical and spiritual consequences of our spiritual hydrophobia that haunt us and make our lives miserable. They're tormentors of the body, the soul and the spirit.

Tormentors of the Body

One day a man entered a doctor's office with his 14-year-old son. The father told the doctor, "I only came to get more pills for my wife's colitis." The boy immediately piped up, "Well, dad, who has mom been colliding with now?" Is there any connection between physical colitis and Christian colliding? A study at a hospital revealed through personal interviews with patients suffering from colitis that resentment was their most prominent personality trait, occurring in 96% of the patients. Other diseases symptomatic of spiritual hydrophobia are toxic goiters, high blood pressure, and heart attacks.

One elderly lady walked into the office of Dr. McMillan, author of *None of These Diseases*,[11] and discovered her systolic blood pressure, which usually hovered around 120, had suddenly jumped to 230. Inwardly, the doctor was concerned, but outwardly he calmly said, "Your blood pressure is up today." With a smile she answered, "I can easily account for that. I just had a heated argument with another patient in your waiting room." Think of that. A cultured, intellectual woman was willing to risk blowing her cerebral fuse to get even with another patient in the waiting room. That's a high price to pay for getting even.

Even the Bible speaks of these chemical changes in the body caused by emotional stress. One guilt test in the Old Testament

---

[11] S. I. McMillan, *None of These Diseases* (Old Tappan, NJ: Fleming H. Revell Company, 1984), 111-12.

is illustrative. To test a woman's guilt, if unfaithfulness has been suspected, take her to the temple and have her drink a mixture of dust and water. If she was guilty, the potion would rot her thigh. Apparently, some germs won't even travel without the chemical condition caused by the guilt (Num 5:11-31).

Our emotional stress from bitterness and resentment elicits certain hormones from the pituitary, adrenal, thyroid, and other glands. This chemical imbalance can cause disease in any part of the body. Refusing to forgive a brother can cause physical fatigue and loss of sleep. We might try to hide our resentments, but soon they will be etched into our eyes and facial muscles as permanent reflections of our inward feelings.

Not only does the body suffer from an unforgiving spirit, the soul suffers as well.

Tormentors of the Soul

Emotions are affected by depression. Sometimes depression is caused by the emotional drain of trying to hold a grudge. As we become weary when our physical strength leaves us, so we become depressed when our emotional energy is exhausted. Mental anguish is another tormentor of the soul. Dr. McMillan says:

The moment I start hating a man, I've become his slave. I can't enjoy my work anymore because he controls my thoughts . . . The man I hate hounds me wherever I go. I can't escape his tyrannical grasp on my mind. He may be many miles from my bedroom, but more cruel than any slave driver, he whips my thoughts into such a frenzy my inner spring mattress becomes a torture rack. I can't even enjoy food. A T-bone steak with baked potato and ice cream for dessert might as well be stale bread and water. I chew the food and swallow it, but the man I hate will not allow me to enjoy it. Maybe that's why Solomon wrote: better a dish of vegetables with love, than the best beef served with hatred.[12]

Yes, both the body and the soul are tormented when we channel an unforgiving spirit into a grudge. However, perhaps the most serious of all are the tormentors of our spirit.

Tormentors of the Spirit

We have seen from this parable the most devastating of all results coming from an unforgiving spirit. If we will not forgive our brother's repeated offenses, then God will not forgive us. What does that mean? If I'm not willing to remove the barrier of fellowship caused by my brother's offenses against me by forgiving him those offenses, then God cannot do the same for me. Just as there will be a barrier to fellowship between my offending brother and me, so there will be a barrier to fellowship between God and me. But take careful note: this is on a fellowship level, not a relationship level. The brothers are still brothers; that is their relationship. That will be their relationship forever. Nothing can change that. It's their fellowship that is at risk, not the relationship. So it is between us and God. He is our heavenly Father. We are His children, born into His family. That relationship is not threatened when we sin and offend Him, but our fellowship is broken. Until the fellowship is restored, the tormentors take over.

How does that work? Very simple. Anger, hate, jealousy, strife —these are emotion-packed words. When I hate my brother, he becomes an emotional focus around which my thoughts converge. Most of us are only capable of one emotional focus at a time. That's why Christ says we cannot serve God and money at the same time. We will either love one and hate the other or vice-versa. We can't have an emotional focus on both at the same time. So it is with our brother. I cannot have an emotional focus of hate for my brother and

---

[12]   Ibid., 116.

one of love for my Father in heaven at the same time. I cannot love God and hate my brother simultaneously. Hatred toward my brother wipes out any love for God. In 1 John 4:12-21 it says, if we love one another, God dwells in us and His love is perfected in us . . . If a man says he loves God and hates his brother, he is a liar. We cannot do both. Because of the barrier between us and our brother, there is also a barrier between us and God.

The result? Guilt, first of all. Our conscience will torment us. This guilt will come directly from the present sin of not forgiving my brother, but there is an implication here that the sins of our past which were removed as a barrier at one time will come back to haunt us. Remember the servant was forgiven the insurmountable debt, but he was turned over to the tormentors again for that debt when he would not forgive his brother. Guilt will overwhelm us. We will stumble along, walking in darkness. John says, ". . . he that hates his brother is in darkness and walks in darkness and knows not where he goes because the darkness has blinded his eyes" (1 Jn 2:11). This darkness so shrouds our view of God that we wonder sometimes if we ever knew Him. For this reason, many doubt their salvation in the first place, if they believe in eternal security, or think they lost it if they don't believe in eternal security. In his darkness, the unforgiving man has no desire for the Bible because it just increases his guilt.

It's a pretty high price to pay for getting even with someone, isn't it? Well, we have looked at the Cause and the Consequences of spiritual hydrophobia. What then is its cure?

III. ITS CURE

After spotting some of the symptoms, we may suspect that we suffer from spiritual hydrophobia. How can it be treated? I think it's all right here in this passage. We can, of course, go a long way toward the cure if we realize the cause. When we sense our anger rising, we must ask ourselves, "why?" Why am I angry? What personal rights am I protecting? What personal goal is blocked? Remember:

selfishness is the root cause of an unforgiving spirit, and hence, spiritual hydrophobia. Here are three suggestions to help overcome an unforgiving spirit.

A. Remember God's Compassion

The primary prevention or treatment for this disease is seen in the contrast between the two debts. The King in His great grace and love forgave $15,000,000, an insurmountable debt owed by the servant. The servant in his selfishness was unwilling to forgive $200, a small debt. Surely anyone with a grudge or bitterness in his heart would be cut to the quick. How could we possibly refuse forgiveness after having been forgiven so much? "Should you not also have had compassion on your fellow servant, even as I had pity on you?" (Mt 18:33). But in the heat of battle we forget what the Lord has done for us. Our eyes are on our own personal loss or embarrassment or injured feelings. But the cure, my friends, is, as with many spiritual problems, to keep our eyes upon Jesus. If we truly understand the greatness of His love and mercy when He removed our debt, we cannot help but overlook the sins of others against us.

1 John 4:10 captures perhaps the most beautiful expression of God's love demonstrated in our midst when He forgave our sins: "Herein is love, not that we loved Him, but He loved us, and sent His Son to be the propitiation for our sins." Love should have originated from us because of all He has done for us by virtue of creation and the provisions for life (common grace). He had no reason to love us, and we resisted Him, were ungrateful, and were unfaithful. But love in Christ originated with Him. This itself is utterly fantastic. Best of all, not only did He love us first, but He had to penetrate a barrier to get there. His Son became the propitiation (satisfaction of God's justice) for our sins. So, much to our amazement, God originated love. Then He surmounted the obstacle of sin to express that love.

It is this type of love which is matured in us when we forgive or seek forgiveness from our brothers or sisters. We love our wives, but they love and respond to us. We love our children, but they are our children. To fully appreciate God's love we must find a person unnecessary to us, with nothing to offer us, and with an unresponsive spirit toward us, perhaps even someone who erects barriers of offense against us. Then to love this person and surmount the barriers he has erected; this is what God did for us. Not that the offending brother loves us, but that we love him. Not that he made it easy to love, but that we removed the barrier by forgiving him. This is love, and God is love. So, if we are willing to reflect on the great love of God which forgave our insurmountable debt, a forgiving spirit will cure us of spiritual hydrophobia if we have been bitten, or prevent us from getting it if we have not. It's both the antidote and the vaccination.

B. Remember their Situation

Are they ignorant? "Well, of course they are ignorant; they don't agree with me," you say. No, I don't mean ignorance in a general sense but as it pertains to the offense. We think of Jesus' words on the cross: "Father, forgive them **because** they know not what they do." (Lk 23:34) The people were acting on inadequate information. That is often the case. We don't have all the facts. This is especially important when it comes to rumors. One pastor I know was the victim of malicious rumors started by one person. It came to light that the rumors were unfounded, but much discord had been sown among the brethren. Considerable damage had been done, and the pastor was deeply hurt. But he forgave the offending brother because he realized this brother was acting from ignorance. He didn't know what he was doing.

That is one reason it is so important to observe 1 Timothy 5:19 carefully: "Do not receive an accusation against an elder except from two or three witnesses." Notice it says we are not even to "receive" accusations without witnesses. Although the situation was not a church setting, take the Judge Cavanaugh hearings, for example. This nominee to the US Supreme Court was accused of sexual misconduct that allegedly occurred forty years before the accusation was made. When the hearing committee heard the accusation, they should have called for witnesses. No witnesses. Next case. You don't even receive the accusation. You give it no merit. Think of all the pain an innocent wife might have avoided. And two little girls. And the whole nation, for that matter. The entire episode was a historic low point in our justice system.

Are they sick? It is easier to forgive someone if they are sick. By sick, I am referring to some sort of psychological problem. In Martha Stout's book *The Sociopath Next Door,* she claims that 15% of adults around us are sociopaths. I always had the misconception that sociopaths were either in jail or belong there. But, no, says Stout. She describes a sociopath as an often gifted, even charismatic character, who runs roughshod over people in order to get his or her way or to gain power without any guilt whatsoever. No conscience. That's the essence of the sociopath or the psychopath. The latter is much rarer (thank God). But chances are you know a sociopath. You may even work with one. You can spot the symptoms from the body bags lying around him. Wherever he goes results in damage. But he is oblivious, along with those he has duped into his point of view. Though it is extremely difficult to forgive this kind of person, it helps to realize they are sick in the sense that they are not even aware of their Machiavellian behavior.

C. Remember the Consequences

If we don't forgive, He won't forgive. Not only does this parable teach this, but so does the Sermon on the Mount. Remember how Jesus taught us to pray: "Father, forgive us our sins even as we forgive others their sins." The word for "sin" here (*opheilēma*) is not the normal word for sin (*hamartia*). The NKJV even translates it as "debt," for that is the normal meaning of *opheilēma*, a debt of money. But that makes no sense in this context. BDAG correctly says in a religious context it just means "sin." In the parallel passage (Luke 11:4) we find the word *hamartia* instead of *opheilēma*. It would seem that God's forgiveness of our sins is dependent on our forgiveness of the sins of others against us.

Of course, this is exactly what the verses immediately following the "Lord's Prayer" instruct: "For if you forgive men their trespasses, your heavenly Father will also forgive you. But if you do not forgive men their trespasses, neither will your Father forgive your trespasses." This time the word for "trespasses" is *paraptōma*, another common word for "sin." The little word "for" at the beginning of these verses tells us Jesus is explaining what He meant in the prayer about forgiving others so God will forgive us. There is no way to escape this truth. The context puts the focus on our sins. If we do not forgive others' sins against us, God will not forgive us our sins.

This makes absolutely no sense unless: 1) Our entrance to heaven requires more than simple faith in Jesus and His work on our behalf; or 2) The forgiveness here is for Fellowship, not Relationship. We choose number 2 since number 1 contradicts so many passages that make faith in Jesus the only requirement to spend eternity with our Maker.

CONCLUSION

Peter asked the Great Physician how many times he should forgive his brother. The answer? As many times as God has had to forgive us. Spiritual hydrophobia involves anger, hatred, jealousy, wrath, and bitterness against our Christian brother or sister, and is a dreaded disease. The cause? An unforgiving spirit motivated by selfishness. Its consequences? Physical disease, mental anguish, and spiritual darkness. Its cure? Remember the great love of God, which has forgiven us our many offenses.

A little boy was once asked his definition of forgiveness. After a moment's thought he replied, "It is the odor flowers give off when trampled on." I like that. Being trampled on–humbled–is often the price we pay when we forgive or seek forgiveness. But remember, we pay a steeper price to get even.

Sometimes I think animals are smarter than people. In one of Dale Carnegie's books, he tells of a trip to National Yellowstone Park. During the tour, their guide showed them the infamous grizzly bear, which is able to overtake any animal in North America with the possible exception of the buffalo or the Kodiak bear. As Mr. Carnegie sat in the stands and watched the grizzly eat, he noticed only one animal brazen enough to eat side-by-side with the bear. It was our friend the skunk. The bear easily could've killed the skunk. And undoubtedly the grizzly resented the skunk for its impudence and longed to get even. But he never did. Why? Because he knew the high price he'd pay to get even. Yes, sometimes I think animals are smarter than humans. Far better to be trampled on and come out smelling like a rose than to get even and come out smelling like a skunk. I leave you with just one question: Is there anyone you would like to bite today? If so, turn your eyes upon Jesus.

"HEAVENLY HORTICULTURE"
John 15:1-6

INTRODUCTION

As your life nears its final chapter, what will be the sum total of its significance? More and more people are searching for a purpose and meaning to their existence. They want their lives to really count. How can we be assured of lives that really count? It helps to have a well-defined purpose. A cattleman shared this bit of wisdom from his days on the ranch:

One morning I watched a couple of cowpunchers going out to bring in a wild steer from its range in the mountains. They took along one of those grey, shaggy little donkeys—a burro. Now, a big three-year-old steer that has been running loose in the timber is a tough customer to handle. But these cowboys had the technique. They got a rope on the steer and then tied him neck and neck, right up close, to the burro.

When they let go, that burro had a bad time. The steer threw him all over the place. He banged him against trees, rocks, and into the bushes. Time after time they both went down. But there was one great difference between the burro and the steer. The burro had an idea. He wanted to go home. No matter how often the steer threw him, every time the burro got to his feet, he took a step closer to the corral. This went on and on, and after about a week the burro showed up at the ranch headquarters. He had with him the tamest, sorriest looking steer you ever saw.

And so, like the steer, one can have a lot of beef and brains, but it all amounts to very little unless there's some worthwhile and well-established purpose directing all these resources. By contrast, the little burro lacked much when it came to size and weight, but it put all it had in one direction and kept on going. Hence, it's not so much one's size as it is his determined direction that counts.

There are many Christians who act just like that wild steer. They seem to lack any direction or purpose. They say, "I have faith in Christ. Isn't that enough?" Yes, my Christian friend, faith is enough, enough to get one eternal life. But no, my Christian friend, saving faith alone is not enough to give one purpose in life. Christian faith gets the ball rolling, but Christian fruit is at the end of the bowling alley. Christ says as much in John 15:16: "You did not choose Me, but I chose you and appointed you that you should go and bear fruit, and *that* your fruit should remain . . ." The Greek word which is translated "chosen" or could be translated "elected" (*eklegomai*) is followed up by the word **"that."** Purpose. God had a definite purpose in mind when He chose us. And He would be far happier, I'm sure, with a little burro than a wild steer. And His purpose for us is quite well-defined, isn't it? It's that we might bring forth fruit.

Interesting, isn't it, that Jesus doesn't say we were chosen so we can go to heaven? It doesn't say we were elected to simply spend eternity with our Creator, magnificent as that thought is in itself. No, this verse completely circumvents the point in time when we became believers. This verse speaks of God's choice for us before we believed, and then it speaks of God's purpose for us after we believed. It doesn't even mention, let alone emphasize, the point of salvation. Not only is this true of this verse, but let me go further, I think it's true of the entire New Testament. Its emphasis is not on "getting saved," so to speak, but rather it's on bearing fruit. It's not on justification; it's on sanctification. Take the Great Commission, for example. At the end of Matthew 28 Christ does not say, "Go into all nations and make a bunch of converts." No, He says, "Go, therefore, and make disciples of all nations," and He defines that not just as baptizing but also teaching them to observe all the things Christ has commanded.

And so, the man or woman or child who says, "I'm saved, I've got it; this is what it's all about," has completely missed the biblical emphasis as to why God chose us. He chose us that we might bring forth fruit. That's His purpose for us as Christians. It's not just to sit in a church pew and sing, "When the roll is called up yonder, I'll be there." It's that we might glorify the Father by bearing fruit right here, and right now. Of course, that leads us to the question of what we mean by fruit. If we aren't careful, we will leave the impression that the person with the most converts is the most important to God. But there's nothing in this passage that defines fruit as converts. As we read the New Testament, it would seem that there is more emphasis on our character than on our accomplishments. If that's true, then we should probably include the fruit of the Spirit in our understanding of fruit: love, joy, peace, longsuffering, kindness, goodness, faithfulness, gentleness, and self-control (Gal 5:22). This fruit puts a spotlight more on our being than on our doing. And any Christian regardless of race or gender has just as much opportunity to demonstrate the fruit of the Spirit as anyone else.

The next question is obvious: how do we go about bearing this fruit? We find the answer to that question in John 15:1-6. We are trying to answer the question of how we can bear fruit that will remain forever. It is easy to think that all the words spoken in John 13 through 16 take place in the Upper Room. Not so. At the end of John 14 Jesus knew the Jewish authorities had been alerted by Judas, so He arose with His disciples to go to the Garden of Gethsemane where He would be betrayed. Along this walk, Jesus taught them through the vine illustration. Our passage unfolds in two sections: the Divine Side of Fruit Bearing (1-3) and the Human Side of Fruit Bearing (4-6).

I. THE DIVINE SIDE OF FRUIT-BEARING 15:1-3

"I am the true vine, and My Father is the vinedresser. Every branch in Me that does not bear fruit He takes away; and every branch that bears fruit He prunes, that it may bear more fruit. You are already clean because of the word which I have spoken to you.

A. Picture of Fruit-Bearing 1

Perhaps as they pass through the gates of Jerusalem, Jesus looks at the golden vine engraved on the gate. This vine was a symbol of Israel. In Psalm 80:8-16 we read about the vine as a symbol of Israel. This symbol appeared on the coins during the Maccabean period some 150 years before Christ. The vine was to Israel as the eagle is to America. The eagle symbolizes freedom. The vine symbolized fruit. Israel was God's chosen vine. The vine was selected to bear fruit, but as Isaiah 5:1 reads, Israel, like a vine, had been planted and cultivated but she bore only wild grapes. God's winepress was never used. Israel was a barren vine. And so, the one which should have symbolized fruitfulness, soon symbolized barrenness.

In the wake of Israel's foolishness and folly Jesus walks along and says, "I am the true vine." The language in which our New Testament was written (common, street Greek) has two different words that mean "true." The one used here carries the flavor of that which is genuine, authentic, or real (*alēthinē*). And Jesus, with Israel in mind, says, "I am the real vine. Israel is barren. She cannot bear fruit. But I can. I am a genuine, authentic vine which will produce fruit for God." In other words, "I am the real deal." And so, Jesus imagines Himself as the Vine and His Father as the husbandman, or the fruit farmer who will attend to the vine. But there is a prerequisite for fruit-bearing.

B. Prerequisite for Fruit-Bearing 2

To bear fruit, the branch must be in the vine. This term "in Me" is rather important in this passage as we shall see. First and foremost,

70

it is a technical phrase used throughout the New Testament to refer to a Christian during the Church Age. We mention the Church Age because that began with the sending of the Holy Spirit at Pentecost, and it was the Holy Spirit that placed us "in Christ" (1 Cor 12:13). It doesn't refer to any particular type of Christian. He or she can be a baby Christian, an immature Christian, a spiritual Christian, or a carnal Christian. But if he is a Christian, he is "in Christ."

Romans 11 speaks of the grafting of the Gentiles into the olive tree; the point being, before any fruit can be born, we must be in Christ. So, I do not want to minimize "salvation truth" or "relationship truth" in any way. It is perhaps the greatest miracle of all. But salvation (justification) is only the first step down a path leading to a meaningful, purposeful, fruit-bearing life. Salvation is the prerequisite; sanctification is the purpose.

C. Procedure for Fruit-Bearing   2-3

1. Propping the Branch   2a

After providing us the prerequisite for fruit-bearing, we then find the procedure for fruit-bearing in the rest of verse 2. At this point we must pay very careful attention. John 15 is a crucial chapter for our Christian lives, but it is also a very controversial chapter, because the imagery invoked can be bent a number of different ways. In other words, we can make it fit our theology rather than allowing it to help shape our theology. Nevertheless, we will attempt to show how a clear understanding of the Relationship/Fellowship distinction gives us an approach that is most consistent with the rest of the NT.

Verse 2 is a case in point: "Every branch in Me that does not bear fruit He takes away; and every *branch* that bears fruit He prunes, that it may bear more fruit." If being in the vine means to be "in Christ," which means to be a Christian, then what happens when this branch is taken away? Does this mean the Christian loses or forfeits his eternal relationship with Christ because he isn't bearing fruit? Many Christian groups believe this. But perhaps there is another way to understand the imagery here. This verse is not intended to be a threat; rather, an encouragement.

Let's look closely at the imagery. Let's have a lesson in horticulture, the science of producing fruit or vegetables. Specifically, what do we know about vineyards during the time of Christ? The first step in preparing a vineyard was to dig a trench about one yard wide all around the proposed area. Next, a hedge of thorn bushes and stones was laid in the trench to keep out pesky insects and animals. Then the land was dug up so young vines could be planted. They were usually arranged in rows about eight feet apart. One of the challenges for the vinedresser was cold soil. The vine will drop its blossom if exposed to cold soil at night. This is the reason in times before vines were supported by poles and wires, vinedressers would prop up the vine off the ground.

We propose that this practice is what Jesus refers to in this verse. The word translated "take away" in our English text is *airō*. This Greek word does frequently mean "to take away," but its basic meaning and most frequent use is "to take up, raise up, or lift up." When Jesus addressed the palsied man in Matthew 9, He said, "Arise, take up your bed, and go into your house." The word translated "take up" was *airō*. When Jesus said, "Take up your cross and follow Me," He used *airō* again. When Jesus "lifted up" His eyes in John 11, the text used *airō*. So, "to take up, raise up, lift up" is a very normal meaning of the word used here and may well fit a horticulture context better than "take away."

Unfortunately, because of their theological background, many translators use "take away," which would suggest a person can lose their salvation. However, the sequence of earthly horticulture commands the image of preparing the soil, planting the vine, lifting up the branches, pruning the branches, washing the branches to protect them from insects, and finally gathering much fruit. If we look closely, this is the sequence here. The young branches not producing fruit are lifted up on support poles to protect their blossoms from the cold night soil. Then came the pruning, the washing (v. 3), and finally the great harvest (v. 8). So, that's earthly horticulture, but we would suggest that Jesus is making a parallel truth with heavenly horticulture.

God doesn't look down at a branch not producing fruit and just take it away. Why, it hasn't even been pruned yet. We're looking at a tender, young branch just growing from the vine. It hasn't produced any fruit yet, but it's growing. In order to encourage the production of fruit, the farmer lifts it up, and raises it out of the dirt and mud in which the vine has been crawling. This is what our heavenly Father does. He encourages fruit production by lifting us up, and supporting us to carry our burden. When we carry all our own weight, we're barely able to keep out of the dirt and mud of this earth, barely able to keep our head up. We can't produce fruit because we're burdened with our own problems and can think only of ourselves. But in love our heavenly Father reaches down and lifts us up:

> He gives power to the weak,
>   And to *those who have* no might He increases strength.
> Even the youths shall faint and be weary,
>   And the young men shall utterly fall,
> But those who wait on the Lord
>   Shall renew their strength;
>   They shall mount up with wings like eagles,
>   They shall run and not be weary,
>   They shall walk and not faint (Isa 40:29-31).

Need a boost? Feet stuck in the mud? Wait upon the Lord. It's a promise. It means nothing until we believe it. But if we do, His love will lift us up and give us all the support necessary to bear fruit. It's like the old chorus I used to make fun of before I was grafted into the vine: "Love lifted me, love lifted me; when nothing else could help, love lifted me." That's heavily horticulture. He won't take you away. He'll lift you up. He's very patient and encouraging as He waits for us to produce fruit. And once we start producing fruit, what does He do? After the propping comes the pruning.

2. Pruning the Branch 2b

God purges every branch that brings forth fruit that it may bring forth more fruit. The word used for pruning is *kathairō*, and it literally means "to clean or to purge." We derive a number of English words from this Greek word, like catharsis, which is a sort of purging of our emotions. In this context, he refers to the pruning and washing process. Each spring the farmer prunes his vines. He wants to make the branch more fruitful. Now this doesn't mean the branch itself is cut off. This is a fruit-producing branch. What the farmer does is cut off the excess offshoots and leafage which drains the branch of sap that could otherwise be used to make more fruit. In other words, the farmer wants all of the energy flowing in that branch to be directed into fruit-producing activity.

How often our Christian lives become cluttered with activities that produce no fruit. Lest you misunderstand, let me remind you that the fruit may include the fruit of the Spirit already mentioned. We mentioned the fruit of the Spirit from Galatians 5:22, but Ephesians 5:9 expands the fruit of the Spirit to include goodness, righteousness, and truth. Romans 1:13 indicates that lives changed for Christ are also fruit. With this understanding, all Christians have equal opportunity to bear fruit. Men don't have a corner on the fruit market because they are usually the preachers, teachers, and evangelists. There need be no women's liberation movement in Christian circles. There is equal opportunity for all to bear fruit. In fact, as I watch some young mothers with their children, I sometimes think their opportunities to bear the fruit of long-suffering, justice, goodness, and faith are greater than men have in their work. At any rate, it's these Christlike attitudes that are the fruit we are primarily to bear.

But how often we channel much of our time and energy into fruitless endeavors, into areas that sap our spiritual strength and rob us of Christlike attitudes. How about it, my Christian friends, are you involved in activities that frustrate the potential fruit you might bear? If so, then God wants to prune. He wants to cut out those activities so you can produce more fruit. How does he do it? Verse three tells us.

The disciples are already "clean," which is the adjectival form of the verb translated "prune" in verse 2. God says they have already passed through the spring pruning and washing with insecticide. How does He do it? Through His words. It's with the Word of Christ, the Word of God that this pruning and washing process goes on. The Word of God is sharper than any two-edged sword. It cuts, and at times it hurts. That is one form of God's discipline that is designed to bear fruit. Hebrews 12:11 says, "Now no chastening seems to be joyful for the present, but painful; nevertheless, afterward it yields the peaceable fruit of righteousness to those who have been trained by it." So as we read the Word of God at home, as we study it at church, the Father is cleansing, He is pruning. Yes, it cuts; it hurts. But it's His Heavenly Horticulture. It's necessary if we want to produce fruit up to our greatest potential.

In 15:1-3 we see the Divine side of fruit-bearing. In 15:4-6 we see the human side. On the divine side we see that Jesus is the vine and our union with Him makes fruit-bearing possible. That's a prerequisite. We also see that the Father tends to the branches by lifting them up to promote fruit-bearing and pruning them to increase fruit-bearing. Well, if He does all that, what are we supposed to do? What's the human side of fruit production?

II. THE HUMAN SIDE OF FRUIT-BEARING   15:4-6

Abide in Me, and I in you. As the branch cannot bear fruit of itself, unless it abides in the vine, neither can you, unless you abide in Me. "I am the vine, you *are* the branches. He who abides in Me, and I in him, bears much fruit; for without Me you can do nothing. If anyone does not abide in Me, he is cast out as a branch and is withered; and they gather them and throw *them* into the fire, and they are burned.

75

A. Our Responsibility   4

Only one thing is asked of us. We must abide in the Vine. All we have to do is stay close to the Vine. That's all a branch can do. The Vine provides the sap of life. The farmer does all the support and pruning and washing. All the branch has to do is stick close to the Vine. Here we see two parallel truths: Relationship and Fellowship.

"IN CHRIST"	"ABIDING IN CHRIST"
Relationship	Fellowship
Union	Communion
Justification	Sanctification

When someone is "in Christ," they have an eternal relationship with God. But someone who is in Christ is not necessarily close to Christ. If they are living in a manner displeasing to their heavenly Father, they will not be enjoying their relationship at all. In other words, there will be no communion with one another—no fellowship. A failure to make this distinction between Relationship and Fellowship has wreaked havoc in the Church for centuries.

But what does it mean "to abide" in Christ? We are never exhorted to be "in Christ," but we are exhorted to "abide in Christ." The end of verse 3 said the disciples were "clean" because of the word Jesus had spoken unto them. They were in close communion with Him. Now all they had to do was remain there. But how does one do that? For one thing, 1 Thessalonians 5:19 tells us not to quench the Spirit. Don't do things that would keep the sap from flowing. An orange tree doesn't get up in the morning and do calisthenics to produce fruit. It just lets the sap flow. When the Holy Spirit prompts us to do something and we resist, then we are quenching the Spirit. And 1 John 1:7 claims, "But if we walk in the light as He is in the light, we have fellowship with one another, and the blood of Jesus Christ His

Son cleanses us from all sin." As long as we walk in obedience to the light (our understanding of God's Word), then we have fellowship with Christ, and He keeps on cleansing us from all the sins in our life we aren't even aware of. His blood provided for our Relationship with Christ, and His blood provides for our Fellowship with Christ.

But why should I focus on staying close to Jesus? That would seem obvious, but it leads us away from our responsibility to His results.

B. His Results   5-6

1. Fruitfulness   5

At the end of verse 6 it says, "For without Me you can do nothing." Does that mean we can't get up in the morning without Christ? Does it mean we cannot do our work at the office without Him? Does it mean we can't get a college degree or do housework or make a scientific discovery without the Vine? No, it means we cannot produce spiritual fruit without Him. We cannot produce fruit that will last forever. Remember, verse 16 says we were chosen to produce fruit. It's to be fruit that is spiritual and will remain forever. But what if we don't abide in Him?

2. Fruitlessness   6

a. Loss Today   6a

If we don't abide in Him, our usefulness ends. We refer here to usefulness for God's kingdom program. How can we work for His kingdom if we are so consumed with our own? Spiritual atrophy sets in. We may leave our first love (Jesus) like the Ephesians in Revelation 2:4. Like Demas, we might leave God's work because of our love for this present world (2 Tim 4:9). If we persist in going our own separate way, then after much warning and without any repentance, we will be gathered like a useless branch and burned. This is where it is important for us to remember that the truth of the Upper Room Discourse is primarily about Fellowship, not Relationship. It is not warning us that if we don't get with the program, He will cut us off and send us to burn in hell. Fellowship and communion are in view, not Relationship and union.

b. Loss Tomorrow 6b

But if this burning does not refer to burning in hell, what burning is John talking about? To understand it we should look only briefly at 1 Corinthians 3:12-15:

> Now if anyone builds on this foundation *with* gold, silver, precious stones, wood, hay, straw, each one's work will become clear; for the Day will declare it, because it will be revealed by fire; and the fire will test each one's work, of what sort it is. If anyone's work which he has built on *it* endures, he will receive a reward. If anyone's work is burned, he will suffer loss; but he himself will be saved, yet so as through fire.

Here it says the deeds of the Christian are tried by fire at the Judgment Seat of Christ (2 Cor 5:10; Rom 14:10-12). The fruit of the Spirit will pass through the fire like gold, silver, and precious stones. It will remain forever. But the work of the flesh will be burned up. Like this useless branch in John 15 the useless Christian will be saved (justified), "yet so as through fire." In other words, his place in heaven (salvation) is intact but his fruit does not remain. It's burned up. So, in verse 6 the useless branch which is burned refers to the believer who continuously resists the methods of Heavenly Horticulture. Finally, he's taken away to be burned, not in hell, but in the fire referred to in 1 Corinthians 3.

CONCLUSION

Therefore, the message is: **ABIDE IN CHRIST**. You have an eternal Relationship with Christ if you have received Him as your Savior. This is a matter of Fellowship. If you stay close to Him, production of fruit is automatic. Stick close to the Vine and you have a great purpose. You will be doing what you were chosen to do, not simply go to heaven, but to bear fruit that will remain forever.

Would you like to have a more meaningful life? In 1979 a study was done among teenagers in Sweden, who were asked to respond to the statement, "I think the following could give my life more meaning." Of those surveyed, 87% thought that meaning could be found in a good job; 85% thought it could be found in a marriage partner, and 84% thought it could be found in sports and recreation. Obviously, there is some overlap in these percentages. But only 15% thought that reading the Bible and prayer could help, and another 15% indicated alcohol could help. About 80% considered the question of the meaning of life important, yet 80% considered it unimportant whether Jesus existed as a man on earth or not. Also, 85% considered it unimportant whether Jesus is the Son of God or not. A full 75% concluded that the question of God's existence is unimportant for having a meaningful life.[13] That was forty years ago. In America, we are usually a generation behind Europe. I wonder if the attitudes of Swedish young people forty years ago are about the same as American young people today.

Bob Buford began a ministry to men having mid-life crises. Not all of these men were out buying sports cars and gold chains and having affairs. Many of them were quite successful, traditional, and faithful. But that was just the problem. They had reached all their goals for success but still felt empty. So, Bob showed them how to move from the success of the first half of their lives to significance in the second half of their lives. His ministry? Halftime. To quote him:

> Halftime is a season of life that offers the opportunity to look back on what you have accomplished, understand who you are, and then redirect your time and talent for an even more purposeful Second half. More than 12,000 people turn 50 each day in America. A Harvard MetLife study shows that

---

[13] Jim Peterson, *Living Proof* (Colorado Springs: NavPress, 1989), 35.

more than half of these individuals want more meaning and significance in the second half of their lives.[14]

It was Henry David Thoreau who observed: "Most men live lives of quiet desperation." The internal angst of emptiness can eat away at a man's soul until there is little left except scraps for the vultures of time. Billy Crystal expresses this futility in an old movie called *City Slickers.*

Billy plays the part of a bored baby boomer who sells radio advertising time. One day he visits his son's school to talk about his work along with the other fathers. He suddenly lets loose a deadpan monologue to the bewildered youngsters in the class:

"Value this time in your life, kids, because this is the time in your life when you still have your choices. It goes by fast:

- When you're a teenager, you think you can do anything, and you do.
- Twenties—are a blur.
- Thirties—you raise a family, you make a little money, and think to yourself, "What happened to my twenties?"
- Forties—you grow a little potbelly, and you grow another chin. The music starts to get too loud, and one of your old girlfriends from high school becomes a grandmother.
- Fifties—you have minor surgery-you call it a procedure, but it's surgery.
- Sixties—you will have a major surgery, the music is still loud, but it doesn't matter because you can't hear it anyway.
- Seventies—you and your wife retire to Fort Lauderdale. You start eating dinner at two o'clock in the afternoon,

---

[14] Bob Buford, *Half Time* (Grand Rapids: Zondervan, 2004), 29.

your lunch around ten o'clock, breakfast the night before, spend most of your time wandering around malls looking for the ultimate soft yogurt and muttering, "How come the kids don't call? How come the kids don't call?"

- Eighties—you'll have a major stroke, and you end up babbling with some Jamaican nurse your wife can't stand, but whom you call mama.

Any questions?"

It doesn't have to be that way. When we seek first the kingdom of God and His righteousness (Matt 6:33), instantly our lives find new meaning and purpose. And according to this passage in John 15, the main thing we have to do to fulfill that purpose is to stay close to Jesus. One of my favorite pictures of Jesus is a simple painting I frequently saw when I went door-to-door selling Bibles for the Southwestern Company in Shawnee, Oklahoma, after my first year of college. It showed Jesus as a shepherd in the center of the picture. But what interested me about the picture was not Jesus; it was His sheep. One little lamb was on His lap nuzzling his nose in the palm of the Shepherd. Another one was brushing up besides Jesus' robe. Still others were a few feet away with both their eyes trained upon their beloved Shepherd. But some sheep had turned their heads away from the Shepherd. Still others had followed one green clump of grass after another until they were a long, long way from the Shepherd.

It is these sheep that are in danger. Being short-sighted they can easily fall off a cliff and break a leg. That would make them easy prey for a nearby predator. Only the sheep close to the Shepherd can count on His protection. If God looked down from heaven and wanted to paint you into this picture, where would you be?

Remember: God would rather have a fruit-bearing burro than a bum steer.

"GUESS WHO MOVED"
Luke 15

INTRODUCTION

A bumper sticker on the back of a car read: "If you don't feel close to God, guess who moved." The sticker was right. If I don't feel close to God, I'm the one who has moved, not God. But so often I think the opposite. Somehow, I lose my spiritual ball in the weeds, so I walk around all day looking for God. That closeness I crave is gone, and I can't seem to get it back. What to do? Luke 15 tells us what to do. It reminds me of the instructions on the inflator to my space-saving tire in the trunk of my car. When my spiritual life has a flat tire, and I can't figure out what to do, these instructions help me get my spiritual life rolling again.

The central point of this passage revolves around the tension between Christ and His ever-present harassers, the Pharisees, over how to deal with sinners. The Pharisees were of the opinion that there is great joy in heaven when a sinful Israelite died. He got what was coming to him. According to this view, God loves the righteous man but hates the sinner. That's why they had such a problem with Christ. Jesus received sinful men. He not only accepted them, He ate with them, which indicates He had fellowship with them. Just the name "Pharisee" meant "separatist." Consequently, the God-fearing man should separate himself from sinners. But Christ did not separate Himself; He mixed with sinful men. Who was right? What is God's attitude toward the sinner?

Three parables in Luke 15 are designed to answer that question: the lost sheep, the lost coin and the lost son. Before we get into the three parables, we must define what we mean by the word "lost." Years ago, a preacher friend of mine called and said he was about to preach an evangelistic series on these three parables. He wanted to know what I thought was the best approach to the passage. I responded with three questions. How do you know the sheep was not a sheep? And how do you know the coin was not a coin? And how do you know the son was not a son? It appears to me that the sheep was a sheep, and it was part of a flock of sheep. It doesn't say it was a goat. It appears to me that the coin was a coin and once was on a necklace with a bunch of other coins just like it. There were ten coins, presumably alike. One is lost. (Leon Morris, *An Introduction to the Gospel of Luke*.) Quite often these coins were used to make a necklace or a headpiece. True or not, the lost coin was part of a collection of ten coins. Finally, it appears to me that the son was a son and part of a family just like his older brother. Consequently, I don't think the passage teaches us anything about evangelism. In other words, it's not about Relationship, but it is about Fellowship.

Further support for this view comes from the opening verses of the chapter: "Then all the tax collectors and the sinners drew near to Him to hear Him. And the Pharisees and scribes complained, saying, 'This man receives sinners and eats with them.'" They were okay if Jesus preached to these sinners but eating with them was going too far. Eating in that culture meant fellowship, as it does in many cultures. So, He used these parables to instruct the Pharisees about fellowship.

There is one additional clue that helps us unravel the thrust of the passage. It is the word "repent" and "repentance" (vv. 8 and 10). Although most interpreters associate repentance with coming into right Relationship with God, there is good evidence that repentance is a matter of Fellowship, not Relationship.[15] Just for starters, the reader might consider the fact that the Gospel of John has more to say about how to receive eternal life (Relationship) than any other book in the NT, but it never mentions repentance of man toward God. Not even once. But we know John understands the word for "repentance" or "repent" because in Revelation 2-3 he calls for five of the seven churches to repent. He doesn't question the doctrinal purity of the church at Ephesus. He doesn't question their Relationship with God. He does question their Fellowship with God. They had lost their first love (intimacy, fellowship). How to restore it? Do the "first works," not open the gates of heaven for an eternal Relationship with God (which would be salvation by works), but restore their first love, their fervor for Christ, their intimate Fellowship with Him.

Don't misunderstand and assume we do not believe in repentance. God "commands all men everywhere to repent" (Acts 17:30). "All men" includes believers and unbelievers. Ultimately, God wants more than just a Relationship (Father/Child) with us; He also wants Fellowship with us. Repentance is a requirement for fellowship. I can't knowingly or defiantly practice intentional sin and be in Fellowship with God. I would need to repent, which means the inward resolve to turn from my sins. The actual turning is the fruit of repentance, and the NT uses a different word for this: *epistrephō*, which means "I turn." The former is internal; the latter is externally observable.

In the Luke 15 parable, each of the three—the lost animal, object, or person—was initially in right relationship to the figure representing God. So, Christ was not talking about saved and unsaved, Christian and non-Christian. He was talking about those in fellowship with God and those not in fellowship with God. The hundred sheep were walking with the shepherd–one went astray. The ten coins were equal parts of a necklace–one slipped away. The two sons were home and

---

[15] See an extensive treatment of repentance in David R. Anderson, *Free Grace Soteriology* (Houston: Grace Theology Press, 2018), 125-65.

had the same father—one went away. With this understanding, it is easy to see how Christians could become the lost sheep, the lost coin, or the lost son. Distinguishing between Relationship truth and Fellowship truth is crucial for interpreting and applying the truth of this passage.

So, the Pharisees have in effect challenged Christ. They said "Okay. You claim to be God. But how can God accept unrighteous men as you're doing?" Answer: the lost sheep.

I. THE PARABLE OF THE LOST SHEEP 15:4-7

"What man of you, having a hundred sheep, if he loses one of them, does not leave the ninety-nine in the wilderness, and go after the one which is lost until he finds it? And when he has found *it*, he lays *it* on his shoulders, rejoicing. And when he comes home, he calls together *his* friends and neighbors, saying to them, 'Rejoice with me, for I have found my sheep which was lost!' I say to you that likewise there will be more joy in heaven over one sinner who repents than over ninety-nine just persons who need no repentance.

A. Interpreting the Parable

The key to understanding Christ's point in this parable is understanding sheep. The shepherd's concern centered around the lost sheep. He wasn't worried about those on the right path, but, rather, the one that took the wrong path. So, he retraced his route until he found the bleating sheep. He carried it back to the flock, and all rejoiced. So, our Father in heaven is more concerned over one of His sheep which is going astray than the ninety-nine on the right path. He searches until He finds it and brings it back to the flock. The rejoicing in heaven is great. The point is, God has the loving concern of a shepherd for lost sheep.

B. Applying the Parable

When we commit sins of ignorance, our Father puts on His searchlight in order to find us and bring us home. We may have wandered into a far-off country by some wrongful habit we don't even know about. In His timing, the Holy Spirit will pinpoint the problem, so we can see it and repent. I'm told that in the rare case of a frequent offender, the shepherd may break the leg of a wayward lamb. After making a splint for the lamb, the shepherd would carry that lamb until the leg healed. After the healing was complete, the lamb has learned a valuable lesson: it never wanders far from the shepherd again. Has the Good Shepherd ever had to break your leg in order to deliver you from a particular sin?

But the Pharisees object. They say, "Okay, okay. We see the parallel. But a sheep is an ignorant animal. It has no sense of direction like a dog or cat and is short-sighted. It's easy to see how a sheep could unwittingly stray from the flock as it eats one green clump of grass after another until it suddenly looks up and doesn't know where it is. It got lost out of stupidity, out of ignorance. Many people fall into sin for the same reason. They are ignorant. They don't know any better. Well, we understand how God could still love such men and search them out. But what about sins other than those done in ignorance?" Of course, Christ anticipated their objection. So, He gives us a second parable dealing with a second situation.

II. THE PARABLE OF THE LOST COIN 15:8-10

"Or what woman, having ten silver coins, if she loses one coin, does not light a lamp, sweep the house, and search carefully until she finds *it*? And when she has found *it*, she calls *her* friends and neighbors together, saying, 'Rejoice with me, for I have found the piece which I lost!' Likewise, I say to you, there is joy in the presence of the angels of God over one sinner who repents."

A. Interpreting the Parable

A woman has ten pieces of silver and loses one. The value of the silver pieces was about like a silver dollar in our money today. It's highly doubtful such a diligent search and jubilant rejoicing would go on for a silver dollar. These ten pieces of silver probably made up what is called a semedi, a frontlet worn over the brow of women in the agent world. The frontlet would be like a wedding band to a woman today. Its sentimental value far exceeded its material worth. So, when one coin accidentally came off the chain, the woman swept and sifted through the entire house searching for it.

B. Applying the Parable

So it is that our Father in heaven searches diligently when one of those stamped with His image accidentally falls out of place. And when He restores him to his proper place, there is great rejoicing in heaven. Many children of God get sucked into strongholds of sin without any premeditation on their part. A little girl's father was a pastor. He had four daughters—beautiful little girls. But he abused each one of them. These girls had no idea at the time the future scars they would carry and how they would perpetuate the sin-cycle spinning in their adult lives because of the psychological damage hidden in their hearts. But our Father sees their hearts.

In his book, *Healing for Damaged Emotions*, David Seamands deals with people who have scars nobody else can see. He uses the analogy of those beautiful giant Sequoia and Redwood trees. "In most of those parks," writes Seamands, "the naturalists can show you a cross section of a great tree they have cut and point out that the rings of the tree reveal its developmental history, year by year. Here's the ring that represents a year when there was a terrible drought. Here are a couple of rings from years when there was too much rain. Here's where the tree was struck by lightning. Here are some normal years of growth. This ring shows a forest fire that almost destroyed the tree. Here's another of savage blight and disease. All this lies embedded in

the heart of the tree, representing the autobiography of its growth."
Seamands continues:

> And that's the way it is with us. Beneath the protective bark,
> the concealing, protective mask, are the recorded rings of
> our lives. There are scars of ancient, painful hurts . . . as
> when a little boy rushed downstairs one Christmas dawn and
> discovered in his Christmas stocking an old dirty rock, put
> there to punish him for some trivial boyhood naughtiness.
> That scar has eaten away at him, causing all kinds of
> interpersonal difficulties. And here we see the pressure of a
> painful repressed memory . . . of running after an alcoholic
> father who was about to kill the mother, and then of rushing
> for the butcher knife. Such scars have been buried in pain for
> so long they're causing hurt and rage that are inexplicable.
> In the rings of our thoughts and emotions, the record is
> there; the memories are recorded, and all are live. And they
> directly and deeply affect our concepts, our feelings, our
> relationships. They affect the way we look at life and God, at
> others and ourselves.[16]

These damaged children of God have been the victims, not of
their own willful sins, but the willful sins of others. God has a special
place in His heart for victims. He can see their damaged hearts, and
He desperately wants to bring them home.

But the Pharisees again object. They say, "Okay, okay, we can
understand how God can love and search out one who accidentally
falls into sin. Maybe he knew better, which is more than we can say for
the sheep, but at least his sin wasn't deliberate. We'll have temporary
slips, which, although real, have not been planned or premeditated.

---

[16] David Seamands, *Healing for Damaged Emotions* (Wheaton, IL: Victor
Books, 1981), 12.

And then there are the victims. But look at these people you're eating with. IRS men. They have deliberately become traitors against their own countrymen to enrich Rome and their own pockets. Why, we don't even accept their money in the offering plate, let alone sit down to a meal with them. You can't tell us they're sinning out of ignorance or accidentally. Tell us, then, how does God treat the deliberate sinner?"

III. THE PARABLE OF THE LOST SON   15:11-32

This, then, hits at the very heart of the problem. How can Christ accept these deliberate sinners who have come to Him? Since this is the primary problem, this answer becomes the focus of the chapter. This parable is the longest, which means it is being emphasized. It's the parable of the prodigal son. It really breaks into four parts: 1) the rebellion of the younger son (11-19); 2) the reception of the father (20-24); 3) the reaction of the elder son (25-30); and 4) the rebuttal of the father (31-32).

A. The Rebellion of the Younger Son   11-19

Then He said: "A certain man had two sons. And the younger of them said to *his* father, 'Father, give me the portion of goods that falls *to me*.' So he divided to them *his* livelihood. And not many days after, the younger son gathered all together, journeyed to a far country, and there wasted his possessions with prodigal living. But when he had spent all, there arose a severe famine in that land, and he began to be in want. Then he went and joined himself to a citizen of that country, and he sent him into his fields to feed swine. And he would gladly have filled his stomach with the pods that the swine ate, and no one gave him *anything*.

"But when he came to himself, he said, 'How many of my father's hired servants have bread enough and to spare, and I perish with hunger! I will arise and go to my father, and will say to him, "Father, I have sinned against heaven and before you, and I am no longer worthy to be called your son. Make me like one of your hired servants."'

In the rebellion of the younger son, we see a classic case of the second-born. The first-born child, like the older brother and like Esau, is often one who responds well to authority and is often the more religious. But the second-born fights for acceptance. He wants to prove himself. He wants to make it on his own in the world. He is very competitive. So, the younger brother is unwilling to stay at home and accept the good graces of his father. He takes his inheritance and goes into the world.

Now the father is not legally bound to give him his inheritance. It did not really belong to the son until the death of his father. But the father must have sensed the willful rebellion in his son which must run its course. So, he let him go. He did not try to force him to stay at home. The father let the son exercise his own free will. As such, our Father in heaven will not force us to stay by His side when, by our own free will, we wish to go the way of the world.

But deliberate sin carries its own consequences. Here we see a panorama of degradation as this young son turns from his father by an act of the will. His flesh follows his will just as anyone who turns from God in his mind subsequently fulfills the desires of the flesh. He spends all he has in riotous living. Soon he finds himself in physical need, so he becomes a servant to a citizen of that country. He becomes enslaved to the world.

He is assigned to the most degrading of tasks–he is to feed the pigs. He finally becomes so hungry he wants to eat pig food. From a man of free will to a slave; from a human to a pig. Then and only then did this young son come to himself. He, like Nebuchadnezzar, who had to eat grass like a cow before he came to his senses, realizes that even the servants of his father have a much better life than the servants of the world. So, he decides to return to his father and beg to become one of his hired servants. Likewise, every man who begins to flirt with the world soon becomes its slave.

B. The Reception of the Father   20-24

> "And he arose and came to his father. But when he was still a great way off, his father saw him and had compassion, and ran and fell on his neck and kissed him. And the son said to him, 'Father, I have sinned against heaven and in your sight, and am no longer worthy to be called your son.'
>
> "But the father said to his servants, 'Bring out the best robe and put *it* on him, and put a ring on his hand and sandals on *his* feet. And bring the fatted calf here and kill *it,* and let us eat and be merry; for this my son was dead and is alive again; he was lost and is found.' And they began to be merry.

What was his father doing all this time? Waiting. Patiently waiting. Waiting for his son to come home. Daily his eyes searched the horizon for the lonely silhouette of his son. He knew the world was a stern schoolmaster. He waited. And when this son was a great way off, his father ran to him, embraced him, and had compassion on him. The father did all this even before his son's confession. The fact that he turned homeward spoke for itself. And yet the confession of the son is revealing. Like David, who said, "Against You, You only, have I sinned" (Ps 51:4), the son knew his sin was against God, even though it was seen by his earthly father. And when he came to himself, he saw himself for what he truly was—a weak, sinful person unworthy of his father's favor. But the father's love had no room for personal offenses. He called for all the tokens of sonship—the robe, the ring, the shoes. A fatted calf, perhaps set aside for the time when his son would return, was prepared for a festive celebration.

Thus, Christ has dealt a fatal blow to the attitude of the Pharisees toward their sinning brothers. He handled sins of ignorance with the parable of the lost sheep; accidental sins with the parable of the lost coin; and finally, deliberate, willful sins with the parable of the lost son. Not only did God show His love toward each of these errant animals, objects, or persons, but I think the implication is that God's love increased with the severity of the sin. Think of it. One sheep out of a hundred was recovered. But then one coin out of ten was recovered. But finally, one son out of two was restored. The Pharisees surely thought God's wrath would increase as the seriousness of the sin increased. Instead, it was the intensity of God's love that increased as did the depth of repentance. The man repenting of willful disobedience surely comes with greater contrition of heart than the one guilty of ignorance. The further one has gone from God, the further he must return. The greater the return, the greater the joy in heaven.

C. The Reaction of the Older Brother   25-30

"Now his older son was in the field. And as he came and drew near to the house, he heard music and dancing. So he called one of the servants and asked what these things meant. And he said to him, 'Your brother has come, and because he has received him safe and sound, your father has killed the fatted calf.'

"But he was angry and would not go in. Therefore, his father came out and pleaded with him. So he answered and said to *his* father, 'Lo, these many years I have been serving you; I never transgressed your commandment at any time; and yet you never gave me a young goat, that I might make merry with my friends. But as soon as this son of yours came, who has devoured your livelihood with harlots, you killed the fatted calf for him.'

The Pharisees were like the elder brother. The elder brother blew up at the father's treatment of his wasteful brother. Why? Because he viewed his relationship with his father as one of merits and demerits. He was a son but acting like a servant. "I have served you all these years and never broken your commandments, but a kid was never killed for me. My brother has done all these terrible things and gets a fatted calf. It's just not fair," he says. "I deserved the fatted calf, and my brother deserved nothing." How much the elder brother was tied to the system of works. He did not know what grace was all about.

Brennan Manning, in his gut-wrenching book, *The Ragamuffin Gospel*, writes:

> The gospel of grace continues to scandalize. The legalists, puritans, prophets of doom, and moral crusaders are having a hissy fit over the Pauline teaching of justification by grace through faith. They take umbrage at the freedom of the children of God and dismiss it as licentiousness. They do not want Christianity to help us become whole but to feel wretched under its burden. They seek to intimidate us, to make us afraid, to file through their exclusive pathway of righteousness, and control rather than liberate our lives. Their perverted spirit of legalism would cripple the human spirit and send us sagging under great spools of rules and regulations. The thrilling quality of their dedication—zealotry is always impressive—obscures the fact that they accept the Gospel in theory and deny it in practice.[17]

The greatest tragedy? The elder brothers don't even know who they are. Hint. It is usually someone who hasn't sinned, if you know what I mean.

D. The Rebuttal of the Father   31-32

> "And he said to him, 'Son, you are always with me, and all that I have is yours. It was right that we should make merry and be glad, for your brother was dead and is alive again, and was lost and is found.'"

The father silenced the elder brother with a brief rebuttal: "My son, all I have is yours. Don't act like a slave trying to earn my favor. Just accept the fact you are a son, and all I have is at your

---

[17] Brennan Manning, *The Ragamuffin Gospel* (Colorado Springs, CO: Multnomah Books, 2005), 223-24.

disposal. Don't rob your beleaguered brother of this moment of joy at his return."

And so, Christ tells the Pharisees they have access to all the promises of the covenant relationship they have with God. Why then fall from such grace to a lower system of merits and demerits, a system of works? Such a system breeds comparison, hatred, pride, and false motives for service. But the system of grace breeds acceptance, love, humility, and true motives for service. The Pharisees simply cannot comprehend such a counterintuitive love. They only understand *lex talionis* (an eye for an eye; a tooth for a tooth).

Alan Paton, the great South African writer, tells this story during the days of apartheid ("apartness" in Africaans): A white police lieutenant secretly carried on an affair with a black African woman. This was against the laws of South Africa in every way. Not only was it against the civil law, but in that stern, racist society, it was an abominable sin, an unforgivable sin. The lieutenant was confronted with the charge by his captain. The lieutenant denied the charge, but the evidence was so overwhelming he finally confessed. The captain does what might appear to be a strange thing. He goes to visit the lieutenant's father and tells him about his son's transgression.

The father asked the captain, "Is it true?"

The captain replies, "I fear it is true."

The father insists, "Are you sure?"

The Captain says, "He confessed to me. It's true."

Then there was silence except for the sound of the father's deep breathing. It was like the breathing of some creature in agonizing pain. In the room observing the scene are the lieutenant's mother and his aunt, the father's sister. The father turns to his sister and says, "Bring me the Book." She goes to the bookcase, pulls down the heavy family Bible, takes it to the father, and sets it before him on the table. She wonders what passage he is going to read.

But he doesn't read any passage at all. Instead, he opens the front of the book where the family names have been recorded for 150 years. He takes the pen and ink and crosses out the name of his son, Pieter van Vlaanderen, not once but many times as though to completely obliterate it from the page. Without any anger or despair (at least that anyone can see), without any words, he does the dramatic task. Then he turns to the captain and very humbly asks, "Is there anything more?" The captain knows that this is his cue to leave the house, and he does, offering to the mother any kind of help he might be able to afford. But the father turns abruptly to him and says, "No one in this house will ask for help." So, the captain leaves. Then the father, still sitting at the table, turns to his sister and says, "Lock the door, and bolt it, and bring me the key. The door of our house will never open again." That's the scene. The door is closed forever. The son could never return home.

For some Christians this story presents no problem. The son had sinned. Therefore, he must be punished: *lex talionis*. For these people, it is as if Jesus never told the story of the prodigal son. In the family of God, the prodigal can always come home. The door is never locked. Why? Because Jesus showed us the heart of God. With His own shed blood, He showed us how much God cares about sinners. And He opened the door to forgiveness.

CONCLUSION

What could the Pharisees say? Their entire theology had been ripped to shreds. God loves all sinners, whether their sins are of ignorance, accident, or on purpose, and the rejoicing in heaven grows in intensity as the depth of repentance increases.

Now perhaps someone will object. "I thought all sin is the same in God's eyes," he says. "But you have differentiated between sins of ignorance, accident, and deliberation. Is that valid?" Yes, I think it is. It is true that all sin is equal in God's eyes in one respect. Any sin is enough to condemn us. Any sin is enough to say, "All we like sheep have gone astray." Any sin is enough to say, "All have sinned and fallen short of the glory of God." But it is not true to say sins do not vary in their seriousness. Numbers 15:29-31 makes it clear that God differentiates between unintentional sins and intentional sins. He considers the latter more serious. And He goes further than this.

The OT clearly establishes a table of punishment for different sins. The punishments vary in intensity. The worse the sin, the greater the punishment. For some sins a man was stoned to death; for others he wasn't. This is also true in the New Testament. Certain gross sins are set apart as especially loathsome, and for these, church discipline may be invoked (1 Cor 5:9-13).

This also explains how there will be degrees of suffering for non-Christians in eternity. People have said to me, "You mean my mother, as wonderful a person as she is, will spend eternity away from God the same as Hitler if she does not receive Christ?" Of course, I had to say yes. But there is some recourse in the fact that at the Great White Throne judgment seat (Rev 20:11-13) every unbeliever will be rewarded according to his deeds. That speaks of degrees of punishment. The man of evil deeds will suffer more than the man of good deeds, although both will be separated from God for eternity because they rejected Christ.

Why do I spend time trying to establish categories of sin? Why? Because it impacts the interpretation and application of the entire chapter. For I see God taking a different line of action toward me depending on what type of sin I committed. I see the great line of demarcation running between the unintentional sins of the first two parables and the intentional rebellion of the prodigal son. The emphasis of the first two parables is on the search. The shepherd searches for the sheep until he finds it. The woman searches for the coin until she finds it. But the father does not go out to search for his prodigal son. No–he waits. And if we see our Father in heaven as the primary figure in all three parables, then emphasis in the first two is on the searching father, while the emphasis in the last is on the waiting father. In fact, the prodigal son really isn't a very good name for the third parable. The central figure throughout is the father. His name is mentioned twelve times as he is seen in relation to both the younger and the older son. But the point is, God responds differently according to the sin we have committed. If we have strayed off the right path through our ignorance, like the sheep, or have accidentally slipped off the chain like the coin, He takes one line of action. He starts searching. He searches for us until He finds us and brings us back into fellowship with Himself.

I think all parents have little ditties about their children they love to tell. My mom was no exception. One in which she found particular delight concerned a shopping spree with her rambunctious three-year-old boy. As mom used to tell it, we were in a busy store like Kroger not more than a few minutes before she realized her little bundle of joy was no longer tagging along at her heels. Not overly alarmed, as such disappearing acts were not infrequent on our shopping jaunts, she was sure I would reappear in a moment. But when I failed to materialize after several minutes, she began cruising the aisles in her search. She had scarcely retraced her path more than a couple of sections when a loud, booming voice from the checkout stand halted her search. The strident bellow of her young son filled the store with its mayday call–"Mommy, you are lost; mommy, you are lost." She quickly retrieved me and relieved the other customers of this noisy distraction. Apparently, the store manager found me and set me up on the checkout stand to see if I could spot my mother.

Now, from my point of view there was no doubt about it: mommy was lost, and I was worried. But mommy knew the truth: she wasn't lost; she was searching. It was a little boy who was lost. From then on, she told me always to stay put as soon as I realized she was missing. If I would do that, she assured me she would find me. All I had to do was to sit tight and stay calm. She would find me.

That lesson has benefited me spiritually. For, spiritually speaking, I'm still a child, a child of God. And when I sense my closeness to God is missing, and I don't know why, how easy it is to believe God is lost. Not so; God is not lost; I am. And if I will just calmly stay in one place, He'll find me because He is searching. More than once I've sensed my spiritual lifeboat beginning to sink. It's sprung a leak somewhere, but I don't know where. I search in vain and get more distressed and more discouraged as the boat sinks more and more. This is exactly when I need to relax, sit back, and wait for my heavenly Father to shine His searchlights over the troubled waters until He finds me, picks me up, and together we fix that leak. So it is, when we are spiritually out of it but don't know why. We must not panic. Just wait on the Lord. He promises to keep on searching until He finds us and restores our fellowship.

But if the theme of the first two parables is the "searching father," then the theme of the last parable is the "waiting father." He doesn't search for the prodigal son, does he? Why? Because the sin of the son was not unintentional. It was intentional, deliberate, and premeditated. There's no sense in searching for the prodigal son. If found, he would only flee further and further from his faithful father. No, there's nothing to do but wait.

Now I think there is a real lesson for us here, both in relation to others and with regard to ourselves. With regard to others, many of us know a prodigal son. I'm talking about our Father's spiritual children who have left the happy home of His fellowship. This parable teaches us a very plain truth. The father is not searching; he is waiting and watching. But unfortunately, we set aside this truth and assume we are God's divinely appointed instruments to lead the prodigal child back home. We start searching while God is waiting. No, it's fine for us to search if the sinner has strayed ignorantly from the fold or accidentally fallen into sin. Many times Paul says, "I would not have you to be ignorant, brethren . . ." God would have us dispel ignorance in a tactful way. But this is not recommended in Scripture when the brother has intentionally turned against His Father in heaven. To search for the prodigal son and beg, barter or badger him back to God will only stir up the mud, some of which we may get in our eyes. The Father is waiting. Why don't we? Let's not interfere with God's waiting by our self-appointed searching. With regard to others, then, searching is discouraged.

With regard to ourselves, seeking is encouraged. When I unintentionally sin against God, He sends out His spiritual searchlight to find me, to show me where I went off the path. But when I intentionally turn against Him, He doesn't need to flash His searchlight on my dark path to show me where we parted. I know where. The only thing the Father can do is wait while the consequences of my deliberate sin take their toll and I turn back to Him. But it is precisely at the point when I have been wrestled to the ground by the world, my strength is gone, and I want to say, "Give," that I need to know my Father is waiting. For right at this point, my shame and sense of unworthiness overwhelm me, and I wonder if God wants me back. "Will you take me back? Have I gone too far?" Perhaps I have cursed His very name and dragged His cross in the mud. Will He take me back? Will He accept me? This is when I need to know my Father is waiting. Though I have traveled far from the household of God, He is waiting. He is waiting. Though I have become a slave to this world, He is waiting. Though I wallow in the mud like a pig, He is waiting.

> If your spiritual lifeboat has sprung a leak and you don't know where,
> Then just be calm–God's searchlight will find you there;
> But if your boat has sunk and you know why,
> Then it's time for you to look to the sky.
> How dark the sin, it doesn't matter;
> The Father's waiting, so climb the ladder.
> My Christian friend, is the Father waiting for you?

"KEEP THE OIL BURNING"
Matthew 25:1-13

INTRODUCTION

We have just experienced (2020) the biggest shock wave in the oil patch of the past century. The Saudis decided to flood the market. In a couple of days. the price of oil dropped from around +$35 a barrel to $-37 a barrel. Producers had to pay people to haul their oil away. At the same time, the US stock market experienced its biggest two-day drop in history. Trillions of dollars—gone. The coronavirus just exacerbated the problem as the demand for oil to feed cars and airplanes caused it to drop 30%. We found ourselves in a black hole the dimensions of which are yet to be determined.

But that wasn't the first oil crisis centered in the Middle East. Jesus spoke of just such a crisis in one of His parables. The crisis of this parable, the Parable of the Ten Virgins, only affected a few imaginary bridesmaids, but the truth of this parable could well affect most of the Christian world. However, figuring out just what this truth is presents a daunting task. I don't know of a parable with more divergent interpretations than this one. In fact, after reading ten Bible commentaries, I could not find any two that agreed on interpretation. My interpretation is not something I would go to the wall for, but I do think recognizing the distinction between Relationship truth and Fellowship truth helps. Let's see how.

The story is simple enough. Five of the ten virgins who were to watch for the coming of the bridegroom ran out of oil for their lamps. They found themselves shut out of the celebration. They felt foolish. In a certain way, I know the feeling. Years ago, when I could still play basketball, I was practicing with the high school varsity (the coach was in my church and let me scrimmage with his players). Unfortunately, after trying to block a jump shot, I came down on the shooter's foot and sprained my ankle—badly. A friend took me home, and I immediately iced down the swollen ankle. I sat around feeling sorry for myself but had to get some work done. My office was a converted tool shed behind the house we were renting. Around ten o'clock I told my wife Betty I was going out to the office to work on the bulletin for Sunday and would be back around midnight. I used a broom for a crutch.

While there, a heavy rain flooded the backyard. At midnight I opened the shed's door just in time to see Betty turn out all the lights. It was pitch black. I was using a crutch. About halfway to the house, my crutch hit a soft spot and sank in the mud. I went down with it while emitting a blood-curdling scream. Surely, Betty heard my scream and would come to the rescue. No Betty. So, I crawled through the mud and into the garage. I still couldn't stand up, so I crawled into the house and down the hall toward our bedroom, in the dark.

I think I felt even more foolish than the five virgins who shortly after midnight found themselves shut out of the house with their lights out and no apparent way to get in. My downfall was through carelessness and foolishness. So was theirs. Whereas my foolishness in trying to navigate in complete darkness over wet terrain using a broom for a crutch is obvious, the foolishness of the five virgins is not so obvious.

By the way, such injuries as mine do have their moments of consolation. As I began crawling down the hallway to our bedroom, I was eagerly looking forward to the consoling words and soothing caresses of my tender, compassionate wife. She heard me coming, and as I stepped into the room, she asked, "Did you hear a cat screaming outside as you came in?" I groaned inwardly as I slinked over to my side of the bed to nurse my wounds in silence and self-pity. But back to the parable.

I. THE PARABLE OF THE TEN VIRGINS: ITS EXPLANATION

A. The Setting

This parable is part of the Olivet discourse, which continues all the way through Matthew 25. The discourse concerns the end times, specifically the events immediately preceding and following the second coming of Christ. Beginning in Matthew 24:32 we find a series of parables, or what I like to call a "parabolic parenthesis." It is a parenthesis occurring after the return of Christ to earth and before His judgment of the sheep and goats. These parables answer one of the questions the disciples ask just before He begins the discourse. They wanted to know three things: 1) when would He come back to set up His kingdom; 2) what would be the sign of His coming; and 3) what would be the signs of the end of the age (Matt 24:3)? He then answers those questions in reverse order (a literary technique known as a chiastic construction: a, b, c: c', b', a.'). So, He gives them the signs of the end of the age first (4-28); then He tells them about the sign of His coming (29-31); finally, He is ready to answer the question about "when." "When? I'm not going to tell you when. Only the Father knows that. What I will tell you is what you should be doing while you're waiting for Me to come back." So, in Matthew 24:32-25:30 we have parables telling us what to do while we wait for Him to come back. All of them have a common thread: service. Yes, we are to watch and wait for His return, but that doesn't mean we are to go sit on a hilltop with our rapture robes as the Millerites did on October 22, 1844. No. We are to serve Him. If that is true, it helps interpret the parable. We will learn something about Christian service, not Christian salvation. It comes back to differentiating between Relationship truth and Fellowship truth.

To recap the story, it's a parable about ten virgins who have been chosen to accompany the bridegroom to get his bride. The virgins leave their own homes and go to the home of the bride. There they await the announcement of the bridegroom's arrival. Apparently, he was traveling from some distance. At the announcement of his imminent coming the ten virgins were to take their lamps on poles and lead or escort the bridegroom to the home of the bride where the marriage festivities would take place. The number ten was customary as this was the number required to form a synagogue or to be present at any official, ceremonial, or formal benediction. So, these are what we might call ten bridesmaids. The lamps they carried were usually made of copper. They were round or shaped something like an Aladdin's lamp with the wick coming out one end and a small hole for replenishing the oil supply in the center. The lamps were carried on top of polls.

B. The Situation

All ten virgins left their homes carrying lighted lamps. They went to the home of the bride and waited. But the bridegroom did not come as soon as expected, so they all went to sleep. Then at midnight the call came: "The bridegroom is coming. Go out to meet him." So, they all rose and trimmed their lamps, which meant they took a short wire and knocked off the burnt part of the wick and pulled some fresh wick up from the hole on one end of the lamp.

But then a curious thing happened. The lamps of the five foolish virgins began to go out. The oil containers in these lamps were small. After a time, the oil would burn up and needed replacing. A wise bridesmaid carried extra oil for this purpose. But these five foolish virgins had been careless. They did not count on a delay. They had not brought a reserve vessel of oil with them as the wise virgins had done to replenish the oil supply in their lamps. So, they tried to borrow some from the wise virgins. "Not so," said the wise virgins, "or there won't be enough for us. Go down to the all-night grocery and buy some for yourselves." But while they were gone, the bridegroom came and went into the house of his bride with the five wise virgins and shut the door to begin celebrating. Meanwhile, the foolish virgins returned. Finding themselves left outside in the dark night, they beat on the door, asking to come in. But the master of the house said, "I don't know who you are." Therefore, watch, because you don't know when the Son of Man will return.

C. The Suggestions

This may be the most complex of all the parables. A variety of explanations have been suggested by various expositors. The following are the most popular:

1. **Partial Rapture**—only the spiritual believers will be taken up when Christ comes for His bride. No carnal Christians, that is, believers walking in darkness with known and unconfessed sin in their lives will be raptured. But such a position runs roughshod over many passages of Scripture. The Bible clearly says we're not appointed for "wrath" but for the attainment of salvation. This "wrath" is a reference to the Tribulation as Revelation 6:17, 1 Thessalonians 1:10 and 5:9 indicate. In the classic passage on the rapture (1 Thess 4:13-18) the "dead in Christ" actually precede those who are alive to meet Christ in the air. The phrase "in Christ" refers to those who have been baptized by the Holy Spirit into the body of Christ (1 Cor 12:13). This includes "all" believers without distinction of maturity or spirituality. The Tribulation will be a purging of Israel and unbelieving Gentiles, not the Church.

2. **Loss of salvation**—because they were not faithful. The foolish virgins fell from grace and were excluded from the presence of the Lord. But if that's true, apparently there are some sins not covered by the blood of Christ, and we must live a life of continual good works in order to maintain our salvation.

3. **Baptism of the Holy Spirit**—because some had oil and others didn't. Only those who have the Holy Spirit will be raptured. But this overlooks the fact that all these virgins started out with an initial supply of oil. All their lamps were burning and burning for hours. If the oil represented the Holy Spirit, then they all had the Holy Spirit to begin. Of course, as referenced above (1 Cor 12:13), all believers in the church age receive the baptism of the Holy Spirit. It occurs the moment we believe, just as it did for Cornelius and his family (Acts 10:44-48).

4. **Possessing Christians versus Professing Christians**—the foolish virgins represent those who profess to be believers but have not truly trusted in Christ as their Savior. They are "nominal" Christians, i.e. Christians in name only. However, as pointed out above, if all ten virgins had oil in the beginning, and oil represents the Holy Spirit, then all had the Holy Spirit and would be "sealed for the day of redemption" (Eph 4:30). If they have the Holy Spirit, they are possessors, not merely professors.

D. The Solution

1. **All ten virgins had oil** when they started their service. If oil represents the Holy Spirit, then all ten have the Holy Spirit. Therefore, all ten have been baptized by the Holy Spirit (1 Cor 12:13) and represent genuine Christians (Rom 8:9).

2. **Context**. Just before this parable we see three directives. We should walk with the Lord, watch for the Lord, and work for the Lord. We see one parable dealing with faithful service for the Lord versus unfaithful service. The faithful servant is rewarded, and the evil servant is given his portion among the hypocrites. For him

there's weeping and gnashing of teeth (extreme grief—remember, this is parabolic language). He receives no reward. That is what comes just before the parable of the ten virgins. Both servants represent Christians, but one was rewarded while the other was not.

What follows the parable of the ten virgins? The parable of the talents. Again, it's a parable about working for the Lord, about service. And again, we see servants of the Lord—all believers —two were faithful and received rewards. One was unfaithful and received no reward. So, both before and after the ten virgins we have the Lord's teaching about Christian service in which all the examples possess salvation, but some enter the joy of the Lord and some are left in darkness.

Therefore, we must ask if this approach could hold for the ten virgins. What is the subject? Ten virgins going forth to perform a service for the Lord. So, it is the same subject—service. It is dealing with our present responsibility He has given us while we wait for Him to return. All ten virgins were called into service, and all ten had lamps full of oil initially. So, all ten represent believers, that is, they're saved. So, this fits exactly with what went before and after the parable. And at the end, five of the virgins are enjoying the presence of the Lord and five are not. This is exactly the same as the previous and following parables. Therefore, I submit to you that this parable is another lesson dealing with our work for the Lord and His rewards when He comes. He is expanding on this aspect of faithful service until He comes.

3. But what about the phrase "I do not **know** you"?

    Here, it is important that we remember some of the principles we have learned about parables to answer this. The parable, you recall, teaches truth about only one point, not several. That would be an allegory. So, if this parable is about service, then it's not about salvation. Again, if it teaches truth about Christian service, it doesn't have anything to say about salvation. Some people want to make this parable teach all kinds of things about the Lord's return for his Bride, the Church. Notice the Bride is not mentioned. No, this parable is teaching one main point, not two, or three, or four. And those who were excluded at the end are not shut out of the kingdom of God, but out of the house where rewards are given (Lk 19:15-27; 2 Cor 5:9-10). They do not enter the joy of the Lord. The parable deals with Christian service, not Christian salvation.

This is where understanding how the distinctions between Relationship and Fellowship can play an important role. "I know" = *oida*, which (according to the *Theological Dictionary of the New Testament* I, 69) is quite often a substitute for *egnōka*, which also means "I know." However, it is used in such a way (its perfect tense intensifies the meaning of this stative verb—see 1 Jn 2:3-4 and Jn 14:7) that this knowledge is a deep knowledge, an intensified knowledge, or an intimate knowledge. Hence, He would be saying He is not *close* to them, is not *intimate* with them. This is not a statement of Relationship, but it is a statement of Fellowship. He is not saying He does not have a Relationship with these foolish virgins, but He is saying He is not having Fellowship with them.

II. THE PARABLE OF THE TEN VIRGINS: ITS APPLICATION

Okay. If the sphere of truth is Christian service, what's the point? What is the one main point the parable is trying to communicate? At the end of the parable Christ says, "Watch." Watch what? He is not talking about the signs of Matthew 24 here. He is telling His servants to watch their lamps. Make sure our lamp doesn't run out of oil like these foolish virgins who took no reserves. And what is the oil? It is simply the fuel which keeps the wick burning, which keeps the lights strong. It is that which goes inside the lamp to keep the light of that fire strong. When we run out of oil, the light begins to go out. The point then is simple. We must make sure, we must watch carefully, to see we provide a steady supply of fuel for that fire. Principle:

NO FUEL, NO FIRE; NO FUEL, NO FIRE

At the end Matthew 24 the Lord encouraged them to work for Him while they watch for Him. With the parable of the ten virgins, He also wants them to work for Him while they watch for Him, but He adds a warning. He says don't go headlong into My work carelessly, forgetting to provide plenty of fuel for the fire. If you do, your fire will surely go out, and you will be left in outer darkness, grasping, helplessly crawling toward the house where the rewards are given, empty-handed. I think the songwriter pinned the tail on the donkey when he wrote:

> Give me oil in my lamp,
>> keep me burning.
> Give me oil in my lamp,
>> I pray.
> Give me oil in my lamp,
>> keep me burning.
> Keep me burning to the break of day.

And that's it, my friends. The Lord wants us to keep on burning for Him, keep on as bright lights, beacons of hope in a stormy world until He comes. This is our responsibility—not to let our lamps burn out. But how do we do it? The parable has three suggestions concerning our responsibility to keep our lights burning. Our responsibility is:

1. *INTERNAL.* Oil goes inside the lamp, not outside. That's right. It's internal. Where do we put the oil if we want the wick to burn? Do we just hold the lamp in our hand and put the flask of oil on the shelf hoping the oil molecules drift from the shelf to the lamp? Do we take the oil and spread it all over the outside of the lamp and expect it to burn? No, if the wick in that lamp is ever going to burn, we must put the oil inside the lamp. But how careless we are. We so often are so eager to serve the Lord, or we get so busy doing it, we forget all about our internal responsibility, our inner spiritual life. Without oil, there is an energy crisis. And sure enough, our fire for the Lord begins to grow dim and slowly dies out.

It reminds me of the sheep of Psalm 23:2. "He makes me to lie down in green pastures; he leads me beside the still waters." Sheep are often alarmed by the howl of a wolf. And being skittish animals, they may race back and forth across the pastureland without stopping, slowly depleting all their strength. When that happens, the good shepherd must forcibly make them lie down in green pastures to rest and feed. We're like that. We get so busy that we run to and fro, helter-skelter, until we find the fire burning low. But our parable says, "Don't be foolish; be wise. Watch—pay attention to your inner spiritual life. Check your fuel supply. Don't let your fire burn out."

Burnout is a serious problem in the ministry. I met one minister who was a victim of his own giftedness. He was a great speaker, but that was just the problem. He not only spoke several times a week at his own church, but he received invitations to speak all over America. He told me that for five years when he took time off from the church, he used it to speak at other churches. Finally, it caught up with him. He was trying to minister from an empty lamp, a broken vessel. So, he just quit. He said he would be happy if he never saw a pulpit again for the rest of his life.

So what kind of fuel do we use to keep that fire burning? Of course, there's the fuel of feeding on God's Word, the fuel of prayer and meditation, and the fuel of fellowship with other Christians. They say one log burning by itself soon grows dim, but several burning together make a bright fire. Do you ever have any real Christian fellowship where the sharing goes deep into your experiences with Christ and His Word? That's fuel for the fire. Some of the richest and sweetest times you will have on this earth will be sharing with one another the things of the Lord. It could be with friends from church, a disciple you're making, your children, or your spouse. It is a dimension of living the unbeliever will never know. That's what John wrote about in 1 John 1:3-4. He wanted us to enjoy the fellowship the apostles had with the Father and His Son Jesus Christ. And he said when we experience this, our joy will be full.

But our responsibility is more than just internal. It is also individual.

2. *INDIVIDUAL.* Each individual is responsible for his own fire, his own fuel. When the foolish virgins saw their lights going out, they tried to borrow some oil from the wise virgins, but the wise virgins refused: "Go buy your own," they said. Now, if we didn't understand the parable, we might think these virgins were just a bit stingy. Christianity would teach they should give them not just their coats, but their cloaks also. But that's not the point. The point is that no one else can provide what is our responsibility alone. It's up to us to provide oil for our own fire. We must go buy the oil. Yes, there may be a price today in order to obtain this fuel.

If you have ever done any inductive Bible study, you know there is a price to pay. Most folks don't want to pay the price. They want someone else to do all the work. To them church is like a dairy farm where they can get their milk in neatly dispensed bottles. Obviously, preachers and teachers have a vital part to play in the maturing life of a believer. But the goal of much of their teaching and preaching is to bring their flock to a place in their spiritual lives where they can feed themselves. Too many want to be spoon-fed the rest of their lives. That's okay to start with, but sooner or later a baby learns to feed himself, if he's growing as he should.

Do you want to know if you're a mature, grown-up Christian? It's very simple. Ask yourself this question: have I learned to feed myself? If you can say yes, then that's one indicator that you may be a mature Christian. Some Bible preachers have so mesmerized their followers that they flock day after day to hear their pastor preach, hanging on each word from the preacher's lips as though it were a raindrop of final truth from heaven itself. My friends, those people will always wallow in immaturity until they learn to feed themselves.

You don't have to know Hebrew and Greek to be a workman who does not need to be ashamed, rightly dividing the word of truth (2 Tim 2:15). God did not give us a riddle; He gave us a revelation. He didn't stutter; He spoke. And you don't need a photographic mind to remember a passage once you have studied it for yourself. It is like rewiring an old house with the current left on. You remember every place you make a connection because you get a shock. So, our responsibility is both internal and individual. But our responsibility is more than internal and individual. Our responsibility is also immediate.

3. *IMMEDIATE.* At the end of the parable the five foolish virgins, realizing they have no oil, dash off to get some at the last minute. But the bridegroom comes, and the foolish virgins miss out. They are left in the dark. It is too late to try to replenish their fuel supply at the last minute when they hear the bridegroom has actually come.

I had a college roommate who came to Christ after hearing a message on prophetic events. But his life did not reflect any change of heart. After several months of patiently waiting for him to progress, I asked him what the problem was. I said, "Well, Bobby, if you really believe Christ is coming soon, why don't you get serious about things? Do you really believe these prophetic events will take place?" He replied, "Yes, it looks like they will, but I think I'll just sort of wait around and see. Then, if they do, I'll get serious real fast." Bobby was honest enough to express what lots of people must think.

For if people really, honestly believed Christ is coming soon, I'm convinced they would get serious right now. A lot of folks are just watching as curious bystanders to see if it will all take place. They say to themselves, "Well, I'm going to be in the rapture. Why get all in an uproar? There's nothing to lose." They're forgetting about the careless, foolish attitude of the five virgins who were left standing in the dark while the others were celebrating. Our responsibility is immediate.

The only man who has the right to say that he is justified by grace alone through faith alone and is the man who has left all to follow Christ can't run a car 50,000 miles after the initial supply of oil is used up and then put in some oil after the first symptom that the engine is falling apart. You can't cultivate your devotion for Jesus Christ just before the whole world blows up. The time is now. Our responsibility for providing fuel for the fire, food for our inner spiritual life, is immediate. To wait is too late. So, why wait?

Yes, this parable deals not with salvation, but service. It's not about our Relationship with Christ, but our Fellowship with Christ. It's also a word of warning and personal responsibility. If we would serve in His house, we must first realize it is our responsibility to keep our lamps burning. Our responsibility is **Internal**. In 1 Peter 2:2 we read, "As newborn babes, desire the pure milk of the Word, that you may grow thereby." In Ephesians 3:16 Paul prays for his readers "that He would grant you, according to the riches of His glory, to be strengthened with might through His Spirit in the inner man." And 2 Corinthians 4:16 encourages us: "Therefore, we do not lose heart. Even though our outward man is perishing, yet the inward man is being renewed day by day." If we are to be of any value to Him outwardly, then our inner spiritual life must have plenty of fuel.

Yet our responsibility is also **Individual**. Hebrews 5:12-14a challenges us:

For though by this time you ought to be teachers, you need *someone* to teach you again the first principles of the oracles of God; and you have come to need milk and not solid food.

For everyone who partakes *only* of milk *is* unskilled in the word of righteousness, for he is a babe. But solid food belongs to those who are of full age, *that is,* those who by reason of use have their senses exercised to discern both good and evil.

No one else can adequately supply that fuel; it's up to us.

Finally, our responsibility is **Immediate**. Our passage (Matthew 25:13) concludes: "Watch therefore, for you know neither the day nor the hour in which the Son of Man is coming."

"TRUE SUCCESS"
Philippians 3:1-16

INTRODUCTION

We live in a success-oriented society. Everyone wants to be a success; nobody wants to be a failure. One who is a repeated success develops a healthy self-image and bears a positive attitude toward himself and the world. But the one who is a repeated failure develops an unhealthy self-image and carries a negative attitude toward himself and the world. One's attitude toward himself and the world in very large measure determines the amount of happiness he finds in this life. The man with a negative attitude detests life. The man with a positive attitude enjoys life. And once ingrained, these attitudes seem to be set for life.

Yes, positive and negative attitudes are formed very early in life and are very closely related to the number of successes or failures we experience. If, then, success is so important, it is imperative that we define success. Otherwise, how will we know when we have reached It? John Wooden, arguably the most successful collegiate basketball coach of all time (ten NCAA championships in twelve years), defined success this way: "Success is the peace of mind which is a direct result of self-satisfaction of knowing you did your best to become the best you're capable of becoming."[18] Now that's an interesting definition. The emphasis is not upon comparison with others, the measuring rod most often used by the world, but comparison with oneself. The idea is to do my best to become the best I can be. And although that definition is appealing and contains much truth, it is still inadequate.

What if I set out to become the very best bank robber I am capable of becoming? I might be very successful in my robberies, but would you call my life a success? What if I set out to be the best arsonist or the best assassin or the best drug dealer I'm capable of becoming? Assuming I succeed in reaching these goals, would you label my life a success? I doubt it. You see, success is very much tied to goals. If my life goal is to become the most prolific serial killer of all time, I might reach my goal, but who would call my life a success? Rather, others would label my life a great failure or a great tragedy. So, success is tied to goals, and if goals are so important, it's very important to pick the right goal. That's why I like Earl Nightingale's definition of success. He says: "Success is the progressive realization of a worthy ideal." Notice the word "worthy." Not just any goal brings us the satisfaction of having lived a successful life. It must be a worthy ideal. The most successful man or woman will be the one who progressively realizes the most worthy ideal.

There are many worthy ideals—hundreds. It is a worthy ideal to become a nurse or doctor; a schoolteacher or football coach; a NASA engineer or airline pilot; a housewife or secretary, and so on. But is there one ideal that is the worthiest of all? After all, I only have one life to invest. I can maximize my life by pursuing the worthiest ideal—if possible. So now, in order to determine what true success is and how we can attain it, we must discover what is the worthiest ideal, the highest goal in life. And this is where the Scriptures come in. The most successful life one can live, its worthy ideal and how to get there, is outlined for us in Philippians 3.

---

[18] John Wooden, *They Call Me Coach* (Waco, TX: Word Books, 1973), vii.

In this chapter, we focus on "the prize." As we outlined "A" truth and "B" truth in our chart, there are a number of contrasting but complementary categories that help us understand the Bible. There is truth pertaining to our justification ("A" truth) and truth pertaining to our sanctification ("B" truth); salvation truth versus discipleship truth; relationship truth versus fellowship truth; and many others. One we have not highlighted thus far is the difference between a "gift" and a "prize." As it relates to the title of this book, the "gift" is tied to our Relationship with God. Our Relationship with God is established by His gift of eternal life to all who trust in Jesus Christ as their Savior. But, having given us this incredible gift by His grace, our Lord holds something else before us, something to motivate us to live for Him above and beyond the obvious gratitude we have for One who has given us this gift. That something is the "prize."

Paul speaks about this in 1 Corinthians 9:24-25 when he says: "Do you not know that those who run in a race all run, but one receives the prize? Run in such a way that you may obtain *it*. And everyone who competes *for the prize* is temperate in all things. Now they *do it* to obtain a perishable crown, but we *for* an imperishable *crown*." The word Paul uses for "prize" in this passage is *brabeion*, the word used for the award given to a winner at the Olympic games. That word is used again in Philippians 3:14, its only other use in the NT. Though only employed twice, the word "prize" pictures for us an entire motivational system sanctioned by our Lord (Matt 19:27-30). We call it "rewards." Although our works can do nothing to open the gates of heaven for us (Jesus paid it all), we were created to live a life of good works, which our Lord promises to reward when He comes to review what kind of return He will get from His investment in our lives (1 Cor 3:12-15; Matt 25:14-30).

These rewards are an extension of our Fellowship with Christ. In fact, one of the primary rewards offered in Scripture is a deeper intimacy/fellowship with Christ in the next life in proportion to the intimacy/fellowship we experience with Him in this life (see the rewards promised to the "overcomers" in Revelation 2-3 and how they progressively get closer to the Savior). So, to gain an appreciation for the "prize," let's look at Philippians 3:1-16, one of two passages in the NT that mentions this prize.

The subject of Philippians is Selflessness. This is Paul's emphasis from beginning to end. The first two chapters deal with the Principle of Selflessness, while the last two deal with the Practice of Selflessness. In chapter 3 the Holy Spirit through Paul tells us what true success really is. And, friends, I can't tell you how much this passage has meant in my life. In fact, I say to you without any reservation, the balance of your life will be measured by how well you understand and apply this passage. In these final two chapters, Paul applies the principle of selflessness to three problems in the church: the Legalists, the Libertines, and the Ladies. He faces the legalists in the first sixteen verses. These verses fall neatly into three parts: False Success by the Flesh (1-6); True Success by Faith (7-11); Future Success (12-16).

I. FALSE SUCCESS BY THE FLESH   3:1-6

> Finally, my brethren, rejoice in the Lord. For me to write the same things to you *is* not tedious, but for you *it is* safe. [2] Beware of dogs, beware of evil workers, beware of the mutilation! [3] For we are the circumcision, who worship God in the Spirit, rejoice in Christ Jesus, and have no confidence in the flesh, [4] though I also might have confidence in the flesh. If anyone else thinks he may have confidence in the flesh, I more so: [5] circumcised the eighth day, of the stock of Israel, *of* the tribe of Benjamin, a Hebrew of the Hebrews; concerning the law, a Pharisee; [6] concerning zeal, persecuting the church; concerning the righteousness which is in the law, blameless.

The opening verses are essentially a warning. Paul wants to safeguard his flock from the false philosophy of the world. His words will prove to be a spiritual safeguard for the Philippian Christians. His warning is to beware of dogs, beware of evil workers, beware of the concision. These are three wordplays in that the Jews thought of the Gentiles as dogs, evil workers, and uncircumcised. Paul turns the table on them and claims they are the dogs, the evil workers, and their circumcision is just self-mutilation of the flesh. Paul wants his readers to beware of the Jews who would enter the assembly and pervert the Christian life of the church by telling the new converts they must be circumcised and keep the law of Moses to be successful in the Christian life.

These false teachers put their confidence in the flesh. Three times in these six verses Paul mentions "confidence in the flesh." That repetition helps us focus on his main point: fleshly accomplishments are not true success. Let's say a little more about what we mean by "true" success. Are we saying it is wrong to succeed in our secular jobs? Would it be better to get fired or just fail? Is it wrong to enter college and successfully earn a degree that might lead to a career? Should we flunk out instead? Of course not. We all want to succeed in our life endeavors. No couple stands at the altar in their right minds and plans for a divorce. They envision marital bliss and happiness ever after. No, by true success versus false success we are contrasting the things of our lives that will have an eternal impact as opposed to those that will not. And, of course, there could be some overlap (a person who uses his career to further God's kingdom). I could be a successful heart surgeon and it could be false success by the definition we are using here, or it could be true success if I am able to use my success in surgery to glorify God and contribute to His eternal kingdom. Our successes by the flesh will perish with the flesh; our successes by faith will live on for eternity. "Do not be deceived, God is not mocked; for whatever a man sows, that he will also reap. For he who sows to his flesh will of the flesh reap corruption, but he who sows to the Spirit will of the Spirit reap everlasting life" (Gal 6:7-8). But, back to Philippians.

The false teachers were impressed by family backgrounds, degrees of higher learning, and religious affiliations. Paul says if you want to begin boasting about success in terms of this world, he has been more successful than any of the Jews attacking his congregation. To prove his point he says, "I am a Hebrew of Hebrews." He builds a mountain of pride here with physical characteristics on one side and spiritual accomplishments on the other. "Hebrew of Hebrews" would be right at the top of the mountain. The point is, if success is to be measured in terms of the accomplishments of the flesh, then he is more successful than any of the troublemakers.

But, warns the Holy Spirit, achievements in the flesh are not true success. They are false success. And Paul strictly warns this flock against measuring their life success in terms of the measuring rods of his day. Though these signs of success in Paul's day don't exactly jump out at us as impressive today, they certainly did in his time. Today it would be like saying, "Well, I did Tim Tebow one better in that I won two Heisman Trophies. And did I mention I made my first million in my dorm room while still in college. Then there was my Rhodes scholarship . . ." I think you get the idea.

In our culture, we measure children by four primary things: how smart they are, how good-looking they are, how athletic they are, and how popular they are. Not too far into first grade Johnny knows if he is in the Blue Bird reading group of the Red Bird reading group. Is he chosen first on the kickball team or last? Does he have lots of friends, or is Johnny a loner? His self-image is usually established by age six. But I ask: Is this a fair system? I feel especially sorry for those born with intellectual disabilities. I think of two status-conscious parents whose newborn baby was hopelessly disabled. Both parents were highly educated. Both were professors in well-known colleges. The mother obtained the finest prenatal care. The baby was born in one of the most up-to-date children's hospitals in the world–it served as a training center in pediatrics for a large university medical school. What better place to get started in life?

When the baby was born, it was immediately apparent he suffered from Down's syndrome. The etiology is partially known: apparently, a genetic malfunction causes the child to inherit an extra chromosome. As the problem was explained to the parents, both initially acted as if they were completely in control of the experience. The husband calmly made arrangements to have the child placed in an institution. Against the advice of doctors, they refused to take the child home with them. But their cool control soon turned to bitterness and hate. This couple became more enraged at the hospital, at the doctors, at life, and at God. What sense, after all, did it make to allow a disabled child to be born to them– intelligent, educated people whose reputations could only suffer from having a handicapped kid around?

So, they put their handicapped child in an institution. But within two months they were trying to get him back. Why? Because they had rejected their own offspring, and the guilt was overwhelming. These parents were caught in a bind. On the one hand, they measured success in terms of status and academic achievement, and they felt unable to tolerate the questions that would be raised by the presence of a disabled child. Surely, a disabled child would cast aspersions on their intellectual superiority. They were painfully torn between the need to maintain their status and need to reduce their guilt. Finally, overwhelmed by guilt, they brought him home.

Their mode of child-rearing was pitiful. Afraid to show him to the world, they hid him at home during the early years. Few people knew they had a disabled child, whom they denied any chance for personal or social development. Bitterness and hostility dominated the parents' lives. Repeatedly they asked, "Why is life so unfair to us and to this child?"

It is clear that if success comes chiefly through achievement, then the present standard is unfair to most people. Since many cannot measure up, this criterion becomes oppressive. But even those who do measure up more often than not don't seem to find fulfillment. I was called to our local hospital to visit a pregnant woman who asked for a minister. She introduced me to her husband. He looked emaciated, unshaven, wearing a T-shirt, shorts, and sandals. He introduced himself as Dr. David Hartman. It turns out he had been a professor at Rice University, my alma mater, for about ten years before he quit. He complained of the emptiness he found in pursuing an academic career. I asked him what he does now. He said he just walks the beaches in Galveston and collects driftwood. Fortunately, both of them found a new purpose in life when they trusted in Christ and began working for His kingdom. Dr. Hartman went back into academics but at a Christian institution, LeTourneau University, in Longview, Texas.

You see, my friends, Paul's warning here is similar to his words in Romans 12:2 where he says we are not to be conformed to this world. We're not to let the world squeeze us into its mold. I must confess, I spent twenty years of my life letting the world system do just that. I counted success by my achievements according to the flesh and had done well. But suddenly I realized while still in college the success I sought was a ruse, an ironic deception. For, after all, what does it profit a man if he gains the whole world but loses his own life (Matt 16:26)? A paraphrase would be, "What does it profit a man if he succeeds in gaining the whole world, but never finds and fulfills his purpose in life?" I could become the very best lawyer or doctor or professor or businessman but be a total failure. In fact, I read in the paper just last week the suicide rate among physicians averages twice that of the population as a whole. False success is never fulfilling, and Paul warns us against it.

II. TRUE SUCCESS BY FAITH 3:7-11

[7] But what things were gain to me, these I have counted loss for Christ. [8] Yet indeed I also count all things loss for the excellence of the knowledge of Christ Jesus my Lord, for whom I have suffered the loss of all things, and count them as rubbish, that I may gain Christ [9] and be found in Him, not having my own righteousness, which *is* from the law, but that which *is* through faith in Christ, the righteousness which is from God by faith; [10] that I may know Him and the power of His resurrection, and the fellowship of His sufferings, being conformed to His death, [11] if, by any means, I may attain to the resurrection from the dead.

In verses 7-11 the Holy Spirit tells us what true success is. Paul completely discards any success he's had according to the standards of the world, the achievements of the flesh. He says they're worthless.

He looks at them like garbage, refuse, something to be thrown to the dogs. Rather, he claims the true standard of success is not by the flesh, but by faith. This is a standard that is fair to everyone. Anyone can have faith in the Lord, but not just anyone can be first in his class or captain of the football team or homecoming queen. True success can be attained by anyone willing to trust in the Lord rather than trusting in self.

Paul actually makes the case that accomplishments of the flesh can be a hindrance to true success. The word for "loss" in vss. 7 and 8 is *zēmia*, which can mean "loss," but it can also mean "disadvantage" (BDAG). Sometimes not having those things can be an advantage when it comes to true success. My firstborn is the one who really taught me this verse. Jimmy was born during my second year of seminary. Everything seemed normal until he began to walk. We were living in the seminary ghettos, some low-rent apartments with only an empty parking lot during the day for a playground. Then Betty and I noticed if Jimmy fell down, he would get up, go find the nearest kid and push him or her down. In his mind, if he had fallen down, then someone must've pushed him. Betty, the eldest of six sisters, told me something was wrong. "Wrong?" I asked incredulously. "Something wrong with my boy? Oh, man, the kid's a born linebacker. You watch."

But Betty was right. At age five we had Jimmy diagnosed by a reputable neurologist. She pointed out a number of neurological difficulties. For example, Jimmy could hop on his left foot but not his right. My best sport growing up was baseball. I longed to teach Jimmy how to throw and catch and hit a baseball. But when I tossed him the ball from just four feet away, he couldn't catch it. And when he tried to throw it to me, he would hit his foot. I also wanted to share some things I learned from books with Jimmy, but his eyes wouldn't go across the page, so he had trouble learning to read.

When Jimmy was six years old, he told me he wanted to play T-ball. I thought to myself, "Well, the ball is not moving, just sitting on a rubber pole at home plate, so maybe he can do that." There were twenty-seven kids on the team, but my son was the worst one. I watched practice one day, and his coach, who had been a professional football player, was making fun of him. He couldn't understand a kid with some gross motor issues. I can feel the anger that welled up within me even now. Though I was a pastor, I wanted to jump the fence and slit the guy's throat so fast he wouldn't know until he sneezed. But being the reflective sort, I could see the headlines of the *Conroe Courier* the next day: "Pastor Kills Football Hero at T-Ball Practice." I also noticed that he was bigger and stronger than I was. How much worse the headlines might read if they said this: "Football Hero Kills Pastor at T-Ball Practice." So, I swallowed my anger.

Jimmy walked up to me with his blond hair and big blue eyes. He was crying and said, "Daddy, why can't I do it?" Frankly, I didn't know what to tell him. With difficulty I said, "Well, Jimmy, God made some people good at some things and other people good at other things." With tears dripping down he looked at his feet, then looked back up to me, and said, "But, daddy, God didn't make me good at anything." It was like a knife to my heart. I still tear up as I write these words.

But of our four children, all of whom have trusted Christ as their Savior as far as we can tell, Jimmy displayed the earliest hunger for spiritual things. One night, Betty and I were sitting on the living room couch of the small home we were renting for $125 a month, and we heard Jimmy in his bedroom rocking back and forth on all fours while he hit his head against the wall. As he did so, he kept repeating, "I want a white heart . . . I want a white heart . . . I want a white heart." He had seen a flannel graph presentation of the gospel given at a Good News Bible Club (Child Evangelism Fellowship). Betty and I looked at each other and said, "He's only three years old; that's too young." But he wouldn't stop hitting his head, and he was making a hole in the sheet rock, so we decided to go talk to him.

"Jimmy, why do you want a white heart?" "Because mine is black." "Why is your heart black?" "Because of my sin." "How have you sinned?" "I pulled Christie's (his little sister) hair." "What do you think will make your heart white?" "The blood of Jesus. You are a preacher and you don't know this?" (Just kidding on that last statement.) Betty and I looked at each other again and said, "Well, who are we to say he's too young." Jimmy received Christ that night and was never the same. His neurological difficulties were still there, but it seemed like he had a direct line to heaven.

I remember when Jimmy was five, we were driving one evening to a local lake. He pointed up to the full moon and asked, "Dad, do you see that moon?" "Yes, son, I see it." "That's God's eye; He's watching you." Whoa. So, I slowed down—divine radar in the sky, you know. Jimmy showed me that some of the things we count so dear can be a disadvantage when it comes to knowing Christ. Are you good-looking? Get over it. That could be your stumbling block when it comes to trusting Christ. Are you a good athlete? Get over it. That could be your stumbling block when it comes to knowing Christ. Are you intelligent? Get over it. That could be your stumbling block when it comes to growing as a Christian. Are you rich? Get over it. It's not that there is anything wrong with being rich or good-looking or smart or athletic. God probably gave most of those things to you when you were born physically.

Our problem is that we enter this world with such an extreme sense of insecurity and insignificance that we grab onto anything of the flesh we are good at, and that becomes our source of security or significance or both. It helps take away our inner pain. We must do what Paul did and throw those things on the scrap heap (the word for "rubbish" is *skubala*, which literally means manure) in order to find our security and significance in Christ (see the book of Romans, all of which is about finding our security and significance in Christ: Security [Rom 1-11]; Significance [Rom 12-16]). The "disadvantaged" people like my son actually have some advantages when it comes to knowing Christ. They needn't get over things of the flesh in order to trust Him.

In verses 10 and 11 Paul outlines the goal of true success. Here is the measuring rod of faith. And what Paul lays before us is total conformity to the life of Jesus Christ. At the one-inch mark on the yardstick of faith is to know Him, to have a saving experience with Christ. Paul does not want to be found with his own human righteousness that came from his keeping of the Law, but the true divine righteousness that comes from faith in Christ.

But there are many people sitting in church who have received Christ as Savior but not advanced in their walk beyond babyhood. They're still in their cribs, in their baby clothes and sucking on the milk bottles. To reach the one-foot line on our yardstick of success we must experience the power of His resurrection. That requires even more faith than believing in His death on the cross to pay for our sins. That means allowing the Holy Spirit to use that resurrection power to deliver us from the power of sin (Romans 5-8), not just the penalty of sin (Romans 4). Each advance on the yardstick of true success requires more faith than the last.

At the two-foot mark on our yardstick of true success is to share in His sufferings. That's where spiritual growth stops for many Christians. When we heard the gospel, we were thrilled at the prospect of living forever (Jn 3:16). But if we thought this ticket to heaven would exempt us from the trials and tribulations of this earth, we had a rude awakening in store. James 1:2 tells us to rejoice **when** various trials come our way, not **if** they come our way. To persist after the disease or financial loss or loss of a loved one knocks on our door requires the endurance born of a greater faith than our initial saving faith. In fact, to the one who desires true success in this life, suffering is a privilege (Phil 1:29 and 2 Thess 1:11) and a joy.

The three-foot mark on the yardstick of faith is the hardest of all. It is to die for Him. This is Paul's very desire. He not only wanted to live for Christ, he wanted to die for Him. He wanted to be so closely conformed to the life Christ lived, he actually wanted the privilege of dying as Christ did and then being raised from the dead as Christ was. Phil 3:11 indicates he might not be raised from the dead. Theologians have wrestled with what this could possibly mean. Did Paul lack assurance of his salvation? Did he wonder if he was truly born-again and would go to heaven when he died? No. This is where one's eschatology is important.

You see, Paul lived every moment in light of Christ's imminent return. In other words, Paul believed Jesus could return at any moment. According to Paul, seven years before His actual, visible return to the earth Christ would come for His Church and rapture them to meet Him in the air. But if Paul were raptured, he could never take the ultimate step of faith–to die for his Savior. You remember, it was Saul of Tarsus who was trying to eliminate the early church. He supervised the stoning of the first martyr, Stephen. In so doing, he saw something of a reenactment of Christ's own death. He even heard Stephen asking God not to lay this sin of killing him to their account (Acts 7:60), just as Jesus had said, "Father, forgive them for they know not what they do." Now, that was Christlikeness all the way. Paul thought the greatest privilege he could experience would be to die for his Savior. If he were raptured, that could never happen.

We certainly are not saying you aren't a true success if you don't die for Christ. However, if I were a missionary in Iraq and Isis knocked on my door and asked if I were a Christian, I would like to say that by the power of the Spirit I would say yes. However, knowing that they would kill me if I did not renounce Christ, confessing Him as my Savior would be the biggest step of faith in my whole life. So, when it comes to the yardstick of faith we begin with spiritual birth and end with physical death. The first step of true success is trusting Christ as our Savior. But what is this yardstick, really? It's total conformity to the life of Christ. And that is the most worthy ideal we've been discussing.

To understand this, my friends, is to have a basis for every major decision in life. When facing any major decision, I ask myself, "Will this make me a more godly person? Will this make me more like Christ?" If the answer is no, then I say no to the decision. This yardstick of faith can change your life.

So, we have learned what false success is in verses 1-6 and we have learned what true success is in verses 7-11. But how do we get there? Verses 12-16 discuss the pursuit of true success.

III. FUTURE SUCCESS   3:12-16

¹²Not that I have already attained, or am already perfected; but I press on, that I may lay hold of that for which Christ Jesus has also laid hold of me. ¹³Brethren, I do not count myself to have apprehended; but one thing *I do,* forgetting those things which are behind and reaching forward to those things which are ahead, ¹⁴I press toward the goal for the prize of the upward call of God in Christ Jesus. ¹⁵Therefore let us, as many as are mature, have this mind; and if in anything you think otherwise, God will reveal even this to you. ¹⁶Nevertheless, to *the degree* that we have already attained, let us walk by the same rule, let us be of the same mind.

Paul does not claim to have arrived in the Christian walk. Remember our definition of success: the progressive realization of a worthy ideal. The most worthy ideal, the highest goal for the Christian, is total conformity to the image of Jesus Christ (Rom 8:29). But that worthy ideal is reached progressively. Paul says he is still in pursuit, still following this goal. He wants to apprehend or attain this goal, because it is for this very reason God has attained or apprehended or taken hold of Paul. God did not lay hold of Paul to get him to heaven when he died. He laid hold of him so he could become like His Son. Of course, becoming like His Son includes living like His Son. So, Paul doesn't think of himself as having reached the goal, but he forgets the past and reaches toward the future. He reaches for the mark, the goal, for the prize of the high calling in Christ. He doesn't beat himself over the head with the past. He doesn't dwell on past mistakes, something that could short-circuit his progress. He will not let guilt over his past life before conversion or after conversion get him down. He fixes his eyes on the goal.

A racetrack is in view here in the Greek Olympiad. The word "rule" (v. 16) was the Greek term for the lane markers around the track. The runners are all looking to the finish line. The finish line, the goal line, is conformity to the image of Christ. And a prize, a token of true success, awaits those who have responded to this high calling. These runners don't look back in the race. They keep their eyes on the goal. And this is the race we should all be running if we know Christ. If you are a mature Christian, then you will recognize this as your goal in life. If you have not yet known this, may God reveal it to you. Nevertheless, wherever we are on the racetrack, to whatever point of maturity we have attained, we should all be running the same race, be running by the same rule, having the same goal in mind.

There are some textual differences in the original Greek in verse 16. The text most modern translations use (the Nestle-Aland) leaves out four words included in the Majority Text (which I prefer because it reflects 98% of existing manuscripts of the NT).[19] Here are the words left out: κανονι το αυτο φρονειν. The first word (κανονι) is the word from which we get "canon," as in the canon of Scripture and translated "rule" in the NKJ. As previously mentioned, it was used as the lane markers around the track. Such markers are used today and can be seen in any race between 200m and 800m which would include a bend in the track (two 180-degree bends for an oval 400m track). These lane

---

[19] Textual criticism (the discussion of the Greek text that most accurately reflects the autograph, the original copy) is a discipline unto itself. Those who believe the oldest manuscripts we have will most accurately reflect the autograph follow the Nestle-Aland text and give precedence to the manuscripts discovered in Egypt, which are, on average, the oldest. Others, who hold to the statistical argument that through the process of copying (with the twelve different types of errors made by the scribes) the errors will always go into isolation, prefer the textual tradition that reflects the overwhelming majority of our manuscripts (5,400 and counting). Although these differences affect only about 5% of the entire text and no major doctrine, there are times, such as here in Philippians 3, where our exposition of the text is affected.

markers are used so they can stagger the runners to make up for the longer distance run by people in the outside lanes. There needed to be an adjustment for them so everyone was running the same distance. But if you ran outside your lane, you were disqualified. If you didn't follow any of that, not to worry. Use of this word just reemphasizes the picture of a race Paul is painting.

The last three words simply ask his readers to have the same attitude. The word (φρονειν) means "attitude." It is the keyword for the whole book—ten uses in this four-chapter book and found in every major section of the book. The attitude Paul calls for is the one best exemplified by Jesus in 2:5-11. It was an attitude of "selflessness." That attitude can cure the Legalists (3:1-16), the Libertines (17-21) and the Ladies (4:1-9). Paul wants all of his readers to have the same (το αυτο) attitude of selflessness.

So, what is True Success? It is progressively becoming more like Jesus as we march through life. It is an equal opportunity system. The goal is wide open for anyone who is not intellectually handicapped (and God has a purpose for them—Exodus 4). But I have heard objections to this. "I can't pursue that goal." "Why not?" "Because along the way I have messed up—royally. I can never become like Christ now because I have done . . . or . . . or . . ." I'm disqualified.

Oh, no you are not! Do you love Jesus? Do you currently want to become more like Him? Romans 8:28 says God can work ALL things together for good to those who love God. The "all things" even includes your sins and failures. Don't ask me how, but our God is so great and so sovereign that He can incorporate our sins into His desire for our good and His glory. After all, what put Jesus on the cross? Wasn't it your sins and mine, and the sins of the whole human race? Did good come out of His crucifixion? Your sins and mine, which were future with regard to the time when He died, were included in that payment He made to keep us from hell. In a way only you may understand, He can actually use your sins to make you more like His Son. But that is another discussion.

In 1981 Col. Heath Bottomly gave a commencement address at Dallas Seminary. He was present at the last recorded speech of Sir Winston Churchill. The speech was given in 1959 at Sandhurst, Churchill's alma mater. At 5 PM the cadets marched onto the grass tennis courts and sat in their chairs. They looked sharp in their pristine, perfectly pressed military uniforms. The parents who came dressed for the occasion: the men in their military uniforms if they were veterans and the women with their formal gowns and frilly parasols to deflect the sun. At 5:10 an old Bentley drove onto the campus and made its way to the tennis courts. A rear door opened, and out stepped Sir Winston. The old warhorse trudged up to the battery of microphones and indulged in a pregnant pause. No one thought it necessary to introduce him, so with his steely gaze he looked out at the cadets and said,

"Never give up . . . never give up . . . neeever, neeever give up."

Then there was silence.

Bottomly had one of those parasols blocking his view, so he leaned around it to get a glimpse at an empty podium. His eyes raced over to the Bentley just in time to see Sir Winston slip into the rear seat and close the door. The Bentley slipped off into the evening. Bottomly looked at the old bell tower that housed the campus clock and saw the big hand very deliberately click: 5:18. Sir Winston had come . . . he had spoken . . . and he had left. But his words hung in the crisp air: NEVER, NEVER GIVE UP.

Scripture says, "The just man falls seven times, but he rises up" (Prov 24:16). Jesus will never give up on us (2 Tim 2:13); let's not give up on Him.

CONCLUSION

Bruce Waltke is an OT scholar the Lord used to draw me, or call me, if you will, into full-time ministry. I was at a Campus Crusade for Christ retreat (CRU today) in Wimberly, TX. I was a young, brash, overly confident and quite immature Christian. It was my first Christian retreat. I looked forward to getting to know some "cool" Christians. When the speaker for the retreat was introduced, I almost sank in my chair. He was the opposite of cool: very thick glasses, balding, New Jersey accent. I thought, "Oh, boy. What have I gotten into here?"

But to this day I remember every message Dr. Waltke gave. Riveting doesn't do them justice; spellbinding, maybe. Convicting, certainly. In his last message, he gave an illustration I'll never forget. He said some friends of his took their eight-year-old son on a trip to explore for the tourmaline crystal, something often found in old stone quarries in Maine and California. It was a semi-precious gem worth $500 per carat on average. After spending most of the day without success, they were about to give up when the setting sun produced a gleam from just under the surface of the water on a steppingstone. The boy's mother stooped down, and yes; she could see the crystal protruding from the side of the rock she was standing on.

Excitedly, she bent down and used her pick to slowly pry the gem loose. If it fell into the water-filled quarry, it was gone. She called her young son out and gave him the gem. She told him to go back to the car and put it in the box they had optimistically brought in case they found something. On the way back to the edge of the quarry the little boy was very careful not to fall into the water or drop the gem. But then he saw a frog perched on another rock in the lake and threw the gem at the frog. Skip . . . skip . . . sink . . . gone. You see, the little boy was just too young and immature to recognize the value of the gem he was holding.

Just as we long for our physical children to grow up so they can exchange the toys and video games of life for something of eternal value, God must long for His children to come to an appreciation of what it means to hold fast to His Son and become more like Him. That's True Success. So often we are too immature to recognize the gem we are holding. Jesus is the gem, the cornerstone on which to build a life of true success. He is the "living stone, rejected indeed by men, but chosen by God *and* precious" (1 Pet 2:4). Too often we chase after the cupie dolls of success, the trinkets of this world with all their glitter and allure. Let's grow up. Let's not throw away the most valuable gem we will ever have. Let's not hold onto the Gift and throw away the Prize.

"THE FOUR LAWS OF SPIRITUAL ACCOUNTING"

Matthew 25:14-30

INTRODUCTION

Most Men are unhappy when they're not working, meaning working for a living. Many studies have shown that men who retire at age sixty-five to rest in their nest with the best in the West die within five years. Work gives purpose, meaning, and fulfillment to many. No wonder young people take so many aptitude tests to learn their abilities and potential skills. From the cradle to college the perennial question is, "What do you want to be when you grow up?" This is all well and good, but in the process of settling this seemingly all-important question of "what am I going to be when I grow up?", a far more important question has been overlooked. It is the question, "How am I going to serve God when I grow up?"

It is interesting, isn't it, that the Bible, the guidebook for life, gives little if any counsel as to what professional niche in society we should fill. But it provides significant counsel on helping us find our proper role in serving God in this life. And isn't it interesting that when it comes time for us to give an account of our days on this earth, we have no record that anyone will be asked about his contribution to his profession, but only about his or her contribution to the kingdom of God? God won't ask us how many promotions we got, how many civic awards we received, if we helped our husbands get ahead, or what level of income we achieved. This doesn't mean our professions and how we conduct ourselves on the job are not important. In fact, our place of work can be a platform to contribute to His kingdom in a variety of ways, even if we do no more than an honest day's work to provide for our family. God tells us to do that, whether we are a homemaker or out in the marketplace as a businessman or businesswoman.

But there is a question we will be asked that is often overlooked in many if not most pulpits. It is simply this: "What did you do with the spiritual gifts and opportunities you were given to contribute to the eternal kingdom?" Unfortunately, for most of us, the world today is the main thought; the world tomorrow is an afterthought, something to be considered only as a side issue. But, my friends, I'd like to suggest our contribution to God's kingdom is not a side issue—something to work on if we have time. No, it's the key issue. In light of that, we want to consider a passage on accountability when Christ returns. In fact, I want to introduce you to the "Four Spiritual Laws of Accountability."

To properly interpret this passage, we need to remember our categories of "A" truth and "B" truth:

"A" TRUTH	"B" TRUTH
RELATIONSHIP	FELLOWSHIP
POSITION	CONDITION
JUSTIFICATION	SANCTIFICATION
SALVATION	DISCIPLESHIP
INDWELT BY THE SPIRIT	LED BY THE SPIRIT
ETERNAL	TEMPORARY
SEALED BY THE SPIRIT	FRUIT OF THE SPIRIT
SUB. DEATH OF CHRIST	SUB. LIFE OF CHRIST
GIFT	PRIZE
ACCEPTANCE	APPROVAL

Matthew 25:14-30 is a great lesson to help us distinguish the difference between Acceptance and Approval. In fact, I would go so far as to say that if we don't make this distinction, we may become hopelessly confused by this parable, another parable that appears we have to win God's acceptance by our faithful service (works).

The difference between Acceptance and Approval should be easy for anyone to understand who has been a parent. The typical child desperately wants to be loved by his parents. Unfortunately, too many parents leave their children the impression that they must perform well in order to win their love. These children often feel they never do well enough to win that love. Consequently, they may go through life looking for love in all the wrong places. They never find the security they're seeking.

Wise are the parents who make it clear to their children that their love for them is completely unconditional. That's one of the benefits of being part of a family. As far as we can tell, Jeffrey Dahmer's (the infamous mass-murderer) father was a Christian. He could do nothing but abhor the unspeakable crimes of his cannibalistic son, but he still loved him. Even in prison, he loved him. As a member of the family, Jeffrey had his father's Acceptance. But he did not have his Approval. Acceptance is automatic; Approval is earned. Acceptance is a gift; Approval is a reward. The children who often perform best are those who know they have their parents' love and Acceptance even if they don't perform well.

Our parable is about Approval, not Acceptance. It's about Christian service, not eternal salvation. In context, we have already looked at one of the parables in what I'm calling a parenthesis of parables between the end of the Tribulation and the beginning of Christ's rule on earth for a thousand years (the Millennium). The Tribulation ends when Christ returns to the earth (Matt 24:29-31). Then He judges the Gentiles (Matt 25:31-46) and the Jews (Ezek 20:33-44) before setting up His kingdom. But the disciples want to know when He will return. He doesn't answer their question of "when." He does tell them "what." That is, He tells them **what** they should be doing while they wait for His return. What should they do? Serve Him.

These are Jesus' disciples. They are already saved (justification). The issue for them is not Acceptance. They are in the family. They have one hundred percent Acceptance. But Approval is another matter. For Approval they need to serve Him. Both parables preceding this were about service (Faithful Steward and Ten Virgins). There is no reason to expect this parable to be about anything other than service. These parables teach us to Walk with the Lord, Watch for the Lord, and Work for the Lord. The first parable told them to serve; the second told them to keep their lamps full of oil while they serve, and now this final parable tells them how God has equipped them to serve, and the Approval that will be meted out to those who are faithful to use their gifts and talents to serve while they wait for Him.

So, let's look at the "Four Laws of Spiritual Accounting".

I. THE LAW OF PROPORTIONS   25:14-15

"For *the kingdom of heaven is* like a man traveling to a far country, *who* called his own servants and delivered his goods to them. [15] And to one he gave five talents, to another two, and to another one, to each according to his own ability; and immediately he went on a journey.

Jesus likens our present responsibility to a group of servants who have been entrusted with the goods of their departing master. This is not an unusual case in the Middle East. Quite often the servants are allowed to engage in business enterprises with a percentage of the profits going to their master. And this is the case in verse 14. The italicized words *"the kingdom of heaven"* really don't belong in the text and aren't necessary to understand the passage. In fact, I think they are a little confusing. Christ is simply representing Himself as going on a long journey, but sure to return. In the meantime, which time is the present Church Age, by the way, he imparts some talents to his servants. Note, my friends, he gives these talents to his "own servants." These did not belong to someone else. In accordance with the symbolism of the parable, these servants would represent Christians. The Lord doesn't call unbelievers to serve Him. He calls unbelievers to believe. He calls believers to serve. If, as many suggest, the talents represent spiritual gifts, the Lord does not give spiritual gifts to unbelievers. The gifts of the Spirit are given by the Spirit to those who have the Spirit (1 Cor 12:11; Rom 8:9).

So, the master gives some talents. The talent was a weight measure equal to about 75 pounds. This could be gold or silver, which would be significantly valuable. However, it was the distribution of the talents and what was done with the respective distribution to three different servants that is instructive. Here we come to the First Spiritual Law of Accounting: it is the Law of Proportions. The master gave to each servant according to that servant's ability.

Some people want to know if the talents represent spiritual gifts alone or natural gifts and spiritual gifts. Natural gifts come at physical birth. Spiritual gifts come at spiritual birth. I suggest the talents represent our spiritual gifts because it says these gifts are given to servants already physically alive and according to their ability. Now this word "ability" I would liken to their natural abilities—their natural gifts and talents. It's the Greek word *dynamis* from which we get the English word dynamite.

What does all this mean? Simply this: God apportions His spiritual gifts to men or women according to each person's unique combination of natural abilities, temperament, and opportunities. There are approximately eighteen different spiritual gifts listed in 1 Corinthians 12, Romans 12, and Ephesians 4. These gifts of the supernatural are superimposed over the natural capacities of the believer. If a man is naturally an organized person, a good spiritual gift for him to look for is that of administration. If he has a natural inclination to go around helping people, he should look for the gift of help. If he has a great heart of compassion for those who suffer, he should look for the gift of administering mercy. If he is intelligent, look for the gift of knowledge. If he communicates well, look for the gift of teaching, preaching, or evangelism. You see, God will not give the gift of preaching to the man who was born unable to speak. He won't give the gift of mercy to one who is lacking in compassion and sensitivity. Therefore, our natural abilities can be a guideline to discover our spiritual gifts.

So also our natural temperament. Each person has a unique combination of temperament traits he or she received at physical birth. Understanding one's temperament can be helpful in determining spiritual gifts. Long ago, ancient Greeks tried to group some seventy different temperament traits into four broad categories: sanguine, melancholic, phlegmatic, and choleric. Observation has shown that most of us are a unique combination of these four, with one or two of the four rather dominant. And each temperament type has its strengths and weaknesses. The weaknesses are controlled by the Holy Spirit as one matures in Christ. The strengths are further strengthened. For example, if John Smith is a sanguine type primarily, then he is usually an enthusiastic person, warm, friendly, outgoing and talkative. With strengths like these, he should look for spiritual gifts in the area of evangelism, preaching, or showing mercy. If John is a choleric, then he has strengths of being strong-willed, disciplined, confident, and practical. He should look for gifts in the area of what we would call apostleship or starting new churches or projects for the Lord—missionary work. If John is melancholic, then he is probably very analytical, able to do in-depth research, is loyal, and does most things well. This person should look for the gifts of knowledge, teaching, or the like. And if John is phlegmatic, then his strengths are dependability, leadership, diplomacy, and efficiency. He would probably have the gifts of administration, helps, or pastoring.

So, we see that each of us has unique natural abilities and temperament traits. And God in His wisdom and love has given us spiritual gifts according to these natural characteristics. They are tailor-made to fit us. And this is encouraging. Many of us are like Moses. God calls us for a spiritual task, and we begin making excuses as to why we are not fitted for the task. We tell God we aren't leaders, or we can't speak, or we lack this or that. But God gives His gifts according to our natural abilities. This is the Law of Proportions. He knows our natural abilities better than we do. He created us. He wove us like a piece of embroidery in the womb. He knows our abilities, and He won't call us to a task we aren't equipped to handle. If we shrink back in fear, it's because we have shortchanged ourselves, not because God has. The Law of Proportions is law one. The Law of Addition is law two in the Four Spiritual Laws of Accounting.

II. THE LAW OF ADDITION   25:16-23

> Then he who had received the five talents went and traded with them, and made another five talents. And likewise he who *had received* two gained two more also. But he who had received one went and dug in the ground, and hid his lord's money. After a long time the lord of those servants came and settled accounts with them. "So he who had received five talents came and brought five other talents, saying, 'Lord, you delivered to me five talents; look, I have gained five more talents besides them.' His lord said to him, 'Well *done,* good and faithful servant; you were faithful over a few things, I will make you ruler over many things. Enter into the joy of your lord.' He also who had received two talents came and said, 'Lord, you delivered to me two talents; look, I have gained two more talents besides them.' His lord said to him, 'Well *done,* good and faithful servant; you have been faithful over a few things, I will make you ruler over many things. Enter into the joy of your lord.'

The servants had taken their talents and done with them as they desired. They had free will. But then their lord returned from his journey and called for his servants to get an accounting of what they had done with their talents. In the case of the first two servants, we see the Law of Addition at work. The equation is simple:

x Talents + Faithfulness = Many Rewards + Joy

Let's see how this law works. The servant who had been given five talents had gained five more talents by his faithful service to invest the talents he had been given. The result? Because he had been faithful over a few things, he was made ruler over many. He received rewards. But he received more than that. He also received joy: "Enter the joy of the Lord." But that is not all. He also received Approval: "Well done, good and faithful servant." Those words probably meant more to him than his rewards. We all long for approval from those over us, whether it is a parent, a coach, a teacher, a boss, or even a close friend.

What about the second servant? The second servant gained only two talents. But he had been just as faithful as the first, so he received the same as the first: rewards + joy. Notice exactly the same words of approval are spoken to him: "Well done, good and faithful servant." You see, when he received his two talents, he didn't go into the corner and sulk, saying, "My brother got more than I did." No, he understood the Law of Proportions which gave more talents to his brother would have no effect on his rewards and joy at his lord's return. No, his rewards were dependent on the Law of Addition. If he would add faithfulness to his talents, he would receive rewards plus joy.

So, the principle is simple. The distribution of gifts one has, which cause so much envy, jealousy, pride, and conceit on earth, have no effect whatsoever on one's rewards or joy at the Lord's return. The key word is faithfulness. A man once pondered the question, "Who do you think has been the greatest Christian of God during the 20th century?" A few moments passed while the man reflected on this difficult question. What would you say—Billy Graham? Bill Bright? Mother Teresa? The awaited reply came, "I am sure it is probably someone we've never heard of." You know, that man may be right.

For in the day of accounting God will not ask about our level of accomplishment. He only wants to know if we've been faithful with what we've received. Do you know, I wouldn't be surprised at all to learn the answer to that question is a woman. It's probably some homemaker. As a matter fact, when I think of some of the Christians who have inspired me the most, it hasn't been the men with the large crowds crooning with their golden-tongued oratory. Often, it's been the homemaker faithful to her calling and gifts in spite of deep suffering at the hands of a faithless husband. Remember the all-important question: Have we been faithful?

Okay. We have seen two of the Four Laws of Spiritual Accounting: the Law of Proportions and the Law of Addition. Now we will look at the Law of Subtraction.

III. THE LAW OF SUBTRACTION   25:24-30

"Then he who had received the one talent came and said, 'Lord, I knew you to be a hard man, reaping where you have not sown, and gathering where you have not scattered seed. And I was afraid, and went and hid your talent in the ground. Look, *there* you have *what is* yours.' "But his lord answered and said to him, 'You wicked and lazy servant, you knew that I reap where I have not sown, and gather where I have not scattered seed. So you ought to have deposited my money with the bankers, and at my coming I would have received back my own with interest. So take the talent from him, and give *it* to him who has ten talents. 'For to everyone who has, more will be given, and he will have abundance; but from him who does not have, even what he has will be taken away. And cast the unprofitable servant into the outer darkness. There will be weeping and gnashing of teeth.'

The equation is simple:

x Talents - Faithfulness = Zero Rewards - Joy

This man received one talent. He didn't have to produce as many as anyone else. He had only to be faithful. Instead, he was fearful. Like many Christians who fall by the wayside, this man was not faithful because he had an insufficient understanding of the character of God. He thought God was standing over him with an ax ready to cut his head off at the first, big mistake. No wonder he couldn't move out for God. He was scared stiff. Just so, many if not most abnormalities in the Christian life can trace their root cause back to an incorrect understanding of God's character. That's one reason we tend to become more faithful Christians the more we study God's Word; it increases our understanding of God.

In the case of this fearful, faithless servant, he needed to see that his lord loved him. Have you ever been around an instructor or teacher where you are afraid to try anything or offer a comment or ask a question? If so, then you are afraid because you think he'll chop you up at the sign of ignorance. But if he really loves you, the instructor expects you to make mistakes and wants to help you. That's the way God is. He's not going to cut us down. He's going to build us up and help us along the path when we stumble and falter along the way.

Now, let me briefly answer a frequent question on spiritual gifts. Can we lose our spiritual gifts? Those who think we can use this passage for support. They say that since this servant did not use his gift, it was taken away and given to another. But this misses one important point. The gift was not taken away until the lord returned. As long as the lord was on his journey, the gift was at the disposal of the servant to do with as he pleased. However, the implication is if we don't use our gifts in this life, then we forfeit their use in the next life. They will be taken away and given to those servants who were faithful in this life (v. 29).

Isn't it interesting that the Lord had problems with the servant who had only one talent? You wouldn't expect it. After all, with only one talent to worry about his job shouldn't have been as hard as the other two. But, in fact, I believe it's the same way in the church. It is the person with only one talent who often tells himself how worthless he is. He thinks he has so little to offer. And perhaps he even feels

144

underprivileged or unloved by God because he doesn't have more gifts. Consequently, he says, "What's the use?" and buries the gift he does have. My friend, if that's your problem, then it's not lack of ability that's derailing you. It's lack of availability. We don't find an example of a Christian in the Bible without a spiritual gift (1 Pet 4:11). You may only have one gift, and it may not be the one you want, but if God gave it to you, then don't despise it. It's your responsibility and it's tailor-made to fit you. It's only required that a servant be found faithful. The servant who is faithful with the one gift he has will receive the same reward as the faithful servant with two gifts or five. Again, the key is faithfulness.

But how do we know when we have been faithful? How do we know when we have done what the Lord has called us to do? This question brings us to the fourth law. We have seen the Law of Proportions: spiritual gifts are given to each one according to his or her natural abilities, temperament, and opportunities. We've also seen the Law of Addition: when we add faithfulness to our talent, we receive rewards in addition to joy. Finally, we've seen the Law of Subtraction: if we are unfaithful with the talents we've been given, there are no rewards and no joy. This does not mean no joy in heaven/New Jerusalem. It's after the thousand-year reign of Christ (the Millennium of Revelation 20) that Revelation 21 says there'll be no more sorrow, pain, tears, or death. We will say more about this when we come to the outer darkness at the end of the parable. But it is the fourth law that is the key.

IV. THE LAW OF 100% RETURN   25:20-22

"So he who had received five talents came and brought five other talents, saying, 'Lord, you delivered to me five talents; look, I have gained five more talents besides them.' His lord said to him, 'Well *done*, good and faithful servant; you were faithful over a few things, I will make you ruler over many things. Enter into the joy of your lord.' He also who had received two talents came and said, 'Lord, you delivered to me two talents; look, I have gained two more talents besides them.' His lord said to him, 'Well *done*, good and faithful servant; you have been faithful over a few things, I will make you ruler over many things. Enter into the joy of your lord.'

Notice when the lord called to his servants for an accounting, he did not actually ask the question, "Have you been faithful?" He knew they had been faithful. How? Because of the return on his investment. The first servant was given five talents and made five more. That's a 100% return.

5 Talents + 5 Talents = 10 Talents = 100% Return

The second servant had two talents and made two more. That's a 100% return.

2 Talents + 2 Talents = 4 Talents = 100% Return

And just as the talents are symbolic of spiritual gifts in the parable, so the returns symbolize all our Lord requires for a servant to be found faithful. The Lord wants us to give 100%. The man with two talents did not have to make five talents to be found faithful; he only had to make two. 100% is all we can give. The principle is simple. **Faithfulness is not measured by how much we're getting out of our efforts, but by how much we're putting into our efforts.** It's not what we get, but what we give. The faithful servant will give 100%.

The late Don Shula is the only coach of an NFL team to have an undefeated season. He claimed his success with what has often been called the "No-Name Defense" for its paucity of All-Star caliber players was due to a group of guys who, like himself, would give 100% effort. In his words: "I always wanted to do everything to the best of my ability. I always got upset . . . whenever I thought anyone was giving less than full effort." Now, if a football coach expected 100% from some men chasing a pigskin up and down a field, what do you think the Lord Jesus Christ wants from us? 100%. And 100% doesn't put any pressure on us to measure up to anyone else. It only means doing the best with whatever natural and spiritual abilities God has given us. Douglas Molloch put it this way;

If you can't be a highway, then just be a trail;
If you can't be the sun, then be a star;
It isn't by size that you win or fail;
Be the best of whatever you are.

These are the four laws of spiritual accounting: the Law of Proportions, the Law of Addition, the Law of Subtraction, and the Law of 100% Return. But there is one more aspect of this passage we need to discuss.

CONCLUSION

We would be remiss if we left this passage without some discussion of verse 30: **"And cast the unprofitable servant into the outer darkness. There will be weeping and gnashing of teeth.'"** Surely this must refer to hell. Outer darkness; weeping and gnashing of teeth? Well, one way we learn exegesis is to validate by invalidating. We combine this with the assumption, based on its own claims, that God is the Big Author of all Scripture as He superintends the work of the little authors (Luke, Paul, Isaiah, etc.). Most also assume these men were inspired by God. No, 2 Timothy 3:16 says the Scriptures were inspired by God, not the men. However, 2 Peter 1:21 does tell us the writers of Scripture were "born along" by the Holy Spirit as they recorded the inspired Word. All this to say that an omniscient Being like God is not going to contradict Himself. So, if He says "A" is true in one place in the Bible, then He won't turn around and say "A" is false in another place in the Bible. Let's take an example.

If God says in Ephesians 2:8-9 that we cannot work our way into heaven, then He is not going to say the opposite in another passage of Scripture. That would be contradicting Himself. Therefore, if one passage appears to contradict another, we work with the clear passage to help us understand the less clear passage. Ephesians 2:8-9 is clear. We will not be saved (justification/salvation) by our works. If that is true, then the Parable of the Talents cannot teach the opposite. Yet, if verse 30 is telling us we go to hell if we are not faithful servants of Christ, then that would mean we get to heaven by our good works. Since that is a direct contradiction of Ephesians, we will invalidate the "works" for heaven interpretation of Matthew 25:30.

So, if this verse is not teaching that we go to heaven or hell based on our faithfulness in service or lack thereof, what does it mean? That takes us back to where we began. This parable comes in a series of parables on what we should be doing while we wait for Christ to return. Each says something a little different about serving Him. And we remember that each parable has one main point, not many as in an allegory. That being true, the main point of this parable must have something to do with service. So, we look at what it teaches about the talents and the day of accounting. Not complicated: servants who use their talents faithfully are rewarded and have joy; servants who do not use their talent(s) faithfully are not rewarded and have sorrow.

One big mistake parabolic interpreters can make is to interpret the elements of the parable figuratively (the talents symbolize something), but at the end of the parable switch to a literal interpretation (literal outer darkness). One must either interpret figuratively, figuratively, figuratively or literally, literally, literally. One must be consistent. Thus, if the talents are not taken literally, then the outer darkness should not be taken literally. It symbolizes something, just as the talents symbolize something. Likely the best suggestion for the talents is that they symbolize spiritual gifts (since the natural abilities were given at physical birth) and/or opportunities. Similarly, the best suggestion for the outer darkness is less intimacy with Christ than those who were faithful. And the best suggestion for the weeping and gnashing of teeth is extreme grief and sorrow over a wasted life. It's a big oops.

How long this sorrow lasts and how intense it will be, we simply are not told. We are told that in the eternal state there will be no more sorrow or crying (Rev 21:4). The eternal state would not have much appeal if we thought we would spend eternity weeping and gnashing our teeth. However, the parable certainly teaches those who do not use what God has given to them to serve Him while they wait for His return will not experience the same amount of joy and responsibility during the Millennium as those who were faithful (Rev 21:7, 22:12).

The most fascinating part of this parable for me is wrapped up in the words "joy of the Lord." Imagine what that would be—to enter the joy of the Lord. We are blessed to be able to glean snippets of that joy right now: "the joy of the Lord is your strength." But to enter His joy forever—a continuum not punctuated by dots of depression and loneliness and rejection. Wow!

Albert Einstein plummeted the depth and breadth of the universe, but he could not deal with the uncertainty of particles like bosons and fermions, quarks and squarks. Heisenberg's Uncertainty Principle left him befuddled. "God does not play with dice," he commented as he launched his search for a Grand Unified Field Theory that would combine the certainty of the macro universe with the uncertainty of the micro-universe into a coherent system. He died with equations lying on his bed revealing his unrequited attempt to harmonize the macro with the micro. Likewise, he was a genius when it came to the big picture of mankind and human race and the need for peace, but he was never comfortable with the interpersonal relationships of living with a wife and children. At the end of his life, he was finally trying to reconcile with his 50-year-old son Hans, who became an engineering professor at the University of California/Berkley. He said, "It is a joy for me to have a son who has inherited the main traits of my personality: the ability to rise above mere existence by sacrificing one's self through the years for an impersonal goal."

Einstein believed in an impersonal god–a supreme intelligence. He said, "I am a deeply religious nonbeliever." Thus, the best he could find in this life was to sacrifice himself through the years for an impersonal goal. And I believe there is a measure of joy in such a life. But how much more joy there must be to believe in a personal God and to sacrifice one's self through the years for a personal goal, that is, a goal that involves people. Paul says of the Philippians, "You are my crown of rejoicing."

When we use God's gifts for God's glory by pouring out our lives for God's people, we catch a glimpse of God's joy. What I think He is trying to tell us is that helpers now will be helpers later; servants now will be servants later, but those who do not serve now forfeit the opportunity to serve later.

An old FRAM oil filter commercial was intended to encourage people to get regular oil changes for their cars lest they wind up with a serious engine problem and a big bill. The commercial ended with the statement: "Pay me now or pay me later." The implication was that it would be much cheaper to pay for regular check-ups than for a major car repair. My wife Betty picked up on that statement and amended it a bit, so when I'm slow to respond to one of her requests for help around the house, she would say, "Well, serve me now, or serve me later." Of course, the serving her later comment referred to the next life where the first will be last and the last will be first, meaning if I don't joyfully serve her in this life, I may find myself serving her in the next life. It might be more biblical to say, "If I don't serve Jesus now, I won't be privileged to serve Him later." Finally, if this parable teaches anything about eternity, it is that our future joy is a function of our present service.

So, let me serve you now, so I may have the opportunity to serve you later.

"GOD'S LOVE LANGUAGE"[20]

1 John 2:3-5

INTRODUCTION

Author and marriage counselor Gary Chapman has suggested that husbands and wives have five general ways in which they perceive love from their partner: 1) Words of Affirmation; 2) Quality Time; 3) Receiving Gifts; 4) Acts of Service; and 5) Physical Touch.[21] Usually one of these "love languages" is primary for a husband and wife. Unfortunately, mates usually don't

---

[20] Years ago I wrote a commentary on the most controversial book of the NT, 1 John. It was called *Maximum Joy*, but the subtitle was "Relationship or Fellowship." I explained that most expositors see the book as a test of whether someone is a Christian or not. The issue for them is Relationship; does someone have an eternal relationship with their Creator. This completely ignores the mention of "fellowship" four times in the first seven verses of the book. We approach the book from a viewpoint of how to enjoy fellowship with a God with Whom we already have an eternal relationship. It would be remiss to completely leave out even a chapter on 1 John in light of the title of this book, *Relationship and Fellowship*. Therefore, I am including a chapter from that book.

[21] Gary Chapman, *The Five Love Languages* (Chicago: Northfield Publishing, 1992).

share the same "love language." Like a Russian who speaks only Russian married to a Chinese person who speaks only Chinese, the husband might be saying "I love you" in his language, but his wife does not get the message because she has a different "love language." According to Chapman, marital intimacy is difficult to achieve unless each partner learns to speak the "love language" of his/her mate.

It took me about seven years of marriage before I learned my wife's love language, but I'll never forget it. We had seen and become enamored by the "Muppet Movie." Betty especially identified with Miss Piggy. She had never seen herself so perfectly portrayed in books or on the screen. Now I didn't exactly identify with Kermit the Frog, but if I'm married to Miss Piggy, we can all guess who I am. And I must admit, it is not easy being green. Well, this is all well and good for fun and games, but one night we were lying about a foot apart in our king size bed, lights out, almost asleep, when I hear this strange, squeaky little voice saying, "Kermie, whisper sweet nothings in my ear." Well, how does a real man respond to that? So I just laid there pretending to be asleep. Now, I'm sure some of you are aware that Miss Piggy has a variety of voices. Suddenly, out of the darkness came a guttural command which said, "Noowww!" Well, a real man knows when he is being manipulated, so I began some soft snoring. But Miss Piggy also has a variety of talents. For example, she knows karate. The next thing I felt was a huge karate chop to the ribs attended by the karate call of "Haaayyah!!!"

Guess which love language belongs to Betty? You're right–Words of Affirmation. That's her primary love language–Sweet Nothings. And if I don't know that, I might assume I'm doing the things to show her I love her, when in her eyes I am missing the boat completely. Could it be God has a primary "love language?" Surely there are many ways to show God we love Him, but what if He has a primary love language and I miss it? Could it be that intimacy with Him will be difficult to achieve if I don't learn to speak His love language?

Not long after he had become a Christian, Chuck Colson wrote a book on how we can love God.[22] He interviewed scores of people but he could not come up with a consensus on how to love God. So he made a study on this in the Bible. He finished up his study in the passage we focus on here, 1 John 2, as well as significant cross-reference from the Upper Room. It was his conclusion that God's primary love language is: Keeping His Commandments. Let's see this in 1 John 2:3-5.

The Main Message:

Love = Keeping His Commandments

Now by this we know that we know Him, if we keep His commandments (2:3).

We have already mentioned that 1 John is the most controversial book in the NT. Some see the book's meaning as "tests of life" (Relationship), while others see it as "tests of intimacy" (Fellowship). The passage under consideration heats up the controversy. It would certainly appear that verse three tells us that the way we can be sure that we know Christ as our Savior is if we keep His commandments. In other words, the way to have assurance of one's salvation is to look at the fruit of one's life. If you keep His commandments, then you are a Christian and will go to heaven when you die; if you don't keep His commandments, then you're not a genuine Christian and will go to hell when you die. This all seems rather plain and obvious. In addition, we don't see the word "love" in this verse, a fact which naturally leads us to think this verse isn't teaching anything about love.

---

[22] Chuck Colson, *Loving God* (New York: Harper Collins Publishers, 1983).

Well, let's go back and establish the structure of the passage and the context for the verse. Here again is the outline we're using for 1 John:

1 JOHN
"The Fruit of Fellowship"

I. Introduction: "The Joy of Fellowship"   1:1-4

II. Body: "The Principles of Fellowship"   1:5-5:17

    A. Principles of Fellowship Introduced   1:5-2:27

       1. Right Living-Dealing with our Sins   1:5-2:2

       2. Right Loving-Dealing with our Brothers   2:3-11

       3. Right Learning-Dealing with our Enemies   2:12-27

    B. Principles of Fellowship Developed   2:28-4:6

       1. Right Living–Dealing with our Sins   2:28-3:10a

       2. Right Loving–Dealing with our Brothers   3:10b-23

       3. Right Learning–Dealing with our Enemies   3:24-4:6

    C. Principles of Fellowship Climaxed   4:7-5:17

       1. Right Loving–Dealing with our Brothers   4:7-5:5

       2. Right Learning–Dealing with our Enemies   5:6-13

       3. Right Living–Dealing with our Sins   5:14-17

III. Conclusion: "Encouragement for Little Children"   5:18-21

From this outline we observe that 2:3 begins a new wave or principle of fellowship, just as 1:5 began our first wave or principle of fellowship. The first principle was what we called "Right Living," in which we were introduced to basic principles about dealing with our sins in order to have close fellowship with God, even though we are not sinless after we are justified. In that first section 1:5 gave us a primary message ("God is light"), which was followed by three erroneous responses (1:6,8,10) and their corresponding corrections.

Here in 2:3 the new section also begins with a main message or topic sentence. It is also followed by three responses, which are signified with the words "He who says . . ." in 2:4, 6, and 9. As we mentioned earlier, John loves doing things in threes. This is important. We need to see that 2:3 does not stand alone. It begins a new section. Them's the facts, ma'am, no matter what approach one takes to the book.

And if we follow the responses of 2:4, 6, and 9 through the section which ends in 2:11, it is easy to see that the primary subject of this section is love. John somewhat innocuously begins with the statement about God's commands, but then subtly leads his readers down the commandment trail to the "old" versus "new" commandment Jesus spoke about in the Upper Room: "A new commandment I give to you, that you love one another; as I have loved you, that you also love one another" (John 13:34).

Thus we see that 2:3 is a verse set in the context of love, specifically loving our brothers. As many have observed, "Loving the whole world for me is no chore; my only problem is my neighbor next door." Difficulty with other Christians is one of the big three barriers to fellowship with God in the mind of John. Our personal sin is a huge barrier, for sure (1:5–2:2); so is not loving our Christian brother, which is, of course, a very specific personal sin. And even though 2:3 does not mention the "love of God," 2:5 does. It says our love for God is perfected when we keep His Word, and John will connect our love for God with our love for our brother via God's commandments.

But let's focus on 2:3. How do we answer the interpretation that on the surface this verse appears to teach one may have assurance of salvation if he keeps God's commandments? This gets a bit technical, but it's helpful. Something we cannot observe from the NKJV is that the verbs for "know" in 2:3 are not the same. The root word is the same, but the tenses are different. We cannot see this from the English translation.

The first use of "know" is in the present tense (*ginōskamen*); but the second use of "know" is in the perfect tense (*egnōkamen*). If we miss this deliberate shift on John's part, we miss his intent for the verse. This verb is what is called by Greek grammarians a "stative" verb because it describes a state of being as opposed to an action. In other words, to "know" or to "believe" speak of inner truths but not outward actions.

A Greek grammarian named McKay has written an excellent article dealing with the perfect tense of stative verbs in which he demonstrates that putting a stative verb into the perfect tense has the effect of intensifying the basic meaning of the verb. It's a deeper state of whatever the meaning of the verb is. In this case, the verb means "to know" in the sense of an experience. So putting it into the perfect tense means "to know intensely, "to experience deeply," or "to know fully." It's much like the OT meaning when it says, "Adam *knew* his wife Eve and she conceived and bore Cain . . ." (Gen 4:1) It's an intimate knowledge.

None of the commentators who take the "tests of life" view of 1 John have observed this significant change in the tenses in 2:3. Some other Bible translations have noticed this change, such as the NASB which says, "And by this we *know* that we *have come to know* Him, if we keep His commandments." This does not solve the problem, nor does this translation reflect the perfect tense of a *stative* verb. I hate to belabor this point, but it is crucial, since 2:3 is referenced more than any other "test of life" in 1 John by those who believe this book gauges if you are a Christian or not.

The perfect tense in the Greek language has the basic meaning of "completed action in the past with present results." But, according to its use in context, a typical verb can put its emphasis on the completed action in the past *or* on the present results. When the translator thinks that emphasis is on the completed action in the past, he will translate it with the English word "have" to emphasize the completed action: have heard, have written, have finished, have been sanctified. But when the translator thinks the emphasis is on the present results of the completed action in the past, he translates the verb like an English present tense: "it is finished" (*tetelestai*—Christ's statement on the cross).

But with a stative verb, McKay's point is that it should always be translated with emphasis on the present results. In other words, "have come to know" does not recognize the significance of a stative verb in the perfect tense. A more accurate rendering of the emphasis on the intensified state of experiential knowledge here would be, "And by this we *know* that we *know* Him *intensely.*" And what is an intense knowledge if not deep, intimate knowledge? Once again, the emphasis here is on *fellowship*, not relationship. It is not a test of whether a person is born again; it is a test of whether a person is having close fellowship with God.

In 1:5–2:2 we saw the most common denominator for fellowship with Christ: walk in the light and confess known sins. A brand-new Christian can walk with the Lord and fellowship with Him on this level. In 2:3–11 we have fellowship at a deeper level. Now the Christian is learning His Word (His commandments). When he chooses to obey these commandments, a deeper fellowship awaits.

Once again, we see the dependency of 1 John on John 13–17. John 14:21–24 tells us in no uncertain terms that keeping His commandments is God's language of love. "If you love Me, keep My commandments" (John 14:15). It doesn't get any clearer than that—God's primary language of love is keeping His commandments. But more than that, when we show Him we love Him, He reciprocates. That's what Jesus is trying to say in John 14:21. If we have Jesus' commandments and keep them, then we show Him we love Him. When we do that, He tells us His Father loves us and He loves us and He *will manifest Himself to us!* The word "manifest" means to "make visible." In other words, He reveals a little more of His love He has in the heart for us.

Isn't this exactly the way it works with deepening love in relationships? We don't dump the whole load on the first date. We test the waters. I reveal a little of myself. If she reciprocates by revealing some of her feelings for me, I may reveal a little more of myself. Of course, I am referring to positive feelings. When I was in grammar school, we communicated through emissaries and notes. If I saw a girl I liked, I would write her a note, but I would have my friend Joe deliver it for me. Then he would bring a return note.

On one occasion I sent a note through Joe to a girl named Kathy. With great anticipation, I saw Joe coming back with a return note. If Kathy reciprocated my feelings, we could dispense with the notes and get rid of the middleman. Alas! Kathy's note said, "Sorry, Dave, I don't like you." Well, that kind of response necessitated a return-return note. I sent Joe back with a note that said, "Then I don't like you either."

In love relationships, we reveal a little of ourselves at a time. The sting of rejection is too strong to dump all our feelings at once. Besides, those feelings tend to intensify as each person reveals or makes manifest a little more of him/herself. The Lord is no different. That's one reason He compares His relationship with the Church to a husband/wife relationship (Eph 5:32). I actually believe He loves everyone He has ever created the same because He is omnibenevolent, that is, He does not show partiality (Rom 2:11) and He loves the whole world (Jn 3:16). He causes it to rain on the just and the unjust. But those who see His message of love written on the cross and believe in it experience His love in a deeper way than those who reject this overture of love from the Lord. Yet, even we believers are probably loved by Him more than we will ever know. Nevertheless, as we communicate with Him in His love language (keep His commandments), He reveals more and more of His love for us. It is a growing, dynamic love relationship.

It's probably the same with you and your children. Let's say you have two children. You love them equally. But your firstborn is much more compliant than your secondborn. Your secondborn can't really compete and outdo his older brother who is bigger, stronger, and knows more than he does. So, instead of getting your attention with his good behavior, he goes the other direction and rebels. Well, even though you love them equally, you must display that love in different ways. For the compliant child there are positive rewards. For the rebellious child there is the rod. It grieves you to manifest your love for your rebellious son with the rod (or other negative consequence). You would love to reward him for his good behavior. But you can't;

not until he begins to keep your commandments. Then you can manifest your love for him in a positive way.

THE ERROR

> He who says, "I know Him," and does not keep His commandments, is a liar, and the truth is not in him (2:4).

Again, this verse and the prior are among the numerous "tests of life" (Relationship) found in 1 John by those who count themselves among the Fruit Inspectors in the Church. According to them, anyone who claims to be a Christian but does not keep Christ's commandments is simply a liar, a false professor of Christ.

I won't address the myriad questions this kind of teaching brings to mind concerning how-when-which of the commandments must be kept. Suffice it to say, I do not believe you cannot know you are a Christian until you die with this understanding of the text. You'll always be adrift on a Sea of Subjectivity wondering if you are being faithful enough.

In his early writings, John Calvin did not believe looking at one's fruit could bring any assurance of salvation. He thought we were doomed if we looked to ourselves, at least as far as assurance is concerned. He said we should look to Christ, and that assurance was part of saving faith. But after his death, Theodore Beza assumed control of the Geneva Academy, which trained many pastors for the Continent as well as the British Isles. Beza supported the concept that Christ died only for the elect. If that were so, he reasoned, it would be invalid to look to Christ for one's assurance, since the looker might be among the reprobate (those God predestined for hell, according to Beza) and thus be looking to a Savior who didn't die for him. Well, if we couldn't look to Christ for the assurance of our salvation, we must look to ourselves and our own fruit, said Beza. Thus began what I call the great Fruit Inspecting Industry during the Reformation, practiced to perfection by the English Puritans and brought to America on the Mayflower.

Relationship and Fellowship

According to William Perkins, one of the leading preachers of Puritanism during the days of Beza, there are nine fruits to look for in your introspective endeavors to determine if you really are among the elect and will go to heaven when you die. Here they are:

1. Feelings of bitterness of heart when we have offended God by sin;

2. Striving against the flesh;

3. Desiring God's grace earnestly;

4. Considering that God's grace is a most precious jewel;

5. Loving the ministers of God's Word;

6. Calling upon God earnestly and with tears;

7. Desiring Christ's second coming;

8. Avoiding all occasions of sin;

9. Persevering in the effects until the last gasp of life.[23]

It must be obvious from these fruits that no one could have assurance of his salvation until he died, if, after all, one must persevere in the faith until his last gasp. When will he be assured of his salvation? Obviously, after his last gasp.

Assurance of one's salvation became the preoccupation of the English Puritans who moved to America.[24] Entire volumes of hundreds of pages were written just to help people discern whether they would go to heaven when they died or not. The Puritans dedicated entire volumes to the introspection necessary to ascertain

---

[23] William Perkins, *The Works of that Famous and Worthy Minister of Christ in the University of Cambridge, Mr. William Perkins*, 3 vols. (Cambridge: n. p., 1608–09), 1:115.

[24] Michael P. Winship, *Making Heretics: Militant Protestantism and Free Grace in Massachusetts 1636 – 1641* (New Jersey: Princeton University Press, 2002).

whether one's faith was sufficient to save them. In commenting on his 650-page tome called *A Discourse concerning the Holy Spirit*, John Owen (d. 1683) stated that his main purpose was to help professors of Christ to determine whether or not they were possessors of Christ.[25]

Fruit inspectors all. And, as the early writings of John Calvin pointed out, such an approach leaves one in doom and despair. That is why churches that adopt this approach to the Christian life are so lacking in Joy. How can one have any joy as long as he is looking to his own life and fruit as the source of his assurance as to whether or not he is going to heaven? As Michael Eaton, who grew up in the Westminster Chapel, has observed:

I found myself reading about the deathbed experiences of 17th-century Puritans. I was shattered to discover that their assurance of salvation at such a time was not what I would have expected. Then I came across the remark of Asahel Nettleton . . . which expressed the very essence of everything I felt was wrong with the approach to grace that I had grown up with: "The most that I have ventured to say respecting myself is, that I think it possible I may get to heaven." Surely, I thought to myself, there is more joy and assurance in the New Testament than that! Yet I knew only too well that such introspection and doubt was widespread in the Reformed circles I knew.[26]

Respectfully, I wish to say that the interpretive failure in regard to 1 John 2:3–4 has been to see these verses in their context. All we

---

[25] John Owen, *The Works of John Owen*, 16 vols., vol. 3: *A Discourse concerning the Holy Spirit* (1677; reprint, Edinburgh: Banner of Truth Trust, 1965), 45-47.

[26] Michael Eaton, *No Condemnation* (Downers Grove, IL: InterVarsity Press, 1995), 9.

need to do is see the three repetitions of "he who says . . ." in verses 4, 6, and 9 to know that John is repeating the pattern he established in chapter one with a topic sentence and three responses to it. That would tell us that 2:5 is directly connected to 2:3-4. And though 2:3-4 do not mention "love" directly, 2:5 does. That's the connection—not between keeping His commandments and entrance into life, but keeping His commandments and enjoyment of life (it's Fellowship, not Relationship). And the "know" of 2:4 is again in the perfect tense, which we have explained at length means to know Him intimately, intensely. This, too, has been overlooked by those who hold the "tests of life" view.

Using these verses as a source of assurance can be dangerous. I once had a discussion with a seminary colleague in which I asked him if he were sure he would go to heaven when he died. He assured me he would.

"How do you know?" I asked.

"Because I can look into my life and see evidence of the Holy Spirit at work: my love for God's Word, my love for people, my hatred of sin, and so on," he replied.

"But couldn't you take a serious fall at some point in the future and lose your love for God's Word, His people, and begin to love sin?"

"Of course," he replied, "let him who thinks he stands take heed lest he falls."

"But if you had such a fall, what would that prove?"

"Well," he said, "if I continued in sin it would prove I was never a genuine believer to begin with."

"Then what could we say about your present assurance based on your love for God, His people, and your hatred for sin?" I asked.

The conversation stopped. The answer is obvious. My colleague's present assurance would be false assurance because his subsequent fall and continuance in sin, according to his understanding, would prove he never was a believer. When would such a person know that he is going to heaven or not? Not until he dies is the only consistent answer.

THE CORRECTION

But whoever keeps His word, truly the love of God is perfected in him. By this we know that we are in Him (2:5)

It is so very important to keep this verse connected with the previous. In 2:3 we get the main message of 2:3–11. There are three responses, the first of which is in 2:4. The response is an error, of which 2:5 is the correction. The "but" tells us what follows will be contrasted with what preceded. The point is that the promise here is not that if someone keeps His Word he will gain entrance to heaven or that he is proving that he has already been given his ticket to heaven. Keeping God's Word in 2:5 is not a sign of regeneration; it is a sign that someone loves God. It is straight out of the Upper Room Discourse, where a bunch of believers is huddled up listening to their Coach tell them that He's about to be transferred to another city. They're going to have to make a go of it on their own. What is their response? The same as any group when their coach or pastor leaves to go to another city: "But don't you care about us? Don't you love us?" They're having heart palpitations. So, Jesus speaks to their need: "Let not your heart be troubled . . ."

Perhaps we can assign some spiritual meaning to the secular song entitled "Turn Around, Look at Me":

There is Someone standing behind you;
Turn around, look at Me.
There is Someone to love and guide you;
Turn around, look and see.
There is Someone who'll love you forever;
Turn around, take My hand.
There is Someone who really loves you;
Turn around, look at Me.

If you don't sense the love of God in your life, perhaps it's because you're not keeping His commandments. You're going down the wrong path in life. But He's right behind you, and He really loves you. And He says, "Turn around. Look at Me." He's really there.

The word "keeps" (*tereō*) means a lot more than "has." When we look again at John 14:21, we see that *keeping* His commandments is more than *having* His commandments. "He who *has* my commandments and *keeps* them . . ." Loving is much more than just having His commandments. It's keeping them. This word *tereō* also means more than to just obey. The basic meaning carries the concept of "watching over, guarding, and protecting," as a shepherd watches over his sheep, as a banker his treasure, or a fiancé his bride to be.

One of our church members saw a good illustration of this recently. On a trip to visit her parents in Quincy, Illinois, she was looking out the front window and saw a baby bird which had fallen to the ground. The mother bird was coming down to feed it. She was feeding the birds still in the nest high above the ground, but then she would swoop down to feed the baby bird on the ground. This continued day after day. Finally, Carol observed that the mother bird was building a protective tent over her baby bird so people passing by wouldn't notice it. Her ritual was to feed the little birds above and then fly to the ground and stay a few feet from the "tent" to watch for predators she might have to ward off should they get near her hidden, baby bird. She was protecting, she was guarding, and she was keeping her little one safe.

That's what "keeps" means in our text. It is more than just having a Bible or several of them in one's house. It's to treasure God's Word, to guard it, to protect it. It's to realize that many people in this world don't have this book, have never had a chance to listen to its promises or read it for themselves. Outside of our personal relationship with Jesus, His Word may be the most precious thing we have from Him. The person who "keeps" His Word is the one who has His Word, guards His Word, and cherishes His Word. In this person, the love of God is perfected.

In the person who so keeps God's Word the love of God is *perfected*. This word (*teteleiōtai*) is another verb in the perfect tense in 1 John. Thus, it could be translated as "is perfected," "has been perfected," or "is made complete." It's love in its fullness, its completeness. And John says what is in a state of completeness here is the "love of God." This could mean our love for God or God's love for us. We suppose it means our love for God since this is God's primary love language, that is, the primary way He says we can show that we love Him. But we can't rule out His love for us here, since He promises in John 14:21 to love us back if we demonstrate our love for Him by keeping His commandments. Reciprocal love—our love for Him and His love for us. Love is most complete when it is reciprocated. If it is all one-sided, it is still imperfect and incomplete.

CONCLUSION

In 1 John 2:3, we have the beginning of a new principle for fellowship. We saw "right living" (dealing with our sins) in 1:5–2:2. In 1 John 2:3–11, John looks that "right loving" (dealing with our brother). Here we learn that God's primary love language is to keep His commandments (2:3). If someone says he is close to God but does not keep His commandments, that person is simply lying (2:4). But when a person chooses to keep God's commandments (His Word), the love of God is made complete in that person.

Boris Kornfeld was a Jewish doctor living in Russia.[27] He grew up with Stalin as his god. He was not a practicing or religious Jew. He did not believe in Yahweh of the OT. He believed in Lenin and Stalin and socialism. But one-fourth of the people in the USSR were informants for the KGB. It was a terrorist state. Someone turned Boris in. For what, he did not know.

The KGB whisked him off to one of their prison camps. He was dumbfounded. He had not been disloyal to the state. Lenin and Stalin had been his gods. But there he was, a prisoner of the state. As he sat in his prison camp and witnessed the senseless death and destruction, he threw off the shackles of socialism. He deposed the

---

[27] Colson, 19-25.

gods he was worshiping. He said to himself, "This philosophy of life cannot be true."

Kornfeld listened to other prisoners who had put their hope in Jesus. For a Jew to give up socialism or communism was one thing, but for a Jew to embrace Jesus was quite another. But as he kept hearing about the peace and hope Jesus could bring, Boris decided to try to Jesus as his Messiah. Not long after trusting Christ he was in a Bible study and listened to this passage, which gives God's love language: "If you love me, keep my commandments." Boris Kornfeld knew he wasn't keeping God's commandments. On a regular basis he, as a doctor, would sign slips of paper saying a prisoner was fit to go back to work in the mines when he knew this particular prisoner was not fit at all. This is how the prison system thinned its ranks. They just sent an unhealthy person into hard labor. They rarely came out of the mines alive.

Boris had signed hundreds of these slips, these death warrants. He thought, "I'm not going to sign anymore slips." He knew he was somewhat protected because they needed doctors, but he really did not know what would happen to him. Soon after this decision, he saw an orderly stealing bread. He could overlook it but decided the right thing to do would be to report it. The orderly was put in the stockade for three days, but when released, Boris knew the orderly would be about to get even.

He began sleeping in the hospital to avoid being caught in the darkness by this vengeful orderly. But he also sensed a new freedom he had not experienced before. He thought, "Being willing to die for Christ, being willing to be punished for Christ—all of a sudden I had a freedom and a peace I had never known in my life. I sensed God was with me and I sensed that He loved me in a special way, and all of a sudden, I had to tell someone. I had never told anyone what had happened to me."

A young man came in who had cancer in his intestines. Boris operated on him, and as the young man was coming out of anesthesia, Boris said to himself, "I've got to tell this fellow." So as the young man was coming out of anesthesia and still in a stupor, Boris began to tell his story of peace and of love and the forgiveness of sins through Jesus Christ. The young man missed most of the beginning of Boris's story because of the drugs lingering in his system, but then he began to understand, and Boris just couldn't stop talking. He went on talking for an entire day.

That night the orderly found Boris and hit him on the head six times with a plasterer's mallet, killing him. But the message Boris shared never left the heart of the young man who heard it, the only man who ever heard Boris's message. This message of good news, peace, and forgiveness burned in his soul until he too trusted in Jesus Christ as his Savior. Ultimately, this young man, cured of physical cancer and the cancer of sin, was released from prison. He came to America and wrote a Nobel prize-winning book about his experiences in the Soviet labor camps: *The Gulag Archipelago*. His name? Aleksandr Solzhenitsyn.

"If you love me, keep my commandments."

"WHAT WILL YOU WEAR TO THE WEDDING?"

2 Corinthians 4:16-5:11

INTRODUCTION

Although people on average are living longer than ever, from time to time something comes along to remind us of our mortality. I experienced one of those times recently when I traveled to Oregon for some vacation time. Betty and I joined my sister Jo Anne and brother-in-law Leland in Portland. We were no sooner there when Leland asked me if I'd like to take a little road trip down to Lake Tahoe in California. His father had a condo on the lake we could use. Sure; why not? We arrived about ten in the evening. It was a beautiful, clear night with lots of stars visible to the naked eye. Leland asked me if I'd like to see the stars really well. Sure; why not? So, we walked a short way to a pier that went out into the lake at least a hundred and fifty yards. There was a group of young people partying at the end of the pier. They were whooping and hollering and making all kinds of noise.

I thought they were being kind of obnoxious, so I began whooping back at them as we walked out on the pier. The pier was well-lit with lights about every twenty or thirty yards, and it was probably fifteen feet wide with a three-foot guard rail. Well, we got about fifty yards out on the pier, and these kids at the far end were still yelling and screaming. I thought, "What a bunch of drunks." After a few more steps, we could understand what they were yelling: "BEAR . . . BEAR!" Suddenly, out of the darkness and into the light twenty yards further out on the pier stepped the biggest black bear I had ever seen. It had to be a 500 pounder with its head dwarfed by its bulging shoulder muscles and thick neck. It was coming right toward us. Apparently, the bear was used to patrolling the pier in the evening looking into the trash cans provided for people getting off their boats from some time on the lake. They often threw left-over food into these cans.

Of course, we abruptly turned around and headed for the shore. Twenty yards is nothing for a big bear since they can run faster than any human. Our instinct was to run, but we heard the kids yelling, "Don't run. Don't run." Apparently, trying to run away from a bear signals something primeval within its psyche that says, "Attack." So, we walked briskly, all the while looking back to make sure the bear was not gaining ground on us. My brother-in-law's eyes were bigger than headlights, so I could tell he was scared. As we walked, I began looking for options in case the bear charged. All I could do would be to jump over the guardrail and into the lake.

Fortunately, we made it to shore. I went straight up a small hill before I looked back, while Leland jumped a fence guarding a swimming pool. I watched as the bear reached shore and took a right turn along the shoreline. Apparently, it was not interested in us. When Leland got out of the pool, I said, "Man, I could tell from your eyes you were really scared." He said, "No, not really. I knew all I had to do was to outrun you" (no big feat since I am ten years older than he and have several artificial joints). Though I had encountered many black bears from years of hiking in the Appalachians, this was the biggest I'd ever seen. As my pulse rate slowed down, the whole experience reminded me of my mortality.

After all, we never know when that time is coming. It reminds me of the cowboy who went to heaven, met St. Peter at the gates, and was asked what deeds of merit he might have done to deserve to enter heaven. "Well," replied the weather-beaten cowboy, "I can think of only one thing. On a trip to the Black Hills out in South Dakota I came upon a gang of bikers who were threatening a young woman. I directed them to leave her alone, but they wouldn't listen. So, I approached the largest and most tattooed biker and smacked him in the face, kicked his bike over, ripped out his nose ring, and threw it on the ground, and yelled, 'Now, back off or I'll kick the snot out of all of you." Well, St. Peter was impressed. "When did this happen?" he asked. "Couple of minutes ago," replied the cowboy.

We never know when our time will come. So, as I find myself looking more and more back to what used to be, I began thinking more and more about looking forward to what will be and what might be. I wanted to see more closely what the Bible tells us about our future glorified bodies and the clothes we will wear in the next life. My musings took me to 2 Corinthians 4:16ff. We want to look briefly at *that which is Perishing, that which is Permanent, and that which is Pleasing.* The first part of our study will be a bit morbid, but don't close the book . . . it gets better. This is another study in contrasting categories: Relationship versus Fellowship, or the Gift versus Prize, or Justification versus Sanctification. We will focus on the next life and what the Bible tells us concerning what we can expect because we have believed in Christ compared to what we can expect because we have not only believed in Christ but also walked with Christ. And when we finish up, I want to ask you this question: "What will you wear to the wedding?" referring, of course, to the wedding of Jesus Christ the groom to His bride, the Church. Let's begin by looking at that which is perishing.

I. THAT WHICH IS PERISHING   4:16-18

Therefore we do not lose heart. Even though our outward man is perishing, yet the inward *man* is being renewed day by day. [17] For our light affliction, which is but for a moment, is working for us a far more exceeding *and* eternal weight of glory, [18] while we do not look at the things which are seen, but

at the things which are not seen. For the things which are seen
are temporary, but the things which are not seen *are* eternal.

Billions of dollars have been spent over the last few decades
looking for "extra" dimensions in our universe. Theoretical physicists
like Brian Green (*The Elegant Universe*) and Lisa Randall (*Warped
Passages*) have predicted that our universe has anywhere from
seven to seventeen "curled up" dimensions we cannot observe.
The Large Hadron Collider (LHC) built between 1998 and 2008 by
CERN (Conseil Européen pour la Recherche Nucléaire [European
Council for Nuclear Research]) near Geneva, Switzerland, the largest
machine in the world, was built in part to try to discover a particle
from one of these unseen dimensions. It is the collaboration of over
10,000 scientists, hundreds of universities and laboratories, and 100
countries. With a circumference of 17 miles, the idea is to accelerate
subatomic particles like protons down a tunnel at speeds near the
speed of light in order to cause a head-on collision that can yield
additional particles like quarks and squarks from dimensions of
reality beyond the four we can easily observe (length, width, height,
and time). In 2012 CERN thinks they proved the existence of the
Higgs particle, nicknamed by some the "God" particle (unhappily for
Higgs, who was an atheist). Scientists are still trying to confirm their
2012 results.

So, scientists are conceding that there is much in our own universe with its dark matter, dark energy, and black holes we cannot
see even with our Hubble telescope. Some even talk about a multi-
verse in which we can observe only our universe. Actually, the Bible
spoke long ago about extra dimensions and even a parallel universe,
only these exist in the spiritual world instead of the physical. In 2
Corinthians 4, Paul speaks of that which can be seen versus that
which cannot be seen. The former is temporal, while the latter is
eternal.

The writer to the Hebrews does the same thing in 12:26-28—
"He has promised, saying, '*Yet once more I* shake not only the
earth, but also heaven.' Now this, "*Yet once more*," indicates the

removal of those things that are being shaken, as of things that are made, that the things which cannot be shaken may remain. "Therefore, since we are receiving a kingdom which cannot be shaken, let us have grace, by which we may serve God acceptably with reverence and godly fear." He speaks of a spiritual world that cannot be shaken as opposed to this physical world that can and will be shaken. Like Paul, the author to the Hebrews believes in an unseen world that will be revealed when this world we can see is replaced.

Paul wants to encourage us with these thoughts. "Our outward man" must certainly refer to our physical bodies, which are subject to deterioration, decay, and death. It can be pretty discouraging as we watch our bodies slowly but surely waste away. I was looking at some graduation pictures of my daughter from seminary in 2009 and was amazed at the physical changes in me over the past twelve years: hair from brown to grey, an aortic aneurysm, a paralyzed diaphragm, neuropathy in both feet, an artificial hip, an artificial knee, an artificial shoulder, shingles for life, a stroke in my right optic nerve, and the list goes on. Yes, the physical man perishes, but the spiritual man, "the inward man is being renewed day by day."

What a joy, what an encouragement to sense the refreshing winds of the Spirit as He reenergizes us spiritually every morning. I sometimes look in the mirror and wonder, "Who is that guy?" I look so old and enervated, but inside I feel so alive and energized. How can we not think of Isaiah 40:31—"But those who wait on the Lord shall renew their strength; they shall mount up with wings like eagles, they shall run and not be weary, they shall walk and not faint." This spiritual renewal is a reminder that some things are not affected by the law of entropy. Some things don't wear out. Some things are eternal. Our God is gracious to give us a taste today of what will be our everyday experience tomorrow.

Paul speaks of our present-day sufferings in the outer man as "a light affliction." I must admit, when I see some of the suffering people endure, it is hard to call it a light affliction. My former next-door neighbor and member of my church had a Ph.D. in chemistry from Vanderbilt University and a significant position with Shell Oil in their plastics department. He was the picture of health, playing tennis and jogging regularly. Then he got pancreatic cancer at age forty-three. I wound up doing his funeral nine months later. As a pastor, I saw quite a bit of this. Every year people in my church died of cancer. But I had never had a next-door neighbor waste away in front of my eyes. Bill went from 180lbs to 90lbs over the nine months. At the end he looked, as you can imagine, like one of the victims of a Nazi labor camp. He couldn't even take a bath without an inflatable donut because his protruding coccyx bone hurt him when he tried to lie down in the bathtub.

How can God call this a "light affliction, which is but for a moment?" There is only one way. When the suffering of the temporal is compared to the sublime of the eternal, it seems to be a light affliction and to last but a moment. Paul echoes this perspective when he writes, "For I consider that the sufferings of this present time are not worthy to be compared with the glory which shall be revealed in us" (Rom 8:18). Somehow the suffering of this world when compared to the glory of the next is like trying to compare a thimble of water to the Pacific Ocean or a grain of sand to Mt. Everest. There simply is no comparison.

When Paul says, ". . . we look . . . at the things not seen," he is revealing a choice he has made. He has chosen to switch his focus from this world that is perishing to the world that is permanent. That requires some imagination. We think of Moses who "endured as seeing Him who is invisible" (Heb 11:27). That phrase (τὸν γὰρ ἀόρατον ὡς ὁρῶν) jumps out in the Greek text because of the play on words; Moses could see what cannot be seen. His faith was so strong that the invisible was more real to him than the visible.

It reminds me of a biography on Nickola Tesla I read in high school while making a Tesla coil. It claimed that in the making of over eight hundred patents, he never wrote anything on paper until he submitted the patent. He would just work on things in his head, sometimes for a couple of years, before he submitted his invention on paper. It claimed that when he envisioned alternating current, he was walking down a sidewalk and ran right into a gas light pole. What he saw in his mind was more real than the physical world right in front of him. Would that we could apply that to our Christian lives.

Could it be that we might turn a "light affliction" into a small jewel to adorn one of the crowns we cast at His feet in the next life, a jewel that will glorify Him forever and ever? I find that extremely motivating. So did Moses. Our passage in Hebrews tells us he chose "rather to suffer affliction with the people of God than to enjoy the passing pleasures of sin, esteeming the reproach of Christ greater riches than the treasures in Egypt; for he looked to the reward." What enabled him to endure suffering? "He looked to the reward." That word for "reward" (*misthapodosia*) is unique to Hebrews (2:2; 10:35; and here). It is made up of two words: *misthos* (pay or wages) and *apodosia* (to pay). Rewards are a great motive for enduring suffering in Hebrews. In Hebrews 10 we read,

> But recall the former days in which, after you were illumi-nated, you endured a great struggle with sufferings: [33] partly while you were made a spectacle both by reproaches and tribulations, and partly while you became companions of those who were so treated; [34] for you had compassion on me in my chains, and joyfully accepted the plundering of your goods, knowing that you have a better and an endur-ing possession for yourselves in heaven. [35] Therefore do not cast away your confidence, which has great reward.

How could these Hebrews endure the plundering of their goods with joy? Only one way: they knew they had a better and an enduring possession in heaven. In short, a reward (*misthapodosia*). They were oriented to the next world. And that is what Paul is trying to do with his Corinthian readers - getting them oriented to a world that is not temporary, a world that is eternal. And this leads us to that which is permanent.

II. THAT WHICH IS PERMANENT 5:1-8

For we know that if our earthly house, *this* tent, is destroyed, we have a building from God, a house not made with hands, eternal in the heavens. [2] For in this we groan, earnestly desiring to be clothed with our habitation which is from heaven, [3] if indeed, having been clothed, we shall not be found naked. [4] For we who are in *this* tent groan, being burdened, not because we want to be unclothed, but further clothed, that mortality may be swallowed up by life. [5] Now He who has prepared us for this very thing *is* God, who also has given us the Spirit as a guarantee. [6] So *we are* always confident, knowing that while we are at home in the body we are absent from the Lord. [7] For we walk by faith, not by sight. [8] We are confident, yes, well pleased rather to be absent from the body and to be present with the Lord.

Normally, after a Sunday Morning Service I would wait in the foyer to greet people as they came out. One particular Sunday, a woman I knew quite well was waiting for me. She was a very nice lady but rather embarrassed by her obesity. She asked, "Pastor Dave, have you read the *Left Behind* series by Tim LaHaye?" I said I had read the first volume. She wanted to know if I agreed with it. I replied, "Largely, but not completely." She responded somewhat indignantly, "Then I don't want to be raptured." Nonplussed, I asked why. She said, "'Cause I don't want to stand around naked in front of a bunch of men." Even more nonplussed I queried, "What makes you think you will be standing around naked in front of a bunch of men?" She quickly retorted, "Well, don't you remember the airplane. That guy was sitting in his chair on the plane, and then the rapture took place, and all the chair had in it was his clothes. That means he went up naked." I couldn't keep from smiling, but reassured her, "I'm pretty sure the Lord will provide Rapture Robes for everyone taken up. You won't be standing around naked." Actually, I was more than pretty sure. The passage above guarantees we will all be clothed, and as we shall see shortly, so does the Book of Revelation.

The first few verses of 2 Corinthians 5 use several different words for our earthly and heavenly bodies: 1) house (*oikia*); 2) tent (*skēnos*); 3) building (*oikodomē*); 4) house (*oikia*); and 5) habitation (*oikētērion*) (NKJ) or heavenly dwelling (NIV; NASB; ESV; NRSV). The first two uses refer to our earthly bodies while the next two refer to our spiritual bodies. It is the fifth use that is most interesting. More than interesting, it is fascinating. It says we will be clothed with our "habitation" in the NKJ. The other modern translations cited have heavenly "dwelling." Now, how do you clothe yourself with a dwelling?

The *oikētērion* is not a dwelling; it's clothing. You are clothed with the *oikētērion*. And because we are clothed, "we shall not be found naked." This word is used only one other time in the NT: Jude 6: "And the angels who did not keep their proper domain, but left their own abode, He has reserved in everlasting chains under darkness for the judgment of the great day." Here the word "abode" is *oikētērion*, which by itself might lead us to think this is some kind of angelic dwelling place, especially since the word for house and the word for building above begin with the same three letters: *oik-*. However, when the passage before us speaks of clothing and not being naked, the meaning of a dwelling place makes no sense.

May I suggest the *oikētērion* is what gives our mortal bodies immortality. As 1 Corinthians 15:50-54 tells us:

> Now this I say, brethren, that flesh and blood cannot inherit the kingdom of God; nor does corruption inherit incorruption. Behold, I tell you a mystery: We shall not all sleep, but we shall all be changed—in a moment, in the twinkling of an eye, at the last trumpet. For the trumpet will sound, and the dead will be raised incorruptible, and we shall be changed. For this corruptible must **put on** incorruption, and this mortal *must* **put on** immortality. So when this corruptible has **put on** incorruption, and this mortal has **put on** immortality, then shall be brought to pass the saying that is written: *"Death is swallowed up in victory."*

"O Death, where is your sting?
O Hades, where is your victory?"

The sting of death *is* sin, and the strength of sin *is* the law. But thanks *be* to God, who gives us the victory through our Lord Jesus Christ.

The word for "put on" is *enduō* and is used four times. It speaks of putting on clothes, just as it does in Ephesians 4:24 where it tells us to take off the old man and put on the new man. Ephesians is talking about the clothes of the old man versus the clothes of the new man. The clothes are a metaphor for our conduct. The unbeliever wore clothes unbecoming a child of Christ. The believer is a new man and should wear new clothes, clothes becoming a member of God's family. And so, in 1 Corinthians 15 when it says, "this corruptible must put on incorruption, and this mortal must put on immortality," I believe it refers to the *oikētērion*, that which is incorruptible.

We remember the garden where Adam and Eve originally lived in incorruptible bodies; they could live forever. And they couldn't see or were not aware of their nakedness. Suddenly, after they sinned, they were naked and ashamed. I suggest that it was their *oikētērion* with its beauty and glory that covered their nakedness and would enable them to live forever. When they sinned, that *oikētērion* was taken away. Now they were naked in their corruptible, mortal bodies. But at the rapture this will be reversed. Believers will put on their *oikētērion* and will have glorified bodies that are incorruptible and can live forever. And no one will be naked!

But Jude 6 says the fallen angels left their *oikētērion*. These are those chained and waiting for judgment, not free to roam around planet earth. Why? Because they wanted to intermarry with humans. To do this they had to set aside their *oikētērion* and assume a fleshly body. This was a major violation of their sphere of authority (they left their "proper domain" [NKJ] or "position of authority" [ESV]—*archēn* = rule, authority, office [BDAG]). Because this sin was so heinous in the Lord's sight these angels have been chained up ever since their fleshly bodies were destroyed in the Genesis flood.

This *oikētērion* is very real to me. As a pastor, I have been with many dear friends as their appointment with death got close. With some of them I heard their last words. One in particular named Norm had been a rugged man's man and a golfing buddy. I didn't live next door to Norm, but I saw him often enough that I could see the ravages of cancer as it ate away at him. He had always been proud of his strength and masculinity. But the grim reaper of cancer had reduced all that to a whisper. As he beckoned me close to hear his last words, I vividly remember imaging his *oikētērion* coming down to envelop his mortal body—"that mortality may be swallowed up by life." Of course, I know that won't happen until his resurrection at the rapture, but it was a salve in the midst of grief to imagine that glorious, immortal provision from the Lord covering over his diseased and decaying mortality.

How we long to exchange that which is perishing for that which is permanent. But while we wait for that day, we shouldn't just sit around twiddling our thumbs. Let's consider that which is pleasing.

III. THAT WHICH IS PLEASING   5:9-11

⁹ Therefore we make it our aim, whether present or absent, to be well pleasing to Him. ¹⁰ For we must all appear before the judgment seat of Christ, that each one may receive the things *done* in the body, according to what he has done, whether good or bad. ¹¹ Knowing, therefore, the terror of the Lord, we persuade men; but we are well known to God, and I also trust are well known in your consciences.

This well-known passage on the Judgment Seat of Christ deserves an entire study to bring out its various implications. Items of note are:

- Living a life well-pleasing to God even after we have left our physical bodies (absent)

- Are there punitive damages meted out in light of the words "bad" and "terror"?

- The emphasis on approval instead of acceptance ("well-pleasing")

Though these observations are worthy of extended discussion, I'd like to use this passage to make just one main point: we will be rewarded if we live a life in our physical bodies that is pleasing to Him. Again, this is not living a life pleasing to Him to gain His Acceptance; it is living a life pleasing to Him to gain His Approval. If we don't make this distinction, then we are right back to believing in a works-oriented justification/salvation.

So, we want to highlight one final contrast between the gift and the prize, justification and sanctification, relationship and fellowship, regeneration and rewards. We find this contrast in the Book of Revelation. Here is where we will find a partial answer to the question of what we will wear to the wedding.

A. Our White Robe   Revelation 4:4; 7:13-14

Around the throne *were* twenty-four thrones, and on the thrones I saw twenty-four elders sitting, clothed in white robes; and they had crowns of gold on their heads (Rev 4:4).

Then one of the elders answered, saying to me, "Who are these arrayed in white robes, and where did they come from?" And I said to him, "Sir, you know." So he said to me, "These are the ones who come out of the great tribulation, and washed their robes and made them white in the blood of the Lamb (Rev 7:13-14).

Both passages above describe people in heaven in the presence of God. Although the identity of the twenty-four elders is disputed, we propose the first group wearing white robes (Rev 4:4), are church saints who have been raptured for these reasons:

- They are wearing white robes, which are made white, according to Revelation 7:14, by being washed in the

180

blood of the Lamb. This is "A" truth. His blood gave us a new Position in Christ, a new Relationship with God, the justification of Romans 4.

- The elders are wearing victor's crowns (*stephanous*) as opposed to royal crowns (*diadems*). These are the crowns given to victorious Christians at the Judgment Seat of Christ (Rev 2:10; 3:11; 1 Pet 5:4; 2 Tim 4:8; 1 Cor 9:25).

- The elders sing a song of redemption (Rev 5:9): "You were slain and have redeemed us to God by your blood out of every tribe and tongue and people and nation."[28] Only humans have been offered a plan of redemption.

- These cannot be OT saints or half OT saints and half NT saints because the OT saints are not resurrected until the end of the Tribulation Period (Dan 12:1-3).

The second group wearing white robes washed by the blood of the Lamb was not a raptured group of church saints, but rather saints martyred during the Tribulation Period by the antichrist. They have not yet been resurrected, something that will not happen until the end of the Tribulation (Dan 12:2), but in their spiritual bodies they are wearing the white robes of imputed righteousness, a righteousness that comes by faith, not by works (Romans 4).

So, all believers have been washed clean by the blood of the Lamb and will wear the white robes that symbolize their imputed righteousness given as a free gift when they trust Christ as their Savior. This is "A" truth, but "B" truth is coming. For the white robe given to each Christian is not the end of the story when it comes to what we will wear in eternity. There is also our wedding dress.

---

[28] Some Greek manuscripts do not have "us" (*hēmas*) in their texts.

B. Our Wedding Dress   Revelation 19:7-8

Let us be glad and rejoice and give Him glory, for the marriage of the Lamb has come, and His wife has made herself ready." And to her it was granted to be arrayed in fine linen, clean and bright, for the fine linen is the righteous acts of the saints. Then he said to me, "Write: 'Blessed *are* those who are called to the marriage supper of the Lamb!'"

We have already seen that the return of Christ is portrayed in the Parable of the Virgins as a groom coming to the hometown of his bride to consummate and celebrate their marriage. In the time while the groom is absent, the future bride and groom are engaged. But the celebratory wedding feast will not occur until the groom comes for his bride. And then not everyone is invited to the wedding feast (Matt 22:1-14; Heb 1:9 where the "companions" [*metachous*] are the best friends of the groom, the groomsmen in our culture). These are the close friends of the bride and groom, kind of like our rehearsal dinners. And, according to the text, they are wearing a dress of "fine linen, clean and bright, for the fine linen is the righteous acts of the saints."

Uh, oh. This array cannot be the same as the white robes of Revelation 4 and 7 or else we have a contradiction: the white robes come from the washing by the blood of Christ, but the fine linen is the righteous acts of the saints. The first comes by faith, but the second comes by works. How can we harmonize the imagery? Again, cultural practices of the day help. We need to understand the distinction between the tunic and the toga. The tunic was the white garment worn underneath the toga of a Roman citizen. The toga was an outer garment, something only a citizen could wear. Each toga was unique to the individual.

But the imagery in Revelation goes even further. More than a toga, we have wedding attire. And, of course, the Church is seen as His bride. How does a bride adorn herself for her wedding, and why does she spend so much time and effort doing it? To be pleasing to her groom, of course. How shameful for her to walk down the aisle, so to speak, in tattered attire, hair frazzled, barefoot, smelling like a farm hand.

Let's imagine the scene. A huge crowd of people from every tongue, tribe, nation, and people is gathered outside the entrance to heaven. If it weren't for the brilliant, incorruptible *oikētērion* engulfing the corruptible body of each person, it would be the world's largest nudist colony. St. Peter slips from a side door and calls for attention. His words are short and to the point:

Okay, people, I know all of you would like to enjoy the amenities of heaven. Unfortunately, this is a gated community, and we cannot accommodate everyone. Only those with the correct password will be allowed in. But don't worry, all of you with the correct confession will receive a white robe as you pass by the gatekeeper. No one goes into heaven naked.

Listen up people. The Lord has been preparing your wedding attire ever since you became part of His forever family on earth. Each thread in these linen garments represents an act or attitude of righteousness performed by you while you were on earth. You will be amazed when you see what He has created just for you. And each garment has His own designer label, "JC Light and Power Company." These wedding garments will go on top of your white robes. The robes are your underwear. These beautiful clothes He has made just for you are your outerwear. For those of you who have done nothing to please the groom since your new birth, there won't be any wedding garments. You will have to come to the wedding in your underwear. Well, that about does it. Any questions?

"Can I rent some formalwear? That's what I did for weddings on earth."

"No, I'm sorry, it's taken the Holy Spirit eighty or more years to make some of these wedding garments. And it is custom-made for the person that it belongs to. The time to make these garments was while you were alive on earth. It's too late now."

"Well, what about the password to heaven? I don't want to get that wrong. Brother Pete, reckon maybe I could just slip you a little something on the side and you could whisper that password in my ear?"

"No, again, I'm sorry, but if you don't know the password by now, it is too late. The light from your *oikētērion* will just fade away and you will go naked into the night."

CONCLUSION

Obviously, this isn't exactly the way all this will come down. But most of the claims in our imaginary scene do reflect what we see in Scripture. And my question to you is this: what will you wear to the wedding? The good news: you won't be naked. The bad news: you might have only your underwear. Worse yet, if you don't know the password, you won't have any wear.

But you know, the most fascinating aspect of this passage for me is not the wedding clothes. It is the *oikētērion* of 2 Corinthians 5:2. As I sit with a friend whose outer man is perishing, I think of this passage: The Perishing, The Permanent, and The Pleasing. And I look forward with him to his transition from the Perishing and to the Permanent. I visualize his *oikētērion* coming upon him and absorbing his perishing body. I see his smile of joy and contentment as the groans of pain subside as mortal puts on immortality, corruption puts on incorruption. So, let me ask you,

What will you wear to the wedding tonight?
To be dressed for the Lamb you want to be right.
Do you want to show up with nothing to wear
Because back here on earth you just didn't care?

He gave you His Spirit to help you along,
To give you His power and make you strong.
The time to prepare for this night was back then;
It's too late to think about what might have been.

What will you wear to the wedding tonight?
Will you stand before Him or slink out of sight?
It depends not on caring or sincerity or sharing;
The answer, you see, lies in what you are wearing.

RELATIONSHIP
AND FELLOWSHIP
PART 2

We have suggested that the distinction between a relationship with someone and fellowship with the same is two distinct though interrelated concepts. If we define "fellowship" as enjoying the relationship we have with someone, the concepts are quite simple. I have a son. My relationship with him is a father/son relationship. My son by birth, he will always, for all eternity, be my son; that's our relationship. Nothing can change it. But just because we have this relationship does not mean we are enjoying the relationship. If we have what some would call a harmonious relationship, then we are both playing the same tune; we are in harmony with each other. We call that "Fellowship". Simple as these concepts may be, they are pregnant with theological significance. Eternal security, forensic righteousness, positional forgiveness, reconciliation, propitiation, justification—these and many more crucial doctrines for Christian theology are wrapped into the word "relationship." At the same time the fruit of the Spirit, freedom from the power of sin, the joy of the Lord, interpersonal forgiveness, eternal rewards, redeeming the time, saving the significance of one's life—these and many more benefits accrue to the believer enjoying "fellowship" with his or her heavenly Father.

In the first part of this book, we looked at a number of passages from a homiletical point of view that make more sense when I view them through the lenses of relationship or fellowship. Part 1 is developed from sermons I have preached over the years as a pastor. What I would like to do in this second part of this book is to lay out some of the scholarship behind the sermons. I will return to the OT to show that the concepts of Relationship and Fellowship have always been the way God has intended to relate to his *magnum opus*, man. To do this we will look more closely at two of the covenants God made with man: the Abrahamic and Mosaic Covenants. We will see Israel as a type not of the Church but of the individual believer. We want to show that God deals with individual believers today just as He did with the nation of Israel in OT times. We will propose that our NT theology of the Christian life has its roots in OT theology, specifically the theology of the covenants.

To achieve these goals, we will focus on academic study. Part 2 of this book is written for people with seminary training. It's going to be dry and boring. But no apology. If the scholarship behind the sermons is faulty, then the sermons are faulty as well. But to support the scholarship we must wade into the deep end of the pool with the scholars. With this warning in mind, unless you want to wade through some sluggish waters, I'd just skip this last half of the book. No harm, no foul.

Two pioneer researchers in the study of biblical covenants who stand out in the history of scholarship on the Mosaic and Abrahamic covenants are Meredith Kline and Moshe Weinfeld. Kline wrote his *Treaty of the Great King*[29] in 1963 in order to demonstrate that *Deuteronomy* follows the pattern of the Suzerainty-Vassal treaties of the Hittites very closely. After a king conquered a city or nation,

---

[29] Meredith G. Kline, *Treaty of the Great King.* (Grand Rapids: Wm. B. Eerdmans Publishing Company, 1963.)

he made a treaty with the conquered. He became their lord, their suzerain, and they became his servants, his vassals. He laid out in the treaty what he expected (the stipulations) and the blessings or curses resulting from their obedience or disobedience, respectively. But Weinfeld observed that the Mosaic Law, first given in Exodus and repeated for a second generation in *Deuteronomy* was the only covenant of its type in the OT. The Abrahamic Covenant followed a completely different form of covenant well-known in the Near East called the "covenant of grant." It was a reward for faithful obedience. Weinfeld unpacks this covenant form in his article written in 1970.[30] Since then Weinfeld's work has impacted covenant studies almost as greatly as E. P. Sanders has impacted Pauline studies. According to Weinfeld, the chief difference between the two covenant types is that the Suzerainty-Vassal treaty is a motivation for *future* obedience, while the Covenant of Grant is a reward for *past* obedience. This difference is so significant we will invest considerable time supporting this thesis. Its importance for theology cannot be overemphasized. Our basic thesis is that the Abrahamic Covenant was a reward for Abraham's past obedience, but the Mosaic Covenant was a motivation for future obedience. As such, the Abrahamic Covenant began a *relationship* with Israel that will last eternally while the Mosaic Covenant provided the Israelites instruction on how to enjoy their relationship with Yahweh, that is, how to stay in *fellowship* with Him.

We will begin with the Abrahamic Covenant and then move to the Mosaic. But before we begin, let me again emphasize that our focus is on God in His relationship with the nation of Israel. The justification/salvation of individuals during OT times is a different subject. But to be clear, as dispensationalists we hold that the means of justification/salvation in any of the four OT dispensations

---

[30] Moshe Weinfeld, "The Covenant of Grant in the Old Testament and the Ancient Near East," *Journal of Ancient Oriental Studies* 90 (1970): 184-203.

after Adam's fall (Conscience, Human Government, Promise, and Law) are the same as in the two NT dispensations (Church and Millennium): *sola fide*. But let us begin by establishing these covenant categories.

The Covenant of Grant in the Old Testament

Although royal grants had been observed and documented through archaeology at the turn of 20th century, no one to this writer's knowledge recognized their form in the Scriptures until Moshe Weinfeld. In his work with covenants, Weinfeld was the first to contrast the suzerainty-vassal treaty with the covenant of grant. In his words: "Two types of covenants occur in the Old Testament: the obligatory type reflected in the covenant of God with Israel and the promissory type reflected in the Abrahamic and Davidic covenants."[31] In contrasting the two categories of covenants, Weinfeld comments:

> Both preserve the same elements: historical introduction, border delineations, stipulations, witnesses, blessings and curses. Functionally, however, there is a vast difference between the two types of covenants. While the "treaty" constitutes an obligation of the vassal to his master, the suzerain, the "grant" constitutes an obligation of the master to his servant. In the "grant" the curse is directed toward the one who will violate the rights of the king's vassal, while in the treaty the curse is directed toward the vassal who will violate the rights of his king. In other words, the "grant" serves mainly to protect the rights of the *servant,* while the treaty comes to protect the rights of the *master.* What is more, while the grant is a reward for loyalty and good deeds already performed, the treaty is an inducement to future loyalty.[32]

---

[31] Ibid.,

[32] Ibid.,

These claims are certainly quite sweeping, and Weinfeld offers no complete grants for study to substantiate his claims, although he does list his sources. It would be helpful, then, to review some of these royal grants to see if his claims are correct. Before doing so, however, a brief review of the suzerainty-vassal treaty form will prove helpful for purposes of contrast.

Victor Korošec was the first (1931) to analyze the structure of the Hittite suzerainty-vassal treaties in his *Hethitische Staatsverträge*. He offers the *folgendes Schema*:

1. *Die Präambel des Vertrags enthält den Namen und Titel des Hattiherrschers* (The preamble of the treaty containing the name and title of the Hittite king).

2. *Die Vorgeschichte* (The historical prologue).

3. *Die eigentlichen Vertragsbestimmungen* (The individual stipulations).

4. *Die Bestimmungen über die Niederlegung der Vertragsurkunde im Tempel* (Provisions for placing the treaty papers in the temple).

5. *Die Anrufung des Götter zur Zeugesshaft, unschliessend die Götterliste* (The appeal to the gods for a witness, opening the godlist).

6. *Die Fluch- und Sezensformel* (The curses and blessings).[33]

George Mendenhall adopted Korošec's outline without alteration, and, indeed, Korošec's analysis has been the foundation for all the covenant analyses examined by this writer. He was the

---

[33] Victor Korošec, *Hethitische Staatsverträge*: Ein Beitrag zu ihrer juristichen Wertung, Leipziger rechts wissenschaft Studienliche, 60 (Leipzig: Verlag von Theodreicher, 1931), 12-14.

pioneer. D. J. McCarthy has suggested a variation in the basic schema. According to him:

> ... The document clause to put the treaty in the temple for subsequent readings appears so rarely that it is difficult to consider it a fixed part of the scheme. This would give us the following, slightly revised picture of the treaty forms as a whole:
>
> 1. Titulature:
>
> 2. History:
>
> 3. Stipulations:
>
> 4. List of Divine Witnesses:
>
> 5. Curses and Blessings.[34]

McCarthy believes this form holds true for both the vassal and parity treaties among the Hittites, and since the document clause is not the focus of this study, these five elements set forth by McCarthy will suffice for comparative purposes. Furthermore, the debate as to whether the Hittite or Assyrian treaty pattern was the model for the Mosaic Covenant will not be addressed here. Suffice it to say that the consistent absence of any historical prologues in the Assyrian treaties as well as the conspicuous absence of any blessings amidst the multiplied curses is enough to eliminate the Assyrian treaty pattern for any serious consideration by an unbiased observer. Thus, for the purposes of this study an early date for Deuteronomy and a Hittite model for the treaty form is assumed. With this assumption set forth, Meredith Kline's outline of Deuteronomy illustrates how recent scholars have plugged this covenant into the suzerainty-vassal treaty form of the Hittites:

---

[34] D. J. McCarthy, *Treaty and Covenant,* Analecta Biblica, 21 (Rome: Pontifical Biblical Institute, 1963), 41.

1. Preamble (1:1-5)
2. Historical Prologue (1:6-4:49)
3. Stipulations (5:1-26:49)
   A. The Great Commandment (5:1-11:32)
   B. Ancillary Commandments (12:1-26:49)
4. Sanctions of Covenant Ratification (27:1-30:20)
   A. Ratification Ceremony in Canaan (27:1-26)
   B. Blessings and Curses (28:1-68)
   C. Summons to the Covenant Oath (29:1-29)
   D. Ultimate Restoration (30:1-10)
   E. Radical Decision (30:11-20)
5. Dynastic Disposition (31:1-34:12)[35]

Thus, the entire Book of Deuteronomy has become recognized to be one great suzerainty-vassal covenant. More recent work has refined the outline offered by Kline with considerable benefit in the Stipulations section, but the basic outline still holds. The conclusion is obvious: the Mosaic Covenant was a suzerainty-vassal treaty.

Royal Grants among the Babylonians

But what about the Royal grants? What did they actually look like, and is Weinfeld correct in his contrast between them and the suzerainty-vassal type? To answer these questions, it will be helpful to examine some of these grants. L. W. King was one of the first (1912) to publish the stones and translation of royal grants given to faithful servants in his work *Babylonian Boundary*

---

[35] Meredith G. Kline, *Treaty of the Great King* (Grand Rapids: Wm. B. Eerdmans Publishing Company, 1963), 9-10.

Stones.[36] These boundary-stones (*kudurrus*) are dated from 1450 BCE to 550 BCE, or the entire period of the Babylonian history during which boundary-stones were employed for the protection of private property. These boundary-stones are usually engraved on conical blocks or boulders of stone, and there is little doubt that in many cases they were set up on landed estates, whose limits and ownership they were intended to define and commemorate. Although the actual stones were not intended to mark out the boundary, the formula with which a text usually begins established the limits and orientation of the estate to which it referred; in this sense, the phrase "boundary-stone" may be regarded as an accurate rendering of the word *kudurru*. Seen from a legal standpoint, these stones formed the primary source of information concerning the Babylonian system of land tenure, and incidentally supplied information on the legal procedure in the case of disputes about the private possession of landed estates. King comments:

> The Kudurru-texts had their origin under the Kassite kings of the Third Babylonian Dynasty, and, while at first recording, or confirming, royal grants of land to important officials and servants of the king, their aim was undoubtedly to place the newly acquired rights of the owner under the protection of the gods. The series of curses, regularly appended to the legal record, was directed against any interference with the owner's rights, which were also placed under the protection of the deities whose symbols were engraved on the blank spaces of the stone.[37]

Such a system of invoking divine protection on landed property conferred by the king has no precedent under the Hammurabic Dynasty, nor does the obelisk of Manishtusu, the early Semitic king of Kish, which records has extensive land purchases in Northern

---

[36] L. W. King, *Babylonian Boundary Stones* (London: Oxford University Press, 1912).

[37] Ibid., x.

Babylonia, have any protection in the form of imprecatory clauses or symbols of the gods. Thus, the suggestion is extremely probable that the custom of protecting private property in this way arose at a time when the authority of the law was not sufficiently powerful to guarantee respect for the landed property of private individuals. This would especially apply to grants of land to favored individuals who were settled in a hostile population, especially if no adequate payment for the property had been made by the Kassite king. The disorder and confusion under which the First Dynasty ended must have shaken public confidence and would in itself account for the practice of placing a private property under the protection of the gods. In the actual granting of the land by a king, the area of ground was first selected and marked out by an official known as the *šadid ekli* , while the other officials were associated with the actual measurement of the land so marked out. And on one of the stones, the king himself is recorded to have marked out the land which was then measured by someone else.

The following is an example of one of the grants recorded on the boundary-stones. Some are longer, some shorter. King observes five sections in this particular *kudurru*, which, according to him, was written in the time of Nebuchadnezzar I. The sections are:

1. Col. I, 11. 1-43: Historical introduction setting forth the services rendered by Ritti-Marduk to Nebuchadnezzar during the campaign in Elam, undertaken to "to avenge Akkad" (11.13), that is to say, in retaliation for Elamite raids in Northern Babylonia. The campaign carried out in the summer, the Babylonian army suffered considerably from the heat and from lack of water (11. 14-21). Ritti-Marduk , the Captain of the chariots, did considerable service to the king, both by encouraging the troops on the march (11. 22-27) and by leading the attack against the Elamite Confederation during the battle which was subsequently fought on the banks of the Eulaseus (11. 28-43).

2. Col. I, 11. 44-51: Record of the granting of the charter by Nebuchadnezzar to Ritti-Marduk, in reward for his services, freeing the towns or villages of Bît-Karziabku, of which he was the head-man, from the jurisdiction of the neighboring city of Namar.

3. Col. I, 1. 51—Col. 11, 1. 10: Recital of the terms of the Charter, (i) Conferring on the towns freedom from all taxation, dues, or confiscations on the part of the king's officers or the officials of Namar (11. 51-60): (ii) Securing the freedom of the towns from the *corvée* for public works (Col. II, 11. 1-2): (iii) Freeing the inhabitants from liability to arrest by imperial soldiers stationed in the towns or villages (Col. II, 11. 3-5): and (iv) Preventing the billeting of such soldiers on the towns by providing for their maintenance by Namar (Col. II, 11. 9-10).

4. Col. II, 11. 11-25: Enumeration of the names and titles of thirteen high officials, who were present at the granting of the Charter (11. 11-24) and the name of the engraver of the record (1. 25).

5. Col. II, 11. 26-60: Imprecations intended to prevent any violation of the Charter, or any injury to the record . . . .[38]

TRANSLATION

COL. I.

(1) When Nebuchadnezzar, the exalted and noble prince,
(2) the offspring of Babylon the ruler of kings,
(3) the valiant patesi, the governor of Eridu,
(4) the Sun of his land, who makes his people to prosper,
(5) who protects boundary-stones, who hold fast the boundaries,
(6) the king of justice, who pronounces a righteous judgment,

---

[38] Ibid., xi.

(7)   the strong hero, whose might is devoted to waging war,

(8)   who bears a terrible bow, who fears not the battle,

(9)   who overthrew the mighty Lullubi with the sword,

(10) the conqueror of the Amorites, the despoiler of the Kassites,

(11) the appointer of kings, the prince beloved of Marduk,

(12) –when the king of the gods, Marduk, sent him forth,

(13) he raised his weapons to avenge Akkad.

(14) From Dêr, the city of Anu,

(15) he marched for thirty double hours.

(16) In the month of Tammuz he undertook the campaign.

(17) . . . the axe burned like fire,

(18) and the . . . of the roads scorched like flame.

(19) there was no water in the wells (?), and the drinking supply was cut off.

(20) The splendor of the great horses failed,

(21) and the legs of the strong man turned aside.

(22) The noble king advances, the gods supporting him.

(23) Nebuchadnezzar marches on, he has no rival,

(24) he fears not the difficult country he urges on (?) the yoked horses.

(25) Ritti-Marduk, the head of the House of Bît-Karziabku,

(26) the captain of his chariots, whose place was at the right hand

(27) of the king, his lord, did not . . . him,

(28) The mighty king hastened, and he came to the bank of the Eulaeus.

(29) the kings took their stand round about and offered battle.

(30) In their midst fire was kindled,

(31) by their dust was the face of the sun darkened:

(32) the hurricane sweeps along, the storm rages.

(33) In the storm of their battle

(34) the warrior in the chariot perceives not the companion at his side.

(35) Ritti-Marduk, the head of the House of Bît-Karziabku,

(36) the captain of his chariots, whose place was at the right hand

(37) of the king, his lord, did not . . . him, and drove on his chariot.

(38) He feared not the battle, he went down against the enemy,

(39) and among the enemies of his lord he valiantly forced a way in.

(40) By the command of Ishtar and Adad, the gods who are arbiters of battle,

(41) he turned evil against the kind of Elam, and destruction overtook him.

(42) And King Nebuchadnezzar triumphed,

(43) he captured the land of Elam, he plundered its possessions.

(44) When he had returned to Akkad in triumph and with joy of heart,

(45) Ritti-Marduk, the head of the House of Bît-Karziabku,

(46) whom the king, his lord, had beheld among the enemies and warriors,

(47) concerning the towns of Bît-Karziabku, in the district of Namar, all that there are,

(48) which under a former king had been freed, but through enemies had, contrary to their laws, come under the jurisdiction of Namar,

(49) informed the king his lord, Nebuchadnezzar,

(50) and the king enquired of the judges, and (to) the towns, as in the days of old, (he gave) their freedom

(51) from the whole jurisdiction of Namar, (decreeing) that officers of the king,

(52) and the governor of Namar, and the commandant are not to enter a town;

(53) that the master of the horse is not to bring stallions or mares

(54) into the towns;

(55) that revenue in cattle or sheep is not to be taken for the king or for the governor of Namar;

(56) that a . . . or a homer of cypress is not to be rendered;

(57) that a homer is not to begiven to the tax-gatherer;

(58) that the master of the riding horses is not to enter the towns,

(59) nor to take therefrom mares as riding horses;

(60) that the fences (?) of the plantations and the date-palm groves no man is to cut down;

COL. II.

(1) that they shall not fortify Bît-Shamash nor Shanbasha,

(2) nor build a bridge, nor bank up a road;

(3) that soldiers of Nippur or Babylon, or such soldiers of the king

(4) as are quartered in the towns of Bît-Karziabku,

(5) are not to cause the arrest of any man whether in town or country;—

(6) from all jurisdiction of Namar whatsoever,

(7) Nebuchadnezzar, the king of hosts, freed the towns of Ritti-Marduk,

(8) the son of Karziabku, in the district of Namar, all that there are,

(9) forever, and the soldiers quartered in those towns

(10) he appointed for special maintenance by the governor of Namar and the commandant,

(11) At (the declaration of) the freedom of those towns there are present

(12) Nazi-Marduk, the son of Shaddakna, the priest of Akkad,

(13) Arad-Nanâ, the son of Mudammik-Ada, the administrator of the land,

(14) Marduk-Kudurri-usur, the minister of Bêl,

(15) Tubia-enna, the officer,

(16) Mukkut-issakh, the son of Sapri, the official of the Palace Gate,

(17) Shamash-nadin-shumi, the son of Attailuma, the governor of Ishin,

(18) Bau-shum-iddina, the son of Khunna, the governor of Babylon,

(19) Uballitsu-Gula, the son of Arad-Ea, the provincial governor,

(20) Marduk-mukîn-apli, the son of Tâbumilê, the keeper of the treasure-house,

(21) Arad-Gula, the son of Kalbi, the governor of Ushti,

(22) Tâb-ashâb-Marduk, the son of Esagilzêru, the governor of Namar,

(23) Enlil-nadin-shumi, the son of Khabban, the governor of Khalman,

(24) and Nabû-kudurri-usar, this commandant of Namar,

(25) The scribe who has written this memorial-stone, is Enlil-tabni-bullit, the seer.

(26) Whenever in after time

(27) one of the sons of Khabban, or any other man,

(28) who may be appointed as governor of Namar,

(29) or as prefect of Namar, be he small or great, whoever he may be,

(30) with regard to the cities of Bît-Karziabku,

(31) which the king has freed from the jurisdiction of Namar,

(32) shall not fear the king or his gods, and shall again place them under (its) jurisdiction,

(33) or shall obliterate the name of a god or of the king, which is inscribed (hereon), and shall write another (in the place thereof),

(34) or shall employ a fool, or a deaf man, or a blind man, or a knave,

(35) and shall smash this memorial with a stone,

(36) or burn it in the fire, or put it in the river,

(37) may all the great gods, whose names are mentioned in heaven and earth,

(38) curse that man in wrath. May god and king look upon him in anger.

(39) May Ninib, the king of heaven and earth, and Gula, the bride of Esharra,

(40) destroy his boundary-stone and obliterate his seed.

(41) May Adad, the ruler of heaven and earth, the lord of springs and rain,

(42) fill his canals with mud.

(43) May he set hunger and want upon him,

(44) and may oppression, ruin, and adversity be bound day and night at his side.

(45) May ruin fasten its grip upon the inhabitants of his city.

(46) May Shumalia, the lady of the bright mountains,

(47) who dwells upon the summits, who treads beside the springs,

(48) Ada, Nergal and Nanâ, the gods of Namar,

(49) Sîru, the bright god, the son of the temple of Dêr,

(50) Sin and the Lady of Akkad, the gods of Bît-Khabban,

(51) may these great gods in the anger of their hearts

(52) contrive evil against him.

(53) May another possess the house which he has built.

(54) With a dagger in his neck, and a poniard in his eye,

(55) may he cast himself upon his face before his captor,

(56) and may he spurn his pleading,

(57) and swiftly cut off his life.

(58) Through the downfall of his house may his hands enter the mire.

(59) As long as he lives may he drag sorrow along with him,

(60) and, as long as heaven and earth remain may his seed perish.[39]

From this example taken from the boundary-stones of Babylonia, we see that the basic form of historical prologue, boundary delineations, stipulations, witnesses, and curses is present, just as Weinfeld claimed. But what about the royal grants among the Hittites? Are they similar to those of the Babylonians? And do they differ from the Hittite suzerainty-vassal treaties?

---

[39] Ibid., 29-36.

Royal Grants among the Hittites

Although he has not printed out the texts in full, Hans G. Güterbock has observed the form of the *Landschenkungsurkunden* (land-grant deeds or documents) during the Hittite period. According to him, the grants followed a consistent pattern:

1. The deeds begin with the words: "The seal of *taberna*, the Great King."
2. The land to be given is mentioned along with the person or state to whom it is being donated.
3. The curse clauses (*Vindikationklausel*) come next.
4. A warning is given not to alter the words of the land-grant. "*Die worte des taberna sind aus Eisen, sie sind nich to verwerfen, nicht zu zerbreche; wer (sie) vertauscht, dessen Kopf wird man abschlagen.*" (These words of *taberna* are in iron: they are not to be changed, not to be broken; whoever alters them, his head will be cut off).
5. A final inscription as to the place of writing and the scribe is given (no dates).[40]

The only significant aspects of these grants which differ from the Babylonian are the omission of any stipulations or witnesses. An example of the grants has been published by D. J. Wiseman in his work *The Alalakh Tablets*.[41] In his explanation of the text Wiseman says:

Deed whereby Abban gives Alalah to Iarimlin. Following a revolt Abban conquered the town of Irridi and thereafter exchanging it for the town of Alalah gives Alalah to "Iarimlim,

---

[40] Hans Güterbock, *Siegel aus Bogasköy* (Berlin: Selbstverlage des Herausgebers, 1940), 49.

[41] D. J. Wiseman, *The Alalakh Tablets* (London: The British Institute of Archaeology at Ankara, 1953), 25.

so [n (?) of Hammu] rabi, his servant" whom he "causes to go up to" the temple of Ištar, i.e., installs as ruler. There follow curses against anyone who would break this arrangement or revolt against Iarimlim or his successors.[42]

Here is a literal translation of the grant offered by Wiseman:

When his brother (allies) revolted again Abban their lord (2) Abban the king (?) with the help of IM, (3) Hepat and the divine weapon, went against Irridi, (4) the city of Irridi Abba (n and) his troops conquered. (5) On that day Abban in exchange for (6) Irridi gave a ci[ty . . .] (7) (and) of his own free will Alalah (8) he released (?). On that day Iarimliim, (9) so [n? of Hammu]rabi, the servant of Abban, (10) [to the temple Iarimlim (12) [...] city for city Rev. has given him. He who would alter that which Abban has done (14) and against Iarimlim (15) and his successors does evil (16) may IM tear him to pieces with the weapon which is in his hand, (17) may Hepat and IŠTAR shatter his weapon, (18) may IŠTAR deliver him into the hand of his conquerors, (19) may IŠTAR who makes eunuchs . . . . (20) bind (?) (him) in his privates.[43]

Although this grant does not follow the form outlined by Güterbock detail by detail, the basic outline of historical prologue, boundary of grant, and curses is present. Absent from the *kudurru* form are the stipulations and witnesses already observed.

Royal Grants among the Neo-Assyrians

One final period where royal grants proliferated was the Neo-Assyrian era. J. N. Postgate has done some of the spade work in the

---

Neo-Assyrian grants.[44] He divided the grants into three different categories: (1) grants of land from the king to private individuals as a reward for loyalty and faithful service; (2) grants of land from the king to private individuals made in order to enable them to supply offerings to a temple; and (3) grants of land from the king to priests or temple officials for the benefit of the temple.

It is the first category that is particularly helpful as a parallel to other grants already examined. Postgate comments on these grants that they are legal documents sealed with the royal seal immediately after the superscription as proof of the king's consent. Almost invariably the exemption from various taxes is connected with the grant. In the simple form of the royal grant, the king prepares a document which states that he has presented to the recipient a certain amount of property–which normally includes fields, orchards, houses, and people–and that he has freed this property and the recipient himself from taxes. The document then closes with injunctions to later rulers, curses, and finally the date. There seems to be some variation in the pattern, but these basic elements are usually present. Here are two examples of such grants:

Nos. 9-12: Translation:

1   Aššur-ban-apli, strong king, king of the world, king of Assyria, sovereign, son of Aššur-ah-iddin, king of the world, king of Assyria, sovereign, son of Sin-ahhe-eriba, king of the world, king of Assyria, and sovereign; (impressions of royal seal)

4   I, Aššur-ban-apli, great king, strong king, king of the world, king of Assyria, king of the four quarters, lover of justice, who makes his people content, who always behaves kindly towards the officials who serve him and rewards the reverent who obey his Royal –

---

[44] J. N. Postgate, *Neo-Assyrian Grants and Decrees* (Rome: Pontifical Biblical Institute, 1969), 2.

11 Baltaya, chief of the fodder supplies of Aššur-ban-apli, king of Assyria, one who has deserved kindness and favor, who, from the 'succession' to the exercise of kingship was devoted to his Lord, who served before me in faithfulness, and walked in safety, who grew with a good repute within my palace, and kept guard over my kingship,

21 at the prompting of my (own) heart, and according to my own counsel I plan to do him good, and decreed a gift (?) for him. The fields, orchards, and people which he had acquired under my protection and made his own estate, I exempted (from taxes), wrote down, and sealed with my royal seal; I gave them? to Baltaya, chief of the fodder supplies, who reverences my kingship.

30 The corn taxes of that land shall not be collected, the straw taxes shall not be gathered, the levy on their herds and flocks shall not be levied. Those fields and orchards (error for 'those people') shall not be called up for ilku and tupšikku service or for the levy of the land; they are free from quay and crossing dues . . . they shall not pay . . . or leather taxes . . . his sons? are freed like him . . . permanent ma'uttu . . . before him . . . you will divide, they? will go out.

42 Any future prince from among the kings my sons, whom Aššur nominates for (kingship), do good and show favor to them and their seed. And if one of them? has sinned against the king his Lord, (or) lifted his hand against a god, do not go on the word of a hostile informer, (but) investigate, and establish whether that statement is true. Do not act negligently against the seal, but impose punishment upon him in accordance with his guilt.

52 When Baltaya, chief of the fodder supplies, goes to his fate in my palace with a good repute, they shall bury him where he dictates, and he shall lie where it was his wish. Where he lives you should not disturb him, and you shall not raise

your hand against him, to do him evil, because he is one who has deserved kindness and favor of the king his lord.

60 Whoever disturbs him and removes him from the grave where he is lying, may the king his lord be angry with him and show him no mercy, may he forbid him to walk in temple and palace, and let him shroud his head daylong from the wrath of god and king. May the dogs tear apart his corpse as it lies unburied.

65 Any king or prince who alters the words of this tablet, (may he be cursed by) the life of Aššur, adad, Ber, Enil of Aššur and Ištar of Aššur. A future prince who does not cast aside the wording of this? tablet, Aššur, adad, Ber, Enil of Aššur and Ištar of Aššur will hear your prayer.

72 Ninth day of Arahsamma, limmu of Labasi, chief . . . .

Nos. 13 and 14: Translation: (introduction and conclusion only)
Line numbering according to No. 14

4 After my father and begetter had departed (this life?), no father brought me up or taught me to spread my wings, no mother cared for me or saw to my education

7 Sin-šum-lišir, the GAL SAG, one who had deserved well of my father and begetter, who had led me constantly? like a father, installed me safely on the throne of my father and begetter and? made?? the people of Assyria, great and small, keep watch? over my kingship during my minority, and respected my royalty?

10 Afterwards, Nabu-rehtu-usur, a . . . . who had made revolt and rebellion . . . assembled the people of the city and the land of Aššur . . . . . treaty oath . . . . . . to Sin-šar-ibni, my? official (eunuch?), . . . whom? I had installed . . . the governor of the city of Kar?- . . . with them . . . I made take . . . they were alone in their (hostile?) talk?? . . . battle and war . . . weapons . . . .

15 at the command of Bel and Nabu, great gods my lords,
I ... ... Sin-šum-lišir, my GAL SAG, and the battle troops
of his own estate ... who had stood with him, people ... with
a good name? ... I planned to do them good ... I clothed
them with coloured clothing, and bound their wrists with
rings of gold ... among them ... fields, orchards, houses
and people I exempted (from taxation) and gave to them.

Overall Form of the Royal Grants

What now can be said about the overall form of the grants?
Franz X. Steinmetzer has observed the following elements in *"Die
Grenzsteinurkunden"* (boundary-stone deeds):

A. *Anmerkung formeller Art* (formal descriptive comments)
B. *Beischrift sachlicher Art* (epilogue with technical description)
D. *Datum*
E. *Einleitung* (prologue)
F. *Fluchformel* (curse formula)
G. *Gegensand der Urkunde* (subject of the deed)
K. *Strafeklausel* (punishment clauses)
N. *Name der Urkunde* (name of the deed)
S. *Segensformel* (blessing formula)
V. *Vorgeschichte* (historical prologue)[45]

Steinmetzer traces the boundary-stones in their development
over a one-thousand-year period (1500-500 BCE).[46] He categorizes
the stones in three groups: (1) deeds which are royal grants of land; (2)
deeds which involve lawsuits; and (3) deeds which determine other
legal transactions. During the Kassite time frame (1700-1100 BCE)

---

[45] Franz X. Steinmetzer, *Die babylonischen Kudurru (Grenzsteine) als
Urkudnenform* (Paderborn: Verlag von Ferdinand Schöningh, 1922), 254.

[46] Ibid., 214-15.

the simplest organization among the stones was in the royal grants of land. These were organized simply with elements G-F (see above). The second grouping (lawsuits) added V (historical prologue) and were organized as V-G-F. Steinmetzer calls the V-G-F pattern the kernel (*Keimzelle*) of the boundary-stones. These essential elements, he argues, are found in the oldest stones. As the use of the stones increased other elements were added. First came N (name of the deed), then the epilogue (B). These were added, he suggests, to support the curses. Blessings (S) and witnesses (Z) were included next. He boils all this down to say that the Kassites had two primary intentions for the stones: first to set forth the subject matter of the deed (the gift), and secondly, to guarantee the gift by using religion. The witnesses were then added to make it all legal.

Later, during the dynasty of Isin, other elements were added. But the *"Keimzelle"* of G-F (grant and curses) remained at the center of the stones. Many different combinations (G-S-F-G-G; V-G-Z-F; G-D-Z-F-B; E—G-F-Z-D-A-F; and others) can be observed, but the G-F kernel seems fairly constant. Thus, it would appear that Weinfeld overstates when he claims that both the suzerainty-vassal treaties and the royal grants preserve the same elements: "... historical introduction, border delineations, stipulations witnesses, blessings and curses." The form for the treaty appears much more consistent and set than the form for the grant. Nevertheless, as far as form goes, it is true that some of the grants utilize all of the elements found in the treaties. Therefore, it would seem that Weinfeld's analysis of the form of the grant is essentially correct.

Much more important, however, than the form of the grants is their purpose. Here Weinfeld is quite accurate. The land grants were invariably rewards for faithful service on the part of a vassal to his suzerain. It is worth commenting that a suzerain-vassal relationship was the basis for a grant. In other words, kings did not give grants to anyone but vassals. *The relationship preceded the reward.* It is the reward aspect of the grants along with the parallel terminology between the grants and the covenants with Abraham and David which convince Weinfeld that these covenants are royal grants.

Both Abraham and David loyally served their suzerain. Abraham is promised the land of Israel *because* he obeyed God (Gen 26:5; 22:16; 18), and David is promised dynasty *because* he served God with truth, loyalty, and righteousness (1 Kings 3:6; 9:4; 11:4, 6; 14:8; 15:3, 5). Here are some of the terminology parallels which point to faithful service noted by Weinfeld:

1. "Kept the charge of my kingship" (Ashurbanipal to his servant Bulta) parallels "kept my charge, my commandments, my rules and my teachings" (Gen 26:5).

2. "Walked in perfection" (Aru 15:13-17) parallels "Walk before me and be perfect" (Gen 17:1).

3. "Stood before me in truth" and "walked with loyalty" parallels "who walked before you in truth, loyalty, and uprightness of heart" (1 Kings 3:6).

4. "I am the King...who returns kindness to the one who serves in obedience and to the one who guards the royal command" (Aru 15:6-7; 16:6-7; 18:9-12) parallels "the God...who keeps his gracious promise to those who are loyal to him and guard his commandments" (Deut 7:9-12) and "who keeps his gracious promise to your servants who serve you wholeheartedly" (1 Kings 8:23).

5. "Land" and "house" seem to be the primary gifts given by kings, which parallel the gifts given to Abraham (land) and David (house = dynasty).

6. "Gives it to Adalšeni and his sons forever" (PRU III 16.132:27-38) parallels "for your descendants forever" (Gen 13:15) and "for your descendants after you throughout their generations" (Gen 17:7, 8).

7. "On that day Abba-El gave the city" parallels "On that day Yahweh concluded a covenant with Abraham." According to Weinfeld, on that day has legal implications.

8. The delineation of borders for land grants is a clear parallel.

9. Marriage/adoption terminology used as a judicial basis for the gift of land or dynasty is quite prevalent among the secular and biblical grants.[47]

From the preceding parallels, it has hopefully been established that the Abrahamic and Davidic Covenants are not suzerainty-vassal treaties but rather covenants of grant. By Abrahamic Covenant, it should be noted that this author is referring to Genesis 15 and not Genesis 12. In Genesis 12 there is at least one stipulation regarding future obedience. Abraham had to travel to the land. Any future reward for Abraham was contingent on his going to the land. In fact, it is after he has arrived in the land, built altars, rescued his nephew (a parity obligation in the ancient treaties among co-vassals), and shown his allegiance to the true Suzerain versus the false (the king of Sodom) by paying tribute (a normal vassal obligation) to the Suzerain's representative (Melchizedek) and having a covenant meal with him (bread and wine) that God says to Abraham, ". . . your reward shall be very great" (Gen 15:1). The covenant of grant of Genesis 15 is a reward for past faithfulness to the Suzerain.

It might help to pause just a moment on Genesis 15:1 (אָנֹכִי מָגֵן לָךְ שְׂכָרְךָ הַרְבֵּה מְאֹד). Those with a Reformed bent prefer to translate this: "I am your shield, your very great reward." This is most likely due to the fact that they have a pre-Weinfeld understanding of the Abrahamic Covenant as completely unconditional, a pure act of grace on God's part, a unilateral *berith* (covenant). This is reflected in some of the translations: NIV—"I am your shield, your very great reward." This translation makes God the reward, which is not only an unnatural way to translate the Hebrew, it works against their unconditional understanding of the passage. Kenneth Mathews covers the options well:

---

[47] Weinfeld, 185-200.

The message is expressed by a poetic tricolon. "Shield" (*māgēn*) may be the poetic glue connecting lines one and three. G. Rendsburg finds in the verse a case of janus parallelism; *māgēn* as "shield" parallels the prior line, and its consonants *m-g-n*, meaning "give" (14:20; Prov 4:9), parallel the subsequent line (i.e., reward). The second and third lines can be synonymous (as NIV) in which "shield" is the cause (metonymy) for the "reward," that is, the Lord will bring about his reward (see NJB, NAB). The parallel line thus gaps the subject: "I am your shield//[I am] your very great reward." If interpreted as a synthetic parallelism, the third line adds to the thought of protection, "Your reward [will be] very great" (NIV note, NASB, NRSV, HCSB).[48]

However, just the natural reading of the text would be "your reward will be very great," and this does not need to be tied back to the "shield." The following context defines the reward. It is not Yahweh but rather the forthcoming covenant with all of its attendant blessings. The Abrahamic covenant is a reward. Gentry and Wellum make the same observation when they write:

First, the italicized "am" indicates the verb to be lacking in Hebrew, and the italicized "and" denotes a word not in the original text. The KJV construes as one sentence with "I" as subject and "thy shield" and "thy exceeding great reward" as the predicate. This is not a likely or plausible reading of the Hebrew text. The fact that "and" is also not in the text signals a new, separate sentence in which "your reward" is subject and "very great" is the predicate. The lack of a clause connector ("and") is not unusual in a sequence of nominal sentences. God commands Abram not to be afraid. This is

---

[48] Kenneth A. Matthews, *The New American Commentary, Genesis 11:27-50:26,* 1b (Nashville: Broadman & Holman, 2005), 162.

backed up by two statements: (1) God will protect him, and (2) God will reward him. Both the command and the promises relate directly to the events of chapter 14. Will the "Four Big Bad Boys from the East" be back next year to take their vengeance on Abram? Certainly the fear of reprisal is both real and significant. But your Yahweh will be Abram's shield. He will protect Abram from possible reprisal. Second, at the end of Genesis 14, Abram took none of the spoils of the victory which were his by right. He wanted his sources to come from the Lord and not from the king of Sodom. So Yahweh promises Abram that he will reward him. He is not saying that he, Yahweh, is Abram's reward instead of the spoils of victory. He is saying that he will give something to Abram that will compensate for the fact that he took none of the spoils. The correct rendering is now provided by the ESV: "Fear not, Abram, I am your shield; your reward shall be very great." That this is the correct interpretation is clear from Abram's response. He says, "What will you *give* me?" not "How will you be my reward?" Abram is exasperated: Yahweh has made big promises, but he is anxiously waiting for the beginning of this great nation to reveal itself by the birth of at least *one baby*.[49]

The importance of this cannot be overemphasized. To reward a vassal presumes a suzerain. As mentioned above, since the suzerainty-vassal treaty or covenant was a motivation to future obedience, the covenant of grant was a reward for that obedience. Genesis 15:1 assumes a suzerainty-vassal relationship between God and Abraham that existed before the reward is given. Bruce Waltke recognizes this point:

---

[49] Peter J. Gentry and Stephen J. Wellum, *God's Kingdom through God's Covenants* (Wheaton, IL: Crossway, 2015), 109.

McCarthy emphasizes the important point that the making of a covenant does not initiate a relationship, but rather formalizes and gives concrete expression to one already in existence. In every covenant of divine commitment, the beneficiary first creates a spiritual climate leading to the commitment. As in the royal grants of the Ancient Near East, God also grants gifts pertaining to land and progeny to Noah, Abraham, and David, because they excelled in loyally serving him . . . If a covenant does not establish a relationship, it nevertheless represents the climax of an already existing spiritual relationship . . . *The oaths presume an already existing relationship* . . . In short, the oaths do not initiate a relationship but reciprocate Abraham's loyalty. [50]

This should not surprise us. In Hebrews 11:8 we read, "By faith Abraham obeyed when he was called to go out to the place which he would receive as an inheritance. And he went out, not knowing where he was going." Apparently, Abraham exercised faith in God long before Genesis 15:6. Was this faith not credited for righteousness as well as the faith of Genesis 15:6? It was credited for something, or this pre-Genesis 15:6 faith would not be singled out for commendation by God in Hebrews 11:8. More than likely, the believer is to live a life of faith (Rom 1:17; Gal 2:20; Heb 11:6) from the beginning of his relationship with God until the end of his life. Could it be that every time the believer exercises faith in God it is credited to his account in heaven? Philippians 4:17 would point to just such an account in heaven: "Not that I seek the gift, but I seek the fruit that abounds to your account (εἰς λόγον ὑμῶν)." The word κλέος (BDAG translates this as "credit" in 1 Peter 2:20) also paints the picture of an account in heaven where credits are given for unjust suffering.

---

[50] Bruce K. Waltke, "The Phenomenon of Conditionality within Unconditional Covenants," in *Israel's Apostasy and Restoration*, ed. Avraham Gileadi (Grand Rapids: Baker Book House, 1988), 126-28.

Another passage that would indicate a suzerainty-vassal relationship between God and Abraham before Genesis 15 is Genesis 26:4-5 where it says, "And I will make your descendants multiply as the stars of heaven; I will give to your descendants all these lands; and in your seed all the nations of the earth shall be blessed; because Abraham obeyed My voice and kept My charge, My commandments, My statutes, and My laws." God is trying to persuade Isaac to remain in the promised land and not go down into Egypt. He looks back to His promise to Abraham in Genesis 15 and says this blessing was promised *because* Abraham obeyed his voice, charge, commandments, statutes, and laws. Now, where are all these commandments, statutes, and laws? Some have suggested that they were imposed after Genesis 15. But there is no later record of them. Abraham was obedient in believing his seed through Sarah would be blessed and acted upon it, but this would hardly qualify for "commandments, statutes, and laws." Nor would the potential sacrifice of Isaac.

Acts 7:2 ("The God of glory appeared to our father Abraham when he was in Mesopotamia, before he dwelt in Haran") speaks to a relationship between God and Abraham back in Ur. We know from Hebrews 11:8 that Abraham first trusts in God in Ur. God sees an obedient heart in Abraham and motivates him to future obedience with the promises recorded in Genesis 12:1-3. As Eugene Merrill observes, Genesis 12:1-3 cannot be a covenant since it doesn't follow any known covenant form.[51] However, it could be a précis of a covenant. When we read "commandments, statutes, and laws," we immediately think of a suzerainty-vassal treaty/covenant. But where are these commandments, statutes, and laws? We do not see them outlined while Abraham was in Ur. Nor do we find them listed anywhere in Genesis 12-26. Yet we know they were there somewhere. We know Abraham is a vassal of God when he receives a reward in Genesis 15 and reconfirmed in Genesis 17 and 22. Hence, the "commandments, statutes, and laws" most likely were part of the suzerainty-vassal

---

[51] Private conversation with this author, 1982.

relationship between God and Abraham established before Abraham ever left the land of Mesopotamia. We need to remember the order: vassalage precedes reward. God does not reward people who are not His vassals.

Though the focus of this study is not on the Davidic Covenant, does the same pattern hold? Yes, absolutely. David was under a suzerainty-vassal covenant.[52] That is what the second giving of the law was: Deuteronomy. Because of his faithfulness to keep all the things commanded him "all the days of his life" (1 Kings 15:5), God rewarded David with the promise of a dynasty. The treaty preceded the reward. There must be a suzerainty-vassal treaty before there can be a reward. At the risk of being repetitive, a suzerain only rewards his vassals.

The greatest gift of all was awarded to the greatest Servant of all when Jesus ascended and sat down at the right hand of His Father. When the writer to the Hebrews quotes Psalm 2 ("You are my son; today I have begotten you") and 2 Samuel 7 ("I shall be to him a father and he shall be to me a son"), he was drawing directly from the covenant of grant adoption terminology when the faithful servant is adopted as a son and given a reward. The Suffering Servant is pictured as adopted by the Father and given a name better than the angels: Son. His land grant? Planet Earth. When He sits down at the right hand of the Father, Jesus gets the title deed to our planet to fulfill the dominion the first Adam was charged to fulfill. The Second Adam will claim what is rightfully His as a reward from His Father when He returns to the earth to rule from Jerusalem for a thousand years.

The fact that Jesus becomes the captain of our salvation who wants to lead many "sons" to glory (Heb 2:10) might be an indicator that the Book of Hebrews is written to believers who need to go on to maturity (Heb 5:13ff) and receive their rewards as sons by participating in Christ's dominion reign over the whole earth. The

---

[52] David R. Anderson, *The King-Priest of Psalm 110 in Hebrews* (New York: Peter Lang, 2001), 41.

first ten chapters of Hebrews concern the Superiority of the Faithful Son; the last three chapters concern the Search for Faithful Sons. The entire book might be called "Salvation through Sonship."[53]

Purpose of the Mosaic Covenant

Continuity and Discontinuity

This brings us around to the purpose of the Mosaic Covenant, whether we are talking about the first giving of the law in Exodus or the second giving in Deuteronomy (we will use "Mosaic Covenant" to refer to both). Again, we are looking at this covenant for its significance for Israel as a nation, not for the individuals within the nation. Because the Mosaic covenant is so different from the others (Adamic, Noahic, Abrahamic, Davidic, and New), it is viewed as something of an inconsistency or anomaly among the covenants. Perhaps because of its inconsistency with the other divine covenants, its interpretation also varies widely. In fact, some claim that all the different denominations or branches of Christianity stem from different interpretations of the Mosaic Covenant: "And it is the interpretation of the relation of the old covenant to the new that is the basis of all major divisions among Christians; that is, all denominational differences derive ultimately from different understandings of how the covenant at Sinai relates to us today."[54]

Progressive covenantalists do a good job of comparing the different interpretations of the Mosaic Covenant by approaching the subject from the viewpoint of continuity and discontinuity, meaning how much of the Mosaic Covenant overlaps or is included

---

[53] By "salvation" we are not referring to justification/salvation. We are referring to the "saving of τὰς ψυχὰς" of Matthew 16:24-27, 1 Peter 1:9, and James 1:21. For a fuller explanation see *Saving the Saved* (Houston: Grace Theology Press, 2020), 31-44.

[54] Peter. J. Gentry and Stephen J. Wellum, *Kingdom through Covenant* (Wheaton, IL: Crossway, 2018), 339.

or continues into the New Covenant. The antipodes are Theonomy and Classic Dispensationalism. In the analysis of Wellum and Parker,[55] these two extremes are theological ditches to be avoided. Theonomy promotes total continuity between the Old Covenant and the New. Theonomists like Bahnsen (see *Five Views*)[56] use the tripart understanding of the Law (ceremonial, civil, and moral) to argue that only the ceremonial part of the Law has ceased. They want to carry both the civil and moral divisions into the New Covenant. This means civil laws should be used to govern the different countries of the world. With this approach, all adulterers, rebellious children, homosexuals, and so on, would be executed.

Moving to the right from the theonomists and toward the other extreme (Classic Dispensationalism) are the Covenant theologians. They too recognize three parts to the Law, but they only want to carry the moral division into New Covenant living. They understand a royal moral law that began in the Garden and expresses itself during the Mosaic period through the Ten Commandments. According to Covenant theology, the ceremonial and civil laws ceased when Christ fulfilled the Law (Rom 10:4), and the final and ultimate sacrifice was made at the cross. So only the moral law is carried forward into the New Covenant era. But within the moral law, most of the covenantalists do not observe the Sabbath. To the dispensationalists, who understand the Mosaic Covenant to be a seamless garment that cannot be subdivided (Gal 5:3; James 2:10), this appears to be an inconsistency in their system.

Willem Vangemeren summarizes pre-Weinfeld approaches to the Abrahamic Covenant *vis-à-vis* the Mosaic along the lines of

---

[55] Stephen J. Wellum and Brent E. Parker, *Progressive Covenantalism* (Nashville, TN: B&H Academic, 2016), 71, 85.

[56] Greg L Bahnsen, "The Theonomic Reformed Approach to Law and Gospel," in *The Law, the Gospel, and the Modern Christian: Five Views* (Grand Rapids, MI: Zondervan, 1993), 93-143.

continuity and discontinuity.[57] He cites John Murray as an example of one who sees continuity between Abraham and Moses: "He carefully argues for continuity between the Abrahamic and the Mosaic covenant because under both covenants obedience is an overt evidence of love for God and a condition for blessing."[58] On the other hand, Vangemeren cites Kline as one who understands discontinuity between Abraham and Moses primarily based on form. Kline does not set forth the full characteristics of the covenant of grant as does Weinfeld, but he does see that the "Abrahamic covenant is a 'promise-covenant' in that God made the promise and swore to fulfill it (Gen. 22:16-17)" whereas the law covenant is 'an administration of God's lordship, consecrating a people to himself under that sanctions of divine law.'"[59] Kline saw the Mosaic covenant as inferior to the Abrahamic: it is an "administration of law, bondage, condemnation, and death."[60] It was a parenthesis between two promise-covenants, the Abrahamic and the New. Nevertheless, according to Kline, grace or promise was subject to law: "Coherence can be achieved in Covenant Theology only by the subordination of grace to law."[61]

If these explanations seem somewhat confusing, it is because they are. Trying to subsume the Law Covenant under the overarching Covenant of Grace and then saying that grace must be subordinated to law in order to find coherence leaves the mind spinning. The

---

[57] Willem A. Vangemeren, "The Law is the Perfection of Righteousness in Jesus Christ: a Reformed Perspective," in *The Law, the Gospel, and the Modern Christian: Five Views* (Grand Rapids, MI: Zondervan, 1993), 48.

[58] John Murray, *The Covenant of Grace* (London: Tyndale, 1954), 31.

[59] Meredith Kline, *By Oath Consigned: A Reinterpretation of the Covenant Signs of Circumcision and Baptism* (Grand Rapids: Eerdmans, 1968), 16-17. Note that Weinfeld's seminal article appears just two years later in 1970.

[60] Ibid., 25.

[61] Ibid., 35.

Covenant theologians like to speak of the covenants subsumed under the grand Covenant of Grace as "administrative" periods under grace. This sounds somewhat like dispensations. In fact, in Walter Kaiser's evaluation of Vangemeren he says, "Is [the Mosaic Covenant] a parenthesis, marked by discontinuity in some, all, or none of its substance? If it is totally parenthetical, will not Reformed theology now differ very little, if at all, with a dispensational option?"[62]

The progressive covenantalists of today prefer to see the Mosaic Law as one step in the progressive unfolding of God's *Heilsgeschichte* as opposed to being a parenthesis. Nevertheless, the Mosaic Law is so out of kilter with the rest of the covenants, one strains to see it as a smooth step in the progress of God's redemptive plan for the ages.

Vangemeren winds up being one of those who sees the significance of the Law as something to reveal the sinfulness of man and point out the need for a Savior. This may well be because he interprets the Law primarily in light of the individual rather than the nation:

> Hope only lies in the Gospel, because Moses' law demands perfect obedience and righteousness (cf. Rom. 10:5). The Law is not defective, but people are. They cannot be justified by the works of the law because they fail to keep the law: "The law and the promise do not contradict each other except in the matter of justification, for the law justifies a man by the merit of works whereas the promise bestows righteousness freely."[63] By this Calvin meant that if one kept the law perfectly, one could be justified by law. However, no one could, except for

---

[62] Walter C. Kaiser, Jr., "Response to Willem A. Vangemeren," in *The Law, the Gospel, and the Modern Christian: Five Views* (Grand Rapids, MI: Zondervan, 1993), 73-74.

[63] John Calvin, Calvin's comment on Galatians 3:17, cited by I. John Hesselink, "Calvin's Concept and Use of the Law" (Ph.D. diss.; Basel, 1961), VI, 5.

the Lord Jesus. Every child of God under the old covenant was justified by the promise in Christ. The Law without Christ and the Spirit is dead and brings condemnation.[64]

Generally, the Reformed writers like to divide the Law into three parts: moral, civil, and ceremonial. This subdivision of the Law is not mentioned or recognized in the Bible itself. The Law is viewed as a whole: James 2:9 and Galatians 5:2. Nevertheless, from this subdivision, it is the moral law that these theologians set forth as the common denominator in all ages. In fact, the primary objection of Douglas Moo to Vangemeren's approach is this singling out of the "moral" law as a binding standard for people from the fall to the New Jerusalem. Moo recognizes an "eternal moral will," but he says, "the Mosaic law is not identical with this eternal moral law . . . It is . . . specifically addressed to Israel—and not to the new covenant community."[65]

Moo understands both the law of Moses and the law of Christ to be under the umbrella of eternal moral law, but the former was for Israel while the latter is for the Church (Gal 6:2). "As to the moral law Vangemeren recognizes three uses: (1) the *usus elenchticus* where the Law warns, convicts, and condemns us; (2) the *usus politicus* whereby the Law restrains us by warning us of the consequences for disobedience (cf. 1 Tim. 1:9-10); and (3) the *usus normativus* where the Holy Spirit teaches believers to understand and do God's will." He thinks this third use is the most important.[66]

Moving to the far right, the Classic Dispensationalists (C. I. Scofield and L. S. Chafer), according to Wellum and Parker, teach two ways of salvation: one for those under the Old Covenant and

---

[64] Vangemeren, "Perfection," 50.

[65] Douglas Moo, "Response to Willem A. Vangemeren," in *The Law, the Gospel, and the Modern Christian: Five Views* (Grand Rapids, MI: Zondervan, 1993), 84.

[66] Ibid., 53.

one for those under the New Covenant. The Old teaches salvation by the Law, while the New teaches salvation by grace.[67] As such, these dispensationalists support total discontinuity. That is, nothing from the Old Covenant carries forward to the New since Christ fulfilled the Law by his life, death, and resurrection. This chart may help visualize the different positions on the line of continuity and discontinuity:

Road of Continuity/Discontinuity[68]

←——————— **Continuity**   **Discontinuity** ——————→

Theonomy	Covenant	Progressive	Forms of Dispensationalism		
	Theology	Covenantalism	Progressive	Revised	Classical

Moving to the left from Classical Dispensationalism we find Revised Dispensationalism and then Progressive Dispensationalism. Each of these moves increasingly away from total discontinuity. Whereas the Classical Dispensationalists left the impression, according to Wellum and Parker, that there were not only two different approaches to salvation but two different destinies for the elect (the heavenly Jerusalem for the Church and the earthly Jerusalem for the Jewish remnant), the Revised Dispensationalists (Ryrie, Walvoord, and Pentecost) distanced themselves from any confusion on this issue by combining the elect from all the

---

[67] It must be noted that Ryrie, Pentecost, and Walvoord would never agree that Scofield and Chafer taught two ways of salvation despite some loose comments in the *Scofield Reference Bible*. This note from the 1917 edition of the *Scofield Reference Bible* [C. I. Scofield, *The Scofield Reference* Bible (New York: Oxford University Press, 1917) 115n1] was corrected and clarified in the *New Scofield Reference Bible*: "The point of testing is no longer legal obedience as the condition of salvation, but acceptance or rejection of Christ with good works as a fruit of salvation."

[68] Wellum and Parker, op.cit., 71.

dispensations into one people group during both the Millennium on earth and the New Jerusalem in the eternal state.

Finally, within the dispensational school are the Progressive Dispensationalists, who move even closer to continuity when they claim that David is now reigning in heaven on David's throne as an inauguration of the Davidic Covenant. This is common ground with all stripes of covenantalism, although the Progressive Dispensationalists still see the consummation of the Davidic Covenant fulfilled when Christ returns to literal, earthly Jerusalem to reign for a thousand years before the eternal state begins (Revelation 21). They also cling to the *sine qua non* of all dispensationalism: one program for Israel and another, separate program for the Church.[69]

Of course, the Progressive Covenantalists believe they have arrived at the perfect balance between the extremes. They agree with the covenantalists that the covenants are God's steppingstones across the river of time to set forth the metanarrative for human history. However, they reject the foundation of Covenant theology and its three covenants: Covenant of Redemption before creation, the Covenant of Works prelapsarian, and the Covenant of Grace postlapsarian. Progressive Covenantalists pride themselves on their exegetical methodology, meaning if they do not see it explicitly stated in the text (the Bible), it is not something they want to hang their hats on (one must wonder what they do with the "Trinity," a word not mentioned in the text). Since they do not find these three covenants stated in the Bible, they choose to reject them as the cornerstone of their theology. The same applies for infant baptism; it is not something observed in the Bible, so why use it as a parallel to circumcision?

---

[69] See Craig Blaising and Darrel Bock eds., *Dispensationalism, Israel, and the Church: The Search for Definition* (TN: Zondervan Academic, 1992), Herbert Bateman ed., *Three Central Issues in Contemporary Dispensationalism* (Grand Rapids, MI: Kregel Academic & Professional, 1999), and Robert Saucy, *The Case for Progressive Dispensationalism* (TN: Zondervan Academic, 2010).

Although the comparisons above are helpful in understanding how much of the Law was or was not carried forward from the Mosaic era to the post-Pentecost era, it still does not tell us much about the function of the Law other than to say that some see the moral law in both eras while others see the Law of Moses ending with Jesus and the Law of Christ beginning. So, just what was the function of the Law?

The Function of the Law of Moses

The difficulty theologians have with the Mosaic Covenant is that it does not reflect much grace. It appears to be all about works. Of course, that is an over-simplification in that the prologue of Deuteronomy appeals to gratitude for God's grace (deliverance from Egypt and sustenance in the wilderness) as a motive for obedience. Nevertheless, the vast majority of the treaty tells the Israelites what to do, which we will call works. This covenant is so out of character with the other OT covenants that there is widespread confusion and disagreement about how it should function in the redemptive history of man.

The only other works-oriented covenant in the OT is the one made with Adam before the fall. Because of the requirement of works in both of these covenants many understand the Mosaic Covenant to be a "republication" of the Adamic Covenant, as mentioned above. This causes great consternation for Protestant scholars who believe in *sola gratia, sola fide*. How a works-oriented covenant can fit under a grace umbrella is a question Covenant theologians must answer since they understand an over-arching Covenant of Grace to be God's governing principle from the fall to the eternal state.

Finding a grace explanation for a works-oriented covenant is no problem for some theologians who believe God's grace is actually earned, like C. VanLandingham. Primarily responding to E. P. Sanders and his covenant nomism, he amasses an enormous amount of material from the extra-biblical Jewish literature of the Greco-Roman period to support a works-merited justification at the final judgment. He says, ". . . *eternal* Life is a reward for behavior, not the result of God's mercy for the person who has tried but failed to obey God sufficiently."[70] He quotes Deuteronomy 30:15-19 and then states the obvious:

> These words of the covenant stipulate that proceeding on a path to life depends as much on one's determination as the decision to proceed on the path to death does. One's own actions determine one's reward or requital ... Everything that could be perceived as a gift—land, progeny, peace, prosperity—is part of a *quid pro quo*. These "two ways" of Deuteronomy will signal the way in which God deals with the people in Second Temple Judaism and are, of course, axiomatic for much of the literature of the Hebrew Bible.[71]

Like so many others, he uses typology to transfer the temporal blessings promised to the Jews in the land to eternal blessings in the eternal state. These blessings must be earned. Even though the opportunity to obey the stipulations might be because of the gracious acts of God (Egypt, Wilderness), the condition of obedience to these stipulations must be observed or the promised blessings are forfeited. So, for VanLandingham eternal life is a reward, not a gift. Of course, those in the Reformed camp react strongly to the *quid pro quo* concept, which they see as a retreat to Roman Catholicism. So how do most in the Reformed tradition explain the purpose or function of the Mosaic Covenant?

---

[70] Chris VanLandingham, *Judgment & Justification* in *Early Judaism* and the *Apostle Paul* (Peabody, MS: Hendrickson Publishers, 2006), 46, n, 109.

[71] Ibid., 47.

THE FUNCTION OF THE LAW IN REFORMED THEOLOGY

Most within Reformed theology subsume the Mosaic Covenant under the umbrella of the Covenant of Grace. Since they usually identify only three primary covenants (Redemption pre-creation, Works prelapsarian, and Grace post lapsarian), these other covenants (Noahic, Abrahamic, Mosaic, Davidic, and New) must fit either into or under their three-covenant scheme. Since their Covenant of Grace covers human history from the fall until the return of Christ, somehow, they must work the Mosaic Covenant into a grace understanding.

Meredith Kline shook up the Reformed community when he said in class at Westminster Theological Seminary California that John Murray's understanding of the covenants turns the gospel into "mush."[72] Kline popularized the "republication theory" of the Mosaic Covenant. He divided the covenant into two tiers: 1) Requirements for eternal blessings; and 2) Requirements for temporal blessings. The eternal blessings came by grace, but the temporal blessings came by obedience. Kline ignited a firestorm when he claimed obedience to the stipulations of the covenant were meritorious for temporal rewards. Arguments in favor of the "republication theory" were advanced in a collection of essays published as *The Law is Not of Faith*.[73]

The reaction to Kline and company came swiftly since the thought of anything fallen man can do of a meritorious nature is anathema to those who adhere to the Westminster Standards. Going back to their Augustinian roots, the Westminster divines defined total depravity as total inability. In other words, even the best that fallen man has to offer is tainted by sin. He is incapable of doing anything

---

[72] William Shishko, in Andrew Elam, Robert Van Kooten, and Randall Bergquist, *Merit and Moses: A Critique of the Klinean Doctrine of Republication* (Eugene, OR: WIPF&Stock, Kindle Edition, 2014), 23.

[73] *The Law is Not of Faith*, eds. Bryan D. Estelle, J. V. Fesko, and David VanDrunen (Phillipsburg, NJ: P&R Publishing Company, 2009).

meritorious in God's sight. Andrew Elam, Robert Van Kooten, and Randall Bergquist published *Merit and Moses: A Critique of the Klinean Doctrine of Republication* in order to ring the heresy bell on *The Law is Not of Faith*. Their list of dangerous doctrines spawned by Kline and company when they suggested that one could be rewarded for his good works as set forth in the blessings and other sections of Deuteronomy leaves us aghast. Here are their cardinal doctrines threatened by this leaven of meritocracy:

- Affects God's Transcendence
- Affects God's Justice
- Affects God's Will
- Redefines Merit
- Compromises the Necessity of Christ's Divine Nature in the Atonement
- Compromises the Necessity of Christ's Perfect Active Obedience
- Detracts from Christ's Singular Glory
- Affects the Second Use of the Law—in the traditional paradigm, the second use of the law refers to its function in convincing fallen man of his sinfulness and inability.
- Affects the Third Use of the Law—as a guide for living
- Blurs the Grace-Works Distinction[74]

No doubt these are hefty charges. The accusations become stentorious when it comes to the mere thought that fallen man can do anything meritorious. After all, total inability may just be the foundational doctrine from which the tree of Augustinian/Calvinism grows. If that foundation cracks, then, as the late R. C.

---

[74] *Merit and Moses*, 135-44.

Sproul[75] acknowledged, the TULIP daisy chain will fall into that crack and disappear forever. Yet how can the traditional covenant theologian escape the obvious motivation of Leviticus 18:5—"You shall therefore keep My statutes and My judgments, which if a man does, he shall live by them: I *am* the Lord"? The promise is rather straightforward: do and you shall live. This reads like synergism at the least and monergism at the most, only anthropological monergism—all man, no God.

Nevertheless, these Calvinists admit to nothing of merit for man in Leviticus 18:5. Elam and company have this to say:

> Is our inability to merit God's blessing limited to spiritual blessings and the reward of eternal life? In other words, is there room for the idea that man is able to merit some sort of temporal blessing from God? Our Standards [WLC 193] answer with an unequivocal, "No!" They state that "in Adam, and by our own sin, we have forfeited our right *to all the outward blessings of this life*, and deserved to be wholly deprived of them by God." Not only have we forfeited all temporal blessings, we are unable to "merit, or by our own industry to procure them.[76]

So how do those conforming to the Westminster Standards escape merit in the Law? Simple: it is all in how one defines "merit." Elam *et al* have this to say about merit:

> For a work to be truly and properly meritorious, it must: (1) be absolutely perfect; and (2) be performed by one who is ontologically equal with God (i.e., infinite, eternal, and unchangeable in his being). Adam could satisfy the first condition, as he was created in original righteousness. But only

---

[75]   R. C. Sproul, *Willing to Believe* (Grand Rapids: Baker, 1997), 193.

[76]   *Merit and Moses*, 122-23

Jesus Christ could satisfy the second, since he is both true man and true God, being the same in substance and equal with the Father. This lays the groundwork for the important distinction between Christ's *strict* merit and Adam's *covenant* merit, . . . [77]

The difference between *strict* merit and *covenant* merit is explained this way:

> Covenant merit is assigned to Adam in the covenant of works, whereas strict merit is assigned to Christ in the covenant of grace. What is the difference between the two? Covenant merit is a lesser category of merit when compared to strict merit. Adam's merit is said to be "improper" when it is measured against the standard of Christ's "proper" merit. This designation of covenant merit reflects the ontological considerations which pertain to Adam's status. It seeks to take into account the Creator-creature distinction and God's act of condescension to enter into covenant with Adam. According to the Confession, the establishment of the covenant of works is God's appointed means of condescension, so that man as mere creature may know and enjoy God as his ultimate blessedness and reward.[78]

Herman Bavinck frames it accordingly:

> A creature as such owes its very existence, all that it is and has, to God; it cannot make any claims before God, and it cannot boast of anything; it has no rights and can make no demands of any kind. There is no such thing as merit in the existence of a creature before God, nor can there be since the relation between the Creator and a creature radically and once-for-all eliminates any notion of merit. This is true after the fall but no less before the fall. Then too, human

---

[77] Ibid., 106.

[78] Ibid., 51-52.

beings were creatures, without entitlements, without rights, without merit. When we have done everything we have been instructed to do, we are still unworthy servants (*douloi achreioi*, Luke 17:10).[79]

Francis Turretin gives us five conditions for "true" merit which explain why Adam's merit could never be ontologically equal to Christ's merit:

> (1) That the "work be undue"—for no one merits by paying what he owes (Lk. 17:10), he only satisfies; (2) that it be ours—for no one can be said to merit from another; (3) that it be absolutely perfect and free from all taint—for where sin is, there merit cannot be; (4) that it be equal and proportioned to the reward and pay; otherwise it would be a gift, not merit . . . according to the meaning of the Council of Trent); (5) that the reward be due to such a work from justice—whence an "undue work" is commonly defined to be one that "makes a reward due in the order of justice."[80]

It is most obvious from these definitions that no man before or after the fall could truly "merit" anything from God. Such are the lengths these covenant theologians must go to keep the Law under the umbrella of the so-called Covenant of Grace. And beneath this stratum is the substratum of Augustine's view of total depravity (= total inability). The internecine strife within the Westminster circles might have been easily avoided if they had been aware that Augustine was the first church father in four hundred years to

---

[79] Herman Bavinck, *Reformed Dogmatics*, ed. John Bolt, translated by John Vriend, 2:570 (Grand Rapids: Baker, 2008), quoted by Elam in *Merit and Moses*, 53-54.

[80] Francis Turretin, *Institutes of Elenctic Theology*, ed. James T. Dennison Jr., translated by George Musgrave Giger, 2:712 (Phillipsburg, NJ: P&R, 1994), quoted in *Merit and Moses*, 56.

remove free will from mankind. Furthermore, did they realize that all five points of Dortian Calvinism came from Augustine? And were they aware that Augustine derived his Christian determinism from the pagan religions of Manichaeism, Neo-platonism, Stoicism, and Gnosticism?[81] Probably not. The same verses used by the Dortian Calvinists to defend their "five points" were used before them by the Manicheans to defend their determinism.[82]

Nevertheless, whether one follows the republication theory of the Law or not, it would seem that covenant theologians of every stripe understand the highest purpose for the Law is to show the Israelites the way to eternal life. Calvin himself said, "We cannot gainsay that the reward of eternal salvation awaits complete obedience to the law, as the Lord has promised."[83] However, Calvin's understanding does line up with the "hypothetical" view in that men are not capable of living up to the perfect standard of obedience required for earning eternal life; only Christ could do that. Bryan Estelle, one of the authors of *The Law is not of Faith*, remarks: "The principle of works is re-published at Sinai for a purpose: to drive one to Faith, trusting in God's initiative and provision to accomplish the goal, that is, entitlement to the land of heaven."[84] For him Leviticus 18:5 is a clear soteriological statement.[85] It is interesting that a simple reading of the Law or the entire Torah reveals scant information on how to go to heaven after we die. Enoch made it before he died, but what about the rest of us after we die? I often ask my soteriology students at the beginning of class to get me

---

[81] Kenneth M. Wilson, *Augustine's Conversion from Traditional Free Choice to "Non-free Free Will"* (Tübingen: Mohr Siebeck, 2018), 12-16, 293.

[82] Ibid., 286-98.

[83] John Calvin, *Institutes*, 2.7.3. "Nec refragari licet quin iustam Legis obedientiam maneat aeternae salutis remunerate, quemadmodem a domino promissa est."

[84] Bryan D. Estelle, "Leviticus 18:5 and Deuteronomy 30:1-14 in Biblical Theological Development," in *The Law*, 131.

[85] Ibid., 134.

to heaven from the OT. Some jump immediately to Genesis 15:6. But that passage never mentions heaven. What about Psalm 16? Where is heaven? At first blush what is the message of the Law? Is it not longevity in the land—physical longevity?

Someone will say, "But what about all the typology?" Of course, the typology of the Pascal Lamb *inter alia* points toward the promised Messiah. We know the promised Seed was foremost in Moses' mind because Hebrew 11:25 tells us he chose the reproach of Christ over the riches of Egypt. His Jewish relatives must have shared their hope with him while he was growing up. His faith in the unseen world was so intense we are told he could see the God who could not be seen (τὸν γὰρ ἀόρατον ὡς ὁρῶν ἐκαρτέρησεν). But we would be hard-pressed to find promises pertaining to eternal life anywhere in the Pentateuch, let alone Exodus 20 and Deuteronomy. To say that the highest purpose of something is to reveal a concept it never talks about challenges credulity. It would be like saying the main purpose of the ark, which we know had typological significance, was to be a type of Christ. Really? Wasn't it to save Noah, his family, *et al*, from dying in the flood? Of course, we say, but don't forget the typology. To which we could respond, "Right, but don't forget the main purpose. It wasn't typology; it was to keep the people from drowning."

So too, it would seem obvious that the main purpose of the Law was just what it claims: do this and you will live—physically. Jacob Neusner wrote a book about a Rabbi's conversation with Jesus.[86] Of course, it is an imaginary conversation, but Neusner was attempting to explain the difference between the primary teachings of Judaism and those of Christianity. In this imaginary time with Jesus, the rabbi listens carefully and respectfully, as does Jesus to the rabbi. But at the end of the day, the two go their separate ways, neither having convinced the other to convert to his point of view. Why? According to Neusner, Jesus was a quixotic eschatological prophet concerned

---

[86] Jacob Neusner, *A Rabbi Talks with Jesus* (New York: Doubleday, 1993).

almost entirely with the kingdom of heaven. On the other hand, as a Jewish rabbi who regarded Torah as the ultimate guide for a religious person, his concern was with this life right here and now. The rabbi is somewhat offended by Jesus' attitude of superiority as evidenced by all the "you have heard it said, . . . but I say unto you" statements in the Sermon on the Mount, since Jesus seems to think His way of righteousness is both superior to and supersedes the righteousness of the Torah. The life of this hypothetical rabbi is bound up in the Torah, and the Torah has very little to say about the kingdom of heaven, or life after death—period.

Reformed theology usually acknowledges five purposes for the Law:[87]

1. To reveal those who are in Adam—the relative principle

2. To teach them about their moral ineptitude—the pedagogical principle

3. To present an impossible offer of salvation by works—the hypothetical principle

4. To look to the perfect obedience of Christ—the typological principle

5. To offer relief and forgiveness by Christ's mediation—the complex principle

Will you notice that all five of these purposes are in some way connected to soteriology. But in this study, we are suggesting that none of the above encapsulates the primary purpose of the Law. We do not deny Paul's claims concerning the Law. And we would never deny the beautiful typology that uses physical things to teach spiritual truths. But the primary purpose of the Law

---

[87] Brenton C. Ferry, "Works in the Mosaic Covenant," in *The Law is not of Faith*, eds. Bryan D. Estelle, J. V. Fesko, and David VanDrunen (Phillipsburg, NJ: P&R Publishing Company, 2009), 98.

was something much more obvious. The Abrahamic Covenant established an eternal Relationship between God and Israel, whereas the Mosaic Covenant was given so that Israel could have Fellowship with God. When we use the word "relationship," we are envisioning the familial language used to describe the Yahweh/Israel connection: Father/Son (Hos 11:1). It's a family. And the blood members of a family have an eternal relationship. Notice the word "everlasting" used twice to describe this relationship in Genesis 17:7-8:

> And I will establish My covenant between Me and you and your descendants after you in their generations, for an *everlasting* covenant, to be God to you and your descendants after you. Also I give to you and your descendants after you the land in which you are a stranger, all the land of Canaan, as an *everlasting* possession; and I will be their God" [italics mine].

Even if a father winds up in heaven and his son winds up in hell, their relationship is intact forever: father/son. But just because they have an eternal relationship does not mean they are enjoying that relationship. This is how we define "fellowship"—enjoying the relationship. Israel had an eternal relationship with God (Gen 17:7), but that does not mean she always enjoyed her relationship with Him. That is, she was not always "in fellowship" with Him.

If "fellowship" does not communicate to you, think of the word "communion." Close communion is fellowship. When the Israelites brought male prostitutes into the temple (1 Kings 14:23-24; 2 Kings 23:7, and very likely Ezekiel 8:16) and encouraged barren women to weep for Tammuz and have their firstborn "pass through the fire," she was not in close communion with God. To enjoy her relationship with God, Israel had to be in the land and obey: "'Every commandment which I command you today you must be careful to observe, that you may live and multiply, and go in and possess the land of which the Lord swore to your fathers'"

(Deut 8:1). The Mosaic Covenant told her how to stay in the land, be blessed in the land, be prosperous and have longevity in the land. And God warned her: if she were unfaithful to the stipulations of the Law, He would put her out of the land (Deut 4:25-28). She would not enjoy her relationship with God when she was out of the land.

Among the thousands of words written about the purpose of the Law, there is a paucity of material devoted to the sacrificial system. If anything is written connecting the sacrificial system to the purpose of the Law, the focus is on the typology and the antitypes. And again, of course there is typology in the sacrificial system. But the main purpose of the sacrificial system was not its typology. It was so Israel could maintain her fellowship with God.

Just as justified people in the NT had to have their "feet washed" on a daily basis, so the Israelites who passed "under the blood" when coming out of Egypt needed a way to have their feet washed. As Martin Luther pointed out, one can be justified and at the same time be a sinner (*simul justus et peccator*). How can a person who has been declared righteous in the courtroom of heaven be in need of foot washing? We understand that a person can have all his sins (past, present, and future) forgiven in the heavenly courtroom (Eph 1:7) but remain in need of daily cleansing from sin here on earth. The former deals with one's Position in heavenly places *in Christ*, while the latter deals with one's yet sinful self while trying to walk the walk on earth (one's Condition).

God has made provision for us to have our feet cleansed as we become aware of the filth: 1 John 1:9. As 1 John 1:1-7 clarifies, the subject in 1 John 1 is not our Relationship with God; it is our Fellowship with God. We see the word "fellowship" (κοινωνία) four times in this short pericope. When we are in fellowship with God, our "joy" (1:4) remains full (πεπληρωμένη). This is not forensic forgiveness like Ephesians 1:7. It has nothing to do with future sins. This is fellowship forgiveness for our current condition. The means of forgiveness? The same as with forensic forgiveness: the blood of Christ cleanses us from all sin (1:7).

We see all these elements of Relationship and Fellowship in the Torah. Unless we think in these categories, where the Law fits into the scheme of the covenants can be very confusing. In 1642 Anthony Burgess wrote: "I do not find in any point of Divinity, learned men so confused and perplexed (being like Abraham's Ram, hung in a bush of briars and brambles by the head) as here."[88] Almost two centuries ago John Lightfoot described the revelation of the gospel in the Mosaic Covenant as "dark, obscure, veiled in types and shadows" and "groped after."[89] John Owen said, "This is a subject wrapped up in much obscurity, and attended with many difficulties"[90] And John Ball remarked that the differences in the old and new covenants are explained "so obscurely, it's hard to find out how they [the old and new covenants] consent with themselves in substance." With regard to Calvin's approach to the covenants, Ball observes, "many things herein are spoken truly, but how all these differences should stand, if they be not covenants opposite in kind, it is not easy to understand."[91]

Perhaps it is not that complicated. Perhaps the Mosaic Covenant fits into a different category from the others. Perfect obedience to the stipulations in order to earn eternal life was never an option on the table (the hypothetical option). If it had been, why detail all the instructions on the various sacrifices to be made for various sins. God knew His people were imperfect. He knew they were fallen. But if they did not have some way to deal with their sins in real time, His fellowship with them would be broken. He had an eternal relationship with them (Abrahamic Covenant), but if they persisted

---

[88] Anthony Burgess, *Vindiciae Legis: or A Vindication of the Moral Law and the Covenants* (London: n.a., 1647), 229.

[89] John Lightfoot, *The Whole Works of the Rev. John Lightfoot*, vol. 4 (London: n.a., 1822), 395.

[90] John Owen, *An Exposition of the Epistle to the Hebrews*, vol. 6 (1855; Carlisle: Banner of Truth, 1991), 60.

[91] John Ball, *A Treatise of the Covenant of Grace* (London: 1645), 95-96.

in sin they could not enjoy that relationship (fellowship). Hence, the sacrifices. They fall into two broad categories: thank offerings and sin offerings. Most of Leviticus 1-19 deals with various sin offerings. "And it shall be forgiven him" is a recurring refrain. This is fellowship forgiveness. As Knox Chamblin, a Reformed scholar, observes:

> It is recognized that even the most devout law-keeper shall fall into sin. Thus, the gracious God provides, as *an integral part of his law*, a system of sacrifices and offerings to make atonement for his people's sins and restore them to fellowship with himself . . . [the] "same sacrifices repeated endlessly year after year" (Heb 11:1) . . . will accomplish . . . that purpose for which the Sinaitic Covenant had been established and the Mosaic law given—namely, the deepest mutual knowledge between Yahweh and his people.[92]

Not all sins were forgiven. Numerous sins listed resulted in "he shall be put to death" or "they shall be put to death." If God were to use the Mosaic standard for sexual behavior in today's culture, He would need to wipe out a fair portion of the world's population. Moses would be accused of hate speech and homophobia, not to mention Moses' God. However, the point here is that the Mosaic law was not given to help redeemed people find a relationship with God; they already had one. Again, from Chamblin: "The law is revealed *on* the basis of redemption, not *as* the basis; not as a way to salvation, but as a guide for showing gratitude for salvation that Yahweh has already accomplished . . . The law was a gift of God which was instituted for the joy and edification of the covenant people."[93] But the nation as a whole could be out of fellowship with

---

[92] Knox Chamblin, "The Law of Moses and the Law of Christ," in *Continuity and Discontinuity*, ed. John S. Feinberg (Wheaton, IL: Crossway Books, 1988), 286-87.

[93] Ibid., 284-85.

God, or, individuals in the nation could commit sins that would break their fellowship with God as well. The sacrificial system paved the way for restoration to fellowship.

Another salient feature of the Mosaic Covenant that does not capture much attention among those who write about the covenants is the love element. After all, love is at the very heart of the shema: "Hear, O Israel: The Lord our God, the Lord *is* one! You shall love the Lord your God with all your heart, with all your soul, and with all your strength" (Deut 6:4). Jesus recognized this as the greatest of all the commandments. Never in Genesis do we read about man's love for God or God's love for man. Man's love for God occurs for the first time in the Pentateuch in Exodus 20:6 in the midst of God's giving the decalogue to Moses: "For I, the Lord your God, *am* a jealous God, visiting the iniquity of the fathers upon the children to the third and fourth *generations* of those who hate Me, but showing mercy to thousands, to those who love Me and keep My commandments." Notice the close connection between loving God and keeping His commandments. Is not this what Jesus claimed: "He who has My commandments and keeps them, it is he who loves Me. And he who loves Me will be loved by My Father, and I will love him and manifest Myself to him" (John 14:21)? Exodus 20:6 is the only use of "love" between man and God in Exodus. Could the fact that it is found in the Mosaic Covenant tell us something?

There are only two uses of "love" in Leviticus, and neither is of love between man and God. The first, however, is referenced by Jesus as the second greatest of the commandments: "... but you shall love your neighbor as yourself..." (Lev 19:18). Then in the final book of the Pentateuch, the word "love" appears 17 times in reference to the love between God and the Israelites. So that this emphasis on the love between man and God is not overlooked, here is a list of its uses:

- And because He **loved** your fathers, therefore He chose their descendants after them; and He brought you out of Egypt with His Presence, with His mighty power, driving out from before you nations greater and mightier than you, to bring you in, to give you their land *as* an inheritance, as *it is* this day (Deut. 4:37-38).

- For I, the Lord your God, *am* a jealous God, visiting the iniquity of the fathers upon the children to the third and fourth *generations* of those who hate Me, but showing mercy to thousands, to those who **love** Me and keep My commandments (Deut. 5:9-10).

- You shall **love** the Lord your God with all your heart, with all your soul, and with all your strength (Deut. 6:5).

- Therefore know that the Lord your God, He *is* God, the faithful God who keeps covenant and mercy for a thousand generations with those who **love** Him and keep His commandments (Deut. 7:9).

- And He will **love** you and bless you and multiply you; He will also bless the fruit of your womb and the fruit of your land, your grain and your new wine and your oil, the increase of your cattle and the offspring of your flock, in the land of which He swore to your fathers to give you (Deut. 7:13).

- And now, Israel, what does the Lord your God require of you, but to fear the Lord your God, to walk in all His ways and to **love** Him, to serve the Lord your God with all your heart and with all your soul, and to keep the commandments of the Lord and His statutes which I command you today for your good? (Deut. 10:12-13).

- The Lord delighted only in your fathers, to **love** them; and He chose their descendants after them, you above all peoples, as *it is* this day (Deut.10:15).

- He administers justice for the fatherless and the widow, and **loves** the stranger, giving him food and clothing (Deut. 10:18).

- Therefore you shall **love** the Lord your God, and keep His charge, His statutes, His judgments, and His commandments always (Deut. 11:1).

- And it shall be that if you earnestly obey My commandments which I command you today, to **love** the Lord your God and serve Him with all your heart and with all your soul, then I will give *you* the rain for your land in its season, the early rain and the latter rain, that you may gather in your grain, your new wine, and your oil. And I will send grass in your fields for your livestock, that you may eat and be filled. Take heed to yourselves, lest your heart be deceived, and you turn aside and serve other gods and worship them, lest the Lord's anger be aroused against you, and He shut up the heavens so that there be no rain, and the land yield no produce, and you perish quickly from the good land which the Lord is giving you (Deut. 11:13-17).

- For if you carefully keep all these commandments which I command you to do—to **love** the Lord your God, to walk in all His ways, and to hold fast to Him—then the Lord will . . . (Deut. 11:22-23).

- . . . you shall not listen to the words of that prophet or that dreamer of dreams, for the Lord your God is testing you to know whether you **love** the Lord your God with all your heart and with all your soul. You shall walk after the Lord your God and fear Him, and keep His commandments and obey His voice; you shall serve Him and hold fast to Him (Deut. 13:3-4).

- . . . and if you keep all these commandments and do them, which I command you today, to **love** the Lord your God and to walk always in His ways, then you shall add three more cities for yourself besides these three (Deut. 19:9).

- Nevertheless, the Lord your God would not listen to Balaam, but the Lord your God turned the curse into a blessing for you, because the Lord your God **loves** you (Deut. 23:6).

- And the Lord your God will circumcise your heart and the heart of your descendants, to **love** the Lord your God with all your heart and with all your soul, that you may live (Deut. 30:6).

- See, I have set before you today life and good, death and evil, in that I command you today to **love** the Lord your God, to walk in His ways, and to keep His commandments, His statutes, and His judgments, that you may live and multiply; and the Lord your God will bless you in the land which you go to possess (Deut. 30:15-16).

- I call heaven and earth as witnesses today against you, *that* I have set before you life and death, blessing and cursing; therefore choose life, that both you and your descendants may live; that you may **love** the Lord your God, that you may obey His voice, and that you may cling to Him, for He *is* your life and the length of your days; and that you may dwell in the land which the Lord swore to your fathers, to Abraham, Isaac, and Jacob, to give them (Deut. 30:19-20).

Is it insignificant that there is no other OT book with more than two "love" references between man and God except Psalms? We should agree that the love emphasis in the Mosaic Covenant tells us something about the purpose of the covenant. Even in passages where the word love (אָהֵב) is not used, it is not far away:

Every commandment which I command you today you must be careful to observe, that you may live and multiply, and go in and possess the land of which the Lord swore to your fathers. And you shall remember that the Lord your

God led you all the way these forty years in the wilderness, to humble you *and* test you, to know what *was* in your heart, whether you would keep His commandments or not (Deut. 8:1-2).

What is the point? It should be obvious. The primary purpose of the Mosaic Covenant was to nurture the love between Israel and God. Even most NT books (22 out of 27) either use the verb for "love" (*agapaō*) not at all or only a few times. Outside of John's writings we have Mark (3x), Romans (3x), and Ephesians (4x), before arriving to John's Gospel (20x) and 1 John (9x). And in John's writings most of the uses are in the Upper Room Discourse (16x). Why? Perhaps it is because the Upper Room Discourse and 1 John are about Fellowship, not Relationship. They do not deal with evangelism and salvation. They deal with having joy through intimate fellowship with their Creator. Doesn't deep intimacy (love) lead to joy? Likewise, we are suggesting that the love emphasis in Deuteronomy (far more than any other OT book besides Psalms) indicates that the great purpose of the Law was to show the Israelites how to have Fellowship with the One with whom they already had a Relationship.

Some writers have observed the fellowship purpose of the Law. J. Dwight Pentecost recognizes ten distinct purposes for the Law:

1. It was given to recognize the holiness of God (1 Pet 1:15).

2. It was given to expose the sinfulness of man (Gal 3:19).

3. It was given to reveal God's standard for fellowship (Ps 24:3-5).

4. It was given to teach us how to grow into maturity (Gal 3:24).

5. It was given to unify the nation (Ex 19:5-8).

6. It was given to separate Israel from the other nations (Ex 31:13).

7. It was given to make a provision for sinfulness and thus to restore fellowship (Lev 1-7).

8. It was given to make a provision for worship (Lev 23).

9. It was given to determine whether one was rightly related to God (Deut 28).

10. It was given to reveal Jesus Christ (typology of the Pascal Lamb).[94]

At least two of these purposes listed by Pentecost point to fellowship as among the reasons God gave the Law. Concerning this purpose Pentecost writes: "They were redeemed in order to enjoy fellowship with God. As the redeemed ones faced the question of what kind of life was required of those who walk in fellowship with their Redeemer, the Law was given to reveal the standard God required."[95]

We need to remember that the generation that came out of Egypt was redeemed (Deut 7:8; 9:26; 13:5; 15:15; 21:8; 24:18). Lest it be argued that this redemption was to physical salvation solely, we need only remember that they were delivered or redeemed by the blood of a lamb. The people exercised faith when they placed the blood of a lamb over the door mantle of their homes. In their celebration of deliverance, the Israelites sang: "You in your mercy have led forth the people whom you have redeemed" (Ex 15:13). In appealing to the Israelites to be wise, Moses writes: "Is he not your Father, who bought you" (Deut 32:6). These people were bought and paid for. They were not in need of Relationship truth; they needed Fellowship truth. They had an eternal relationship with God; now they needed to learn how to enjoy that relationship. Wayne Strickland agrees:

---

[94] J. Dwight Pentecost, "The Purpose of the Law," *Bibliotheca Sacra* vol. 128 (Dallas: July/September, 1971): 227-44.

[95] Ibid., 230.

As one studies the Mosaic law, it becomes increasingly clear that its purpose was not to save, for it contains no clear message of salvation or redemption. Furthermore, whatever role the Mosaic law may have had, faith was *not* preempted as the proper response of the individual. The most convincing evidence for this observation is found in Exodus. There God gave his law to an already redeemed or covenant nation (Ex 20). Salvation came to the Hebrews prior to the revelation of the law on Mount Sinai, during their experience in Egypt when they placed blood on the lintels and crossed over the Red Sea. Then we read: "the people feared the Lord and put their trust in him." Such faith rules out the possibility that adherence to the law brought about salvation. Israel acknowledged their spiritual deliverance when they sang with Moses: "In your unfailing love you will lead the people you have redeemed."[96]

Again, Strickland comments in reference to the Law:

The entire life of the Old Testament saint was regulated, including diet and marital relationships. Israel needed such instruction to maintain fellowship with God as his redeemed people. The law therefore functioned as a means of blessing for those already redeemed . . . Disobedience to the law did not remove them from the coveted covenant relationship, for that relationship depended on God's faithfulness. However, disobedience did affect the *enjoyment* of the blessings attendant to salvation. Note, however, that the consequences for disobedience to the law are not stated in terms of eternal condemnation, but

---

[96] Wayne G. Strickland, "Inauguration of the Law of Christ with the Gospel," in *The Law, the Gospel, and the Modern Christian: Five Views* (Grand Rapids: Zondervan, 1993), 233.

rather in terms of physical, temporal punishment (Deut 28:58-62). This also indicates the law did not have Israel's eternal salvation in view. Finally, the law included not only a description of the requirement of holiness, but also the provision for forgiveness for Israel's failure to obey through the prescribed sacrifices (e.g., Lev 1-7). The blood of the sacrifice brought about cleansing, sanctification, and renewed fellowship.[97]

Lest it be argued that only dispensationalists recognize the purpose of fellowship for the Law, here is what Walter Kaiser, a non-dispensationalist has to say about Leviticus 18:5: "In the context of Leviticus 18, the customs of the pagans were contrasted with the happy privilege that Israel had of perpetuating a life already begun by their continuing to do the law. This is similar, then to John 10:10—'have come that they may have life, and have it to the full.'"[98] Again: "The conditionality taught in these texts does not relate to the promise of eternal life or salvation taught in either the Old or New Testament. Instead, the conditions relate to the quality of life lived in the promise and the joy of participating in all the benefits of that promise."[99] Kaiser also made this important observation: "When Israel broke the law of God, they did not thereby forfeit their relationship to the Lord God [Relationship], rather that very law made provision for the forgiveness and removal of all sins (Lev. 16) [Fellowship]."[100]

---

[97] Ibid., 237-38.

[98] Walter C. Kaiser, Jr., "The Law as God's Gracious Guidance for the Promotion of Holiness," in *The Law, the Gospel, and the Modern Christian: Five Views* (Grand Rapids, MI: Zondervan, 1993), 185.

[99] Ibid., 191.

[100] Walter C. Kaiser, Jr (1971), "Leviticus 18:5 and Paul: Do This and You Shall Live (Eternally?)" in *Journal of the Evangelical Theological Society*, 14 (1), 22.

Patrick Fairbairn is another who recognizes the difference between Relationship and Fellowship, even if he did not use those words:

> Neither Moses nor Ezekiel, it is obvious, meant that the life spoken of, which comprehends whatever is really excellent and good, was to be acquired by means of such conformity to the enactments of heaven; for life in that sense already was theirs [Relationship] .... Doing the things, they lived in them; because life thus had its due exercise and nourishment and was in a condition to enjoy [Fellowship] the manifold privileges and blessing secured in the covenant. And the very same may be said of the precepts and ordinances of the gospel: a man lives after the higher life of faith only insofar as he walks in conformity with these; for though he gets life by a simple act of faith in Christ [Relationship], he cannot exercise, maintain, and enjoy it [Fellowship] but in connection with the institutions and requirements of the gospel.[101]

Even Scott Hahn, a graduate of Gordon-Conwell Seminary who converted to Roman Catholicism, recognizes the purpose of the Deuteronomic law as restoration to fellowship: "... the Deuteronomic covenant was ... given for the purpose of restoring (and rehabilitating) the twelve tribes of Israel following their apostasy at Baal-peor."[102] Again Hahn's understanding is very close to that of this author when he writes:

---

[101] Patrick Fairbairn, *An Exposition of Ezekiel* (Evansville, IN: Sovereign Grace, 1960), 215-16 (insertions mine).

[102] Scott W. Hahn, *Kinship by Covenant* (New Haven, CT: Yale University Press, 2009), 68-69.

The gift of life from father to son is unmerited [Relationship], and thereafter a father will love his son unconditionally. Yet it is precisely because of his unconditional love that the father wishes his son to practice the virtues he himself possesses, and thus become like the father and so enjoy deeper communion [Fellowship] with him. When this familial model is applied to the theological concepts of grace in law, we see that the divine grace—the unconditional love of the father—is always primary, and the divine law—the virtue required of the son to be in the image of his father—flows naturally and necessarily from that grace. Once these covenant relations and obligations are reexamined in the light of the natural complexity of kinship relations and obligations, there is no need to posit any inherent tension between unconditional grace and the conditions of law, or between unilateral or bilateral covenant relations.[103]

God had not given up on His promises to the nation via Abraham. While the Hebrew people were in Egypt, Yahweh still had a Relationship with them, but they were sadly out of Fellowship. Berkhof, a respected Reformed scholar, wrote: "It was not the salvation of the Israelite [Relationship], but his theocratic standing in the nation, and the enjoyment of external blessings [Fellowship] that was made dependent on keeping of the law."[104] And Moshe Weinfeld, who certainly had no Christian theological axe to grind as he was not a Christian, observes:

'Life' in the book of Deuteronomy, as in both Israelite and non-Israelite wisdom literature, constitutes the framework of reward . . . 'Life' here denotes 'happiness,' that is to say, life

---

[103] Ibid., 335.

[104] Louis Berkhof, *Systematic Theology* (Grand Rapids: Eerdmans, 1939), 298.

in its fullest sense. Deuteronomy promises life and longevity to the obedient Israelites . . . Addition of the word 'good' indicates the sense in which 'life' is employed in the book of Deuteronomy: it is the 'good life,' i.e. a full life, in brief — a happy life . . . The promise of reward in Deuteronomy is indeed generally expressed in terms of *life and the good* . . . The experience of a good life evokes joyousness within the heart of the individual. This sense or experience of joy is also one of the distinctive features of reward.[105]

To extrapolate the concept of eternal life from all the references to temporal life in Deuteronomy is for many a "bridge too far."

But why have so few keyed in on these nuggets lying openly on the riverbed for all to see? Here are some suggested reasons:

1. They seem to miss the primary distinction between the grants and the treaties proposed by Weinfeld: the Suzerainty-Vassal treaty/covenant was a motivation for *future* obedience, while the Covenant of Grant was a reward for *past* obedience.[106] This distinction alone makes Deuteronomy unique among the covenants unless we agree with those who understand it to be a republication of the Adamic covenant. The Noahic, Abrahamic, Davidic, New—all fall into the grant

---

[105] Moshe Weinfeld, *Deuteronomy and the Deuteronomic School* (Winona Lake, IN: Oxford University Press, 1992), 307-11.

[106] Ibid. Hahn has identified only three contemporary scholars who challenge Weinfeld's work on the grant covenants: G. N. Knoppers ["Ancient Near Eastern Royal Grants and the Davidic Covenant," *JAOS* 116 (1996): 670-91], D. N. Freedman and D. A. Miano ["The People of the New Covenant," in *The Concept of the Covenant in the Second Temple Period* (ed. S. E. Porter and J. C. R. de Roo; JSJSup 71; Leiden: Brill, 2003), 4-5; 7-26]. He answers these challenges summarily (Hahn, 177-79).

category. Thus, we should expect the Mosaic to be unique and should stop trying to force it into the paradigm of the others.

2. They try to explain God's works-standard as a probationary administration of the overarching Covenant of Grace to prove to men that they could not measure up to the standard required for eternal life. But if that were the true purpose of all these "works," why have a sacrificial system? God knew they could not keep the standard. He knew they would sin. So, He made provision for their failures to bring them back into fellowship. By availing themselves of the sacrificial system to maintain fellowship after they had sinned the Israelites were actually keeping the Law! "One of the ways of *doing* the law was to recognize that that same law made provisions for those who failed to keep the law in that it provided for sacrifices and the forgiveness of one's sins."[107]

3. The NT use of Leviticus 18:5 prompts them to see the entire Mosaic Covenant through redemptive eyes. They, like John Calvin, assume "live" in Leviticus 18:5 means "live eternally," a classic case of inserting one's theology into the text. Again, we acknowledge and appreciate the typology that points to the Christ, the Messiah, as the only One who could fulfill the standard and live the perfect life, the righteousness of which would be credited to the heavenly account of any and all who would put their trust in Him. But if you were an Israelite living under the Law of Moses, your primary concern year by year would be whether your offering would be sufficient to clean your sin-slate once a year and whether the Lord would accept the sprinkling performed by the high priest. They

---

[107] Strickland, 191.

felt guilty. They wanted fellowship. The never-ending attempt by Covenant theologians to make the Mosaic Covenant primarily redemptive when it was given to a people already redeemed is the proverbial attempt to put the square peg into the round hole. It simply does not fit.

4. They view the Law through jaundiced eyes. Viewing the Law through the spectacles of the NT can leave one with a negative view of the Law. Supposedly, it was given to condemn; it was given to expose our sinfulness; it was given to reveal our need for a Savior. But nowhere in the OT do we read that the Law was given to condemn. Nowhere do we read that the Law was unattainable. Quite the opposite. As a matter of fact, Paul himself claims that he was blameless regarding the righteousness which is in the Law (Phil 3:6). Of Zacharias and Elizabeth, it is said, "they were both righteous before God, walking in all the commandments and ordinances of the Lord blameless" (Luke 1:6). Even the tenth commandment on covetousness is set in a specific context: "You shall not covet your neighbor's house; you shall not covet your neighbor's wife, nor his male servant, nor his female servant, nor his ox, nor his donkey, nor anything that *is* your neighbor's" (Ex 20:17). Everything forbidden was tied to my neighbor, and much of it was probably sexual in nature. Hence, as given in Exodus, even the moral law was attainable. Why would God give these commandments and explain that they were the key to a good, long, and prosperous life in the land if they could not be kept? The life promised was not eternal life, but temporal life. Those like Kline and Horton who extrapolate eternal life from the temporal promise of Leviticus 18:5 have created an imaginary doctrine from silence. There exists not one redemptive promise in the entire Mosaic Covenant (meaning promise of eternal life).

5. They maintain their focus on the individual rather than the nation. Although covenants such as the Adamic, the Noahic, the Abrahamic, and the Davidic were with individuals, the Mosaic covenant was with a nation:

> The Law was designed for a nation and was therefore administered by the magistracy for the purpose of maintaining social order, religious conformity and national stability. Although it had to be kept by the individual Israelite, it was not designed to be central in a one-to-one personal relationship to God, a relationship of faith, guided by the Spirit.[108]

The Mosaic Covenant must be viewed with eyes to the nation rather than the individual. The Adamic, Noahic, Abrahamic, and Davidic were covenants made with individuals, but not the Mosaic. Moses might have been the mediator of the covenant, but the covenant was made with the nation. If the nation was blessed, no doubt individuals in the nation would be blessed as well. If the nation were cursed and put out of the land, the vast majority of the individuals in the nation would be put out of the land. But it is Israel as a nation that is called "son" by Yahweh.

But someone might object: if Leviticus 18:5 is not soteriological, how does one explain Paul's use of this verse in Romans 10:5 and Galatians 3:12 where surely he attaches soteriological meaning? There are a number of interpretations offered by scholars.

---

[108] Eaton, *Condemnation*, 84.

Romans 10:5

We will look first at Romans 10:5: "For Moses writes about the righteousness which is of the law, *"The man who does those things shall live by them."* Here are some options:

1. The Typological View

This view sees Leviticus 18:5 as physical salvation but typological of spiritual salvation. Since there is nothing in the immediate or distant context that even hints of eternal life, it is conceded that the promise of this verse is longevity in the land with possible overtones regarding the quality of one's existence in the land, in other words, not just a long life but a long life of prosperity, good health, and many offspring. But, since Paul's use of the verse is in a soteriological context (Rom 10:1, 9, 10, 13), he must understand the promise of longevity in the land to bleed over into eternal life (irrespective of whether he understood the verse to be a hypothetical offer or not). With the same *sensus plenior* used to explain Hosea 11:1 ("When Israel *was* a child, I loved him, and out of Egypt I called My son") as a reference to Jesus (Matt 2:15), Paul interprets "shall live" in Leviticus to be a type of eternal life, albeit eternal life achieved by keeping the Law.[109]

The problem with this view is that Paul would contradict himself. He has made the claim that no one can be justified by works of the law (Rom 3:28). If he then holds to an eternal life interpretation of Leviticus 18:5, he must acknowledge two ways of obtaining eternal life (one by law and one by faith) or that Leviticus offers a hypothetical approach to obtaining eternal life (if one could perfectly keep the Law, he could earn eternal life, but no one can do that except Christ). Neither option makes good sense. What would be the point

---

[109] See Anders Nygren, *Commentary on Romans* (Minneapolis, MN: Augsburg Fortress Pub, 1978), 384. The original version of the book was published in 1944.

of holding out a promise of a happy life in the land if that life could only be achieved by keeping the Law to perfection? Since no one can do that, the only life left for the Israelites was one haunted by the curses of Deuteronomy 29.

2. The Hypothetical View

This is a view imposed on Leviticus 18:5 by those who cannot accept that the Law does not have within it an offer of eternal life. As previously mentioned some see two tiers within the law: the physical and the spiritual. On the physical plane, those who keep the Law will have a good or what Weinfeld calls a "happy" life in the land. And on the spiritual plane, those who keep the Law will be rewarded with eternal life after they die physically. This is salvation by works, pure and simple, or as Kline and Horton would have it, a republication of the Adamic covenant, the so-called Covenant of Works.

There is just one problem: fallen man is incapable of keeping the Law perfectly, a requirement for gaining eternal life. Thus, the promise of Leviticus 18:5 is only hypothetical, meaning *if* a person could keep the Law perfectly, he could earn his way to heaven. Of course, he is incapable of such a life of perfection, so the plan of salvation by works was no plan at all. Why, then, make such a gratuitous promise? Obviously, to reveal the imperfection of every person and drive them to the One who could and did keep the Law perfectly. By placing their faith in Him, His perfect righteousness could be imputed to them.

It must be restated that nowhere in Leviticus 18:5 or its context is there any hint that the writer of Leviticus had such thoughts swimming in his brain. The entire hypothetical view is concocted in effort to explain what was happening in Paul's mind when he included this verse in Romans 10, to superimpose some soteriology into the Law, and to neutralize any legitimate implication of salvation by works within the Law. To the unsophisticated reader, the entire proposal appears to suffer from a failure to launch.

3. The Non-Soteriological View of "Saved" in Romans 10

This view rests primarily on some observations concerning the word σῴζειν (to save) or σωτηρία (salvation) in the Book of Romans. In Romans 10:10 we are told that with the heart one believes unto righteousness and with the mouth one confesses unto salvation. The word "unto" is εἰς, which usually has a goal in mind, that is, "with a view to." So, this text really does say that one confesses with the mouth "with a view to" or "with the goal in mind" of salvation. This leaves the obvious dilemma: what if one does not confess with his mouth? Can he go to heaven? If one is honest with the text, he must admit that to be saved one must confess with his mouth. To explain the dilemma as "evidence of salvation" simply circumvents the problem. In Romans 10:10, one absolutely must confess with his mouth to be saved. Of course, this transparent understanding of the text has led many evangelists to the declaration that men and women must respond to an invitation to come to the front and confess Christ with their mouths if they wish to go to heaven.[110]

But for those who can free themselves of the shackles of traditional thinking long enough to explore new solutions to old problems, confession with the mouth is certainly a work. Circumcision was identified as a work by Paul. What are some of the characteristics of a work? It is observable by the naked eye, accomplished by physical means, and performed by a human agent. All these are true of circumcision, but they are also true of confession with the mouth. If circumcision is a work, so also is confession with the mouth. But that means we must perform a work in order to be saved. Since we do not believe in salvation by works (Eph 2:8-10), there must be another explanation. Either confession with the mouth is not a work or it could be that the salvation to which Paul refers in this passage is not reception of eternal life. Perhaps it is in one of the other categories we have already observed to be beyond

---

[110] Ibid., 382-383.

the scope of the spiritual salvation which grants us eternal life, or perhaps it is in a new category, one which we have yet to observe until now.

One way to solve our apparent dilemma is to use our concordance to research other uses of σῴζειν and σωτηρία in Romans (Biblical Theology). The first use we find of the verb σῴζειν is in Rom 5:9. It is used again in the next verse. In both verses, we find that the readers have already been justified (v. 9) and reconciled (v. 10), but they have not yet been "saved" (vv. 9 and 10). In both verses, the justification is in the past and the reconciliation is in the past. These past tenses (aorist participles) place the action of the verbs before the action of the main verbs—"shall be saved." But the salvation spoken of is yet future. The tense of both verbs is future. These people have been justified and reconciled, but they have not yet been saved. If they died before receiving the Book of Romans, they would go to heaven because they had been justified and reconciled. But they would not be saved. We cannot escape this truth. Again, the tense of both verbs for being saved in these verses is future. So once again as in Romans 10:10, we are faced with the fact that "saved" here in Rom 5:9-10 might mean something other than the salvation which takes someone to heaven when they die. What could it mean?

We need to look for other clues. Perhaps it would help to ask ourselves what the Romans were to be saved from. Rom 5:9 tells us exactly what they will be saved from: wrath (ὀργὴ). But what is that? Does not wrath refer to God's judgment on unbelievers for eternity? This is lexically possible, but the key is to establish the meaning of "wrath" in Romans. Once again, we search in our concordance for the first use of wrath in Romans to see if it gives us any clues. It certainly does. The first use of wrath in Romans is found in Rom 1:18. There it tells us that the "wrath" of God "is revealed" from heaven against all ungodliness and unrighteousness of men who hold back the truth in unbelief. The important factor to notice is the present tense of "is revealed" (αποκαλύπτεται). This wrath is presently being revealed from heaven against the ungodliness and unrighteousness of mankind. This is not referring to something that will take place at the Great White Throne Judgment (as a matter of fact, there is no use of ὀργὴ in the NT which links it directly to the Great White Throne). It is in no way connected with eternal judgment in Romans 1:18. This is a present time judgment.

Specifically, this wrath is defined in the rest of Romans 1 as three stages of God's giving sinful man over to the control of his sinful nature as he descends the staircase into the basement of depravity. The phrase παρέδωκεν αὐτοὺς ὁ θεός (God gave them up/over) defines these three stages in vv. 24, 26, and 28. The bottom of the basement is to have a mind that is ἀδόκιμον, "disapproved" or "unable to tell right from wrong." It is total control by the sin nature. That is wrath in Rom 1:18ff.

So let us try it out in Rom 5:9 to see if it makes any sense. "Much more, then, having now been justified by His blood, we shall be saved from wrath [the control of our sinful nature] through Him." Does that make sense? Perhaps. But does it fit the rest of the context? In Rom 5:10, it says that we were reconciled (past tense) through the death of His Son, but we shall be saved (future tense) through His life. If the meaning of wrath in Rom 5:9 is adhered to, then the saving in Rom 5:9 must also refer to being saved from the tyranny of the sin nature in our lives. And this does make sense. We were saved from the penalty of sin by His death, but we shall be saved from the power of sin by His life. We gained eternal life as He became our substitute in death, but we shall enjoy an abundant life as He becomes our substitute in life. "I am crucified with Christ; nevertheless, I live; yet not I, but *Christ lives in me* . . . ." (Gal 2:20). The hardest thing for a non-Christian to believe in is the substitutionary death of Christ, but the hardest thing for a Christian to believe in is the substitutionary life of Christ. Rom 5:10 is about His substitutionary life. In this "swing section" of Romans Paul turns his focus on justification from the penalty of sin to salvation from the power of sin. And being saved in this section is to be delivered from the tyranny of the sin nature in one's life (the wrath of Rom 1:18).

Could this meaning of "saved" fit in Romans 10? In Romans 5, being saved was an advance in the Christian life beyond being justified. Being justified delivers one from the penalty of sin; being saved delivers one from the power of sin. Could these definitions work in Romans 10? Possibly. If one looks at v. 9 as an equation, it would look like this: Belief + Confession = Salvation. The verse also makes it clear that belief is a matter of the heart, whereas confession is a matter of the mouth. One is internal, while the other is external. One is spiritual, the other physical. But v. 10 explains that it is the internal transaction of belief which results in righteousness. This righteousness (δικαιοσύνη) is the same righteousness accorded to Abraham in Rom 4:3 (Gen 15:6), δικαιοσύνη. "Abraham believed, and it was reckoned [imputed = ἐλογίσθη, the aorist tense of λογίζεται] unto him for righteousness." Paul has already established that imputed righteousness is the direct result of faith and faith alone. The verb form for all this is "to justify" (ἐδικαιόω—can you see this is the same root as δικαιοσύνη?). By faith and faith alone, one is justified or credited with the righteousness of Christ. It is a matter of the heart.

But with the mouth confession is made "with the goal of" (*eis*) salvation. Once again, let us suspend our ingrained presupposition that salvation or being saved must be equivalent to justification or the transaction which would put us in heaven if we died. Let us assume for the sake of argument that this salvation is a step beyond justification, just as it was in Rom 5:9-10. Let us adopt the same definition we discovered in the context of Romans 5, that is, to be saved is to be delivered from wrath, the tyranny of the sin nature in one's life (Rom 1:18ff). If this is so, obviously deliverance from the penalty of sin is a prerequisite for deliverance from the power of sin. In other words, justification must precede sanctification. No one will be sanctified who has not already been justified. With this understanding in mind, Rom 10:9-10 tells us that one believes in his heart with the goal of being justified, and he confesses with his mouth with the goal of being sanctified, or saved, or delivered from the power of the sin nature in his life. We propose that this understanding makes sense and fits the following context.

Paul himself wants to prove this point, and he calls upon Scripture to achieve his goal. He equates "calling upon the name of the Lord" with confession with the mouth. We know this because of the common understanding that if A = B and B = C, then A = C. In v. 10 he said that "confession with the mouth" (A) leads to "salvation" (B), and in v. 13 he says that being "saved" (B) comes from "calling upon the name of the Lord" (C); therefore, A = B, B = C, and A = C: Confession with the Mouth = Calling upon the Name of the Lord.

But notice from the progression in vv. 14-15a that calling upon the name of the Lord is a separate, distinct, and subsequent act to believing. This becomes transparent if we follow the progression in reverse: (1) After the sending comes the preaching; (2) after the preaching comes the hearing; (3) after the hearing comes the believing; and (4) after the believing comes the calling upon. The actions here are sequential. The calling upon and the believing are not identical actions, nor are they concomitant. After one believes, he can then call upon the name of the Lord (confess with his mouth the Lord Jesus). But this leaves the obvious question of whether one can believe and *not* call upon the name of the Lord.

In order to answer this question, we once again retreat to our concordance to find other uses of "calling upon the name of the Lord." We discover from its usage in Acts 7:59; 9:14, 21; 1 Cor 1:2, and 2 Tim 2:22, that to "call upon the name of the Lord" is to openly, publicly identify with or to worship Him. Saul of Tarsus found believers because he asked where they were meeting. He was told they were "calling upon the name of the Lord" at the house of Festus. So, off he went to find and persecute them. What we discover, then, from Romans 10:9-10 is that calling upon the name of the Lord (confession with the mouth of the Lord Jesus) is open, public identification with Jesus Christ as one's personal Lord and Savior. John 12:42-43 says one can believe in Him without confessing Him: ". . . even among the rulers many believed in Him, but because of the Pharisees they did not confess *Him,* lest they should be put out of the synagogue; for they loved the praise of men more than the praise of God." And Paul explicitly states that this is an integral step in one's deliverance from wrath, or the power of the sin nature in one's life. The power of Satan is in darkness. But when one comes to the light (Eph 5:11-14), the darkness is dispelled, and the power of the enemy and his accomplice (our sin nature) is defeated. In the terms used in Rom 5:9 and 10:9-10, the justified believer is then "saved." Hence, though confession with the mouth is not an integral part of justification, it is essential for sanctification.[111]

Thus, the point of this entire exercise is to expand our understanding of the terms σῴζειν and σωτηρία. We have done this by studying the words in their immediate contexts. And we have applied the hermeneutical circle to our study. If any part of the text does not harmonize with our understanding of the whole, we must revise the whole until all the parts synchronize.[112] If we want to be accurate in our soteriology, the study of σωτηρία, then it behooves us to be accurate in our understanding of its NT uses. Our aim is to arrive at our Systematic Theology by harmonizing the results of our Biblical Theology. What we will discover is that "God's so great salvation" revealed in the NT is far greater than we ever imagined.

---

[111] See the author's *Portraits of Righteousness* (Lynchburg, VA: Liberty University Press, 2013). Also, this view is alluded to by Robert Jewett, *Romans: A Commentary (Hermeneia: A Critical & Historical Commentary on the Bible)* (Minneapolis, MN: Fortress Press, November 1, 2006), 630.

[112] See E. D. Hirsch, *Validity in Interpretation* (New Haven: Yale University Press, 1967), 173-98.

This salvation has the power to deliver people from sin and death in this life and to a full inheritance in the next.

4. The "Soteriological Influence of The Pharisees" View

With this approach, the soteriological understanding within Judaism shifted over the centuries from faith to works. The Pharisees began an oral tradition during the Babylonian captivity. Their influence gained traction with each generation as the *meturgeman* (Aramaic for translator) stood in the synagogue and paraphrased while the preacher sat and read the Hebrew text. Since Standard Biblical Hebrew (the Hebrew of the OT) was lost as a spoken language during the captivity, the people needed a translator to translate the Hebrew text into Aramaic. These oral translations or paraphrases became the oral tradition promoted by the Pharisees. Ultimately, this oral tradition became more authoritative in the minds of the Jewish people than the written Bible in that they could understand the oral tradition (Aramaic) but not the written word (Standard Biblical Hebrew). By the time of Jesus works of the Law had displaced faith as the requirement for salvation.

Strack-Billerbeck explain the Pharisaic system of merits and demerits:

Jede Gebotserfüllung schließt als ein Akt des Gehorsams gegen den göttlichen Gesetzgeber ein Verdienst des Israeliten vor Gott in sich, ebenso wie jede Gesetzesübertretung eine Schuld vor Gott nach sich zieht. Von den Gebotserfüllungen abgesehen werden Verdienste vor Gott weiter erworben durch Almosen, Fasten, u. besondere Liebeswerke, nicht zuletzt durch das Torastudium. Das Verhältnis, in welchem die Verdienste des Menschen nach Zahl u. innerm Wert zu seinen Übertretungsschulden stehen, stellt den jeweiligen rechtl. Stand des Menschen vor Gott dar: überwiegen die

Verdienste, so wird der Mensch von Gott als ein Gerechter angesehen; überwiegen seine Übertretungsschulden, so gilt er al sein Frevler.[113]

This shift to eternal life resulting from obedience to the Law is reflected in *Targum Onkelos* in which the translator inserted "in the life of eternity" after "shall live in them" in Leviticus 18:5. This is true as well where *Targum Jonathan* cites Leviticus 18:5.[114] Bryan Estelle calls this the "entitlement to heaven" view. Within this view is the hypothetical assumption that Paul understands that the promise here regards eternal life for the one who can keep the Law, but since fallen man cannot do so, people are driven to the One who can: "The principle of works is republished at Sinai for a purpose to drive one to faith, trusting in God's initiative and provision to

---

[113] Hermann L. Strack and Paul Billerbeck, *Kommentar zum Neuen Testament aus Talmud und Midrasch*, Erster Band Das Evangelium nach Matthäus (München: C. H. Beck'sche Verlagsbuchhandlung, 1924), 251. Every fulfillment of the commandment, as an act of obedience to the divine lawgiver, implies a merit of the Israelite before God, just as every violation of the law entails a debt before God. Apart from the fulfillment of the commandments, merits are earned before God through alms, fasting and special works of love, not least through studying the Torah. The relationship in which the merits of man stand in terms of number and intrinsic value to his debt of transgression represents the respective legal status of man before God: if the merits outweigh the debts, then man is regarded by God as a righteous person; if his trespassing debt outweighs, he is considered to be his wrongdoer (translation mine).

[114] Bryan D. Estelle, "Leviticus 18:5 and Deuteronomy 30:1-14 in Biblical Theological Development," in *The Law is not of Faith*, eds. Bryan D. Estelle, J. V. Fesko, and David VanDrunen (Phillipsburg, NJ: P&R Publishing Company, 2009), 138. Estelle does make note that *Targum Neofiti* and *Fragment Targum* do not include this insertion.

accomplish the goal, that is, entitlement to the land of heaven."[115] Such are the lengths to which one must go to find soteriology in Leviticus 18:5.

THE NEW PERSPECTIVE ON PAUL

Of course, we would be remiss if we did not address the "New Perspective on Paul" (NPP) championed by E. P. Sanders, James D. G. Dunn, and N. T. Wright.[116] Sanders led the way with his watershed work *Paul and Palestinian Judaism*.[117] So, what about E. P. Sanders? No question that he infused a wealth of research into the Tannaitic/Rabbinic literature (from 200 BC to 200 AD) in his search for a "scale-in-the-sky" tradition within the Pharisaic community. He especially takes Billerbeck to task as he claims to find no evidence of a works-based approach to entering heaven in any of this literature other that 4 Ezra. He combs carefully through the Qumran literature, the Apocrypha, the Pseudepigrapha, and much more in his search for a legalistic soteriology within 1st Century Judaism.

What Sanders does find is the belief that by virtue of the Abrahamic Covenant anyone born through the lineage of Abraham and Sarah is an heir of eternal life. This is the covenant community. The covenant and physical descendance through Abraham and Sarah guarantee a relationship with God. However, Sanders still has to do something with Deuteronomy and its call for fealty to the Law, i.e., works. So, he describes the Judaist approach to God as "covenant nomism." One gains a relationship with God by being part of the covenant community through physical birth as one of

---

[115] Ibid., 131.

[116] The literature on this subject, both for and against, is voluminous. See a partial list of some of the relevant articles and works in the Bibliography.

[117] E.P. Sanders, *Paul and Palestinian Judaism* (Philadelphia: Fortress Press, 1977).

the descendants of Abraham and Sarah (as opposed to Abraham and Hagar). But works of the Law are required to maintain this relationship. If one is not faithful to the Law, he forfeits his relationship. Thus, according to Sanders, Judaism is not at all legalistic. One is saved by grace (physical birth as a son of Abraham over which no one has control) but that salvation is maintained by works, which are the inevitable result of gratitude toward God for His grace in electing His covenant community. That good works are required to maintain sovereign election by grace without works Sanders explains summarily as a "paradox."[118]

Dunn and Wright also subscribe to this covenant nomism. But what else do the three men have in common? Sanders, Dunn, and Wright come from the same historical-critical school begun by F. C. Bauer. This greatly impacts how they view the evidence, especially when it pertains to the Scriptures. They do not believe the Gospels to be reliable sources. Sanders claims, "We do not know who wrote the gospels . . . . These men—Matthew, Mark, Luke, and John—really lived, but we do not know that they wrote the gospels."[119] Again: "Nothing survives that was written by Jesus himself . . . . The main sources for our knowledge of Jesus himself, the Gospels in the NT, are, from the viewpoint of the historian, tainted by the fact that they were written by people who intended to glorify their hero."[120] That explains why Sanders avoids the Gospels when amassing his evidence from Tannaitic literature. But Sanders is not alone.

Dunn also finds the Gospels unreliable since they were not written by Matthew, Mark, Luke, and John but were freighted by the *kerugma* of the followers of Jesus: "[T]hough a theology of Jesus would be more fascinating [than one of Paul], we have nothing firsthand from Jesus which can provide a secure starting point. The theologies of the Evangelists are almost equally problematic, since their focus on

---

[118] Ibid., 829. Kindle Edition.

[119] E. P. Sanders, *The Historical Figure of Jesus* (London: Penguin, 1993), 63.

[120] Ibid., 3.

the ministry and teaching of Jesus makes their own theologies that much more allusive."[121] Not only does he find the gospels unreliable, but he follows F. C. Bauer's *Hauptbriefe,* meaning he rejects Pauline authorship for Ephesians, Colossians, and the Pastoral Epistles. He thinks the latter were written by Timothy or other pseudepigraphers. The rejection of Ephesians, for which he offers no support, is convenient in that he admits that Ephesians 2:8-9 lends support to the understanding of the traditional Reformation's understanding of *sola fide.*

Wright follows in line with the historical-critical approach to Paul's epistles, drawing on the "undisputed" letters and ignoring the others.[122] He seriously questions whether Paul had anything to do with the Pastoral Epistles.[123] As for the Gospels, Wright reveals his bias by being part of the "Third Quest for the Historical Jesus."[124] This means the quest begun by Wrede and continued through Schweitzer has now morphed again by utilizing more extra-biblical Jewish sources than previous quests. Obviously, the historicity of the Gospels is questioned.

Flowing from their skepticism toward Scripture comes their skepticism regarding the supernatural. Sanders does not believe in the deity of Christ[125] or the virgin birth.[126] Dunn did not believe in the deity of Christ in that he did not think Paul taught a pre-existent

---

[121] James D. G. Dunn, *The Theology of Paul the Apostle* (Grand Rapids and Cambridge: Eerdmans, 1998), 13.

[122] N. T. Wright, *What Saint Paul Really Said* (Grand Rapids: Eerdmans, 1997), 8.

[123] N. T. Wright, *The Resurrection of the Son of God* (Minneapolis: Fortress, 2003), 267.

[124] N. T. Wright, *Jesus and the Victory of God* (Minneapolis: Fortress, 1996), 78.

[125] Sanders, *Historical Figure*, 162.

[126] Ibid., 244.

Christ.[127] As for Wright, he considered the miracles of Christ simply part of the stories told by the gospel writers to create the myth of Jesus (following the trail of Schweitzer[128] *Von Reimarus zu Wrede*).[129] So much for some presuppositions Sanders, Dunn, and Wright bring to their study of Paul and Judaism. What are some of the weaknesses in their approaches, respectively?

Without turning this study into an extended response to the NPP, here are some weaknesses we find in Sanders' work:[130] First, Sanders only deals with the Pauline epistles in the NT. The Gospels and Acts are pregnant with material with clues about the Jewish doctrines of that day. Even different sects of Paul's day in Israel held different understandings about crucial doctrines. For example, at Qumran we find support about four different identities for the Messiah: the Messiah of Moses; the Messiah of Aaron; the Messiah of David; and the Messiah of Israel.[131] But when we get to Jerusalem, the Pharisees had no hesitancy in identifying their future Messiah as one from the lineage of David (Matt 22:41-46). However, Sanders does not draw on any of the gospel material, since he thinks they are all pseudepigraphical. Thus, he conveniently overlooks the parable of the Pharisee and the sinner

---

[127] Dunn, *Theology of Paul*, 293.

[128] Albert Schweitzer, *Von Reimarus zu Wrede: Eine Geschichte der Leben-Jesu-Forschung* (Tübingen: Mohr/Siebeck, 1906).

[129] N. T. Wright, *Jesus and the Victory of God* (Minneapolis: Fortress, 1996), 424-26.

[130] For a critical evaluation of the NPP, see D.A. Carson, *Justification and Variegated Nomism* (Ada, MI: Baker Academic, 2001/ 2004), vol. 1 & 2. Also see John Piper, *The Future of Justification* (IL: Crossway Books, 2007), Mark Husbands and Daniel J. Treier eds., *Justification: What's at Stake in the Current Debates* (Downers Grove, IL: IVP Academic, 2004), Seeyon Kim, *Paul and the New Perspective: Second Thoughts on the Origin of Paul's Gospel* (Grand Rapids, MI: Eerdmans, 2001).

[131] Randall Price, *Secrets of the Dead Sea Scrolls* (Eugene, OR: Harvest House Publishers, 1996), 303-05.

(Luke 18:9-14). Here is a Pharisee who trusted in himself as being righteous. To justify himself he begins listing his good works: absence of immorality, fasting, and tithing. He does not look to God's mercy as the tax collector does but trusts in his own good works. Jesus flatly declares this Pharisee as unjustified even though he is from the seed of Abraham (a child of the covenant) and has many good works.

Even in the Second Temple literature Sanders references, he blithely overlooks synergistic material which vitiates his thesis. Daniel W. Waldschmidt comments: "The New Perspective does not take sufficient account of the fact that there are also statements of synergism in Second-Temple Jewish literature. For example, Sirach 3:3, 29 says, 'He who honors his father atones for sins. ... Water quenches a flaming fire, and alms atone for sins.'"[132] Preston Sprinkle sees good works in Sirach opening the door to God's mercy:

> Judgment of according to works is consistently affirmed throughout Sirach, and the nature of reward stems from a *Deuteronomic* view of retribution. For Sirach, "on the day of death . . . one's deeds are revealed," and the Lord will "reward individuals according to their conduct" (Sir 11:26-27). God "judges a person according to one's deeds" and "everyone received in accordance with one's deeds" (Sir 16:11, 14). On judgment Day, God "does justice for the righteous and executes judgment" when "he repays mortals according to their deeds, and the works of all according to their thoughts" (Sir 35:22, 24). The theme of judgment according to works is pervasive and clear . . . [133]

---

[132] Daniel W. Waldschmit, "Hermeneutics of the New Perspective on Paul," Wisconsin Lutheran Seminary Symposium (September 20, 2016): 5.

[133] Preston M. Sprinkle, *Paul & Judaism Revisited* (Downers Grove, IL: InterVarsity Press, 2013), 217. Sprinkle gives many other examples of judgment according to works from the *Psalms of Solomon, The Wisdom of Solomon,* and *4 Ezra* (217-27).

Moisés Silva notes that Sanders quotes these passages in his discussion of Sirach, but "astonishingly, Sanders overlooks altogether the theological implications of those statements ... Sanders offers no explanation for—indeed, shows no awareness of—what looks like a fairly blatant view of self-salvation."[134] And none other than D. A. Carson observes: "For example, personal worth and meritorious works can be evidenced in *Judith* and *Tobit*; personal faithfulness can be seen in *Additions to Esther*; and *4 Ezra* exhibits an overwhelming emphasis on meriting salvation through obedience to the Law while marginalizing God's grace."[135]

When one looks at the pseudepigraphical writings, like *1 Enoch*, there is mention over and over of those who will spend eternity with God: the elect and the righteous ones. The "righteous" or "righteous ones" are mentioned 78x. There is no mention of the Abrahamic covenant or Abraham in the entire book of *1 Enoch*. The word "faith" occurs once. The word "saved" occurs several times, but always connected to those who have lived righteously. "Gentiles" are not excluded. Sanders spends most of his discussion trying to figure out who "the elect and the righteous ones" are. Without any mention of Israel, he concludes that the elect and righteous are those faithful to Israel through keeping the Law. The soteriology of *1 Enoch* might best be expressed by this statement: "Be righteous and you will live forever." In short, there is little if anything in *1 Enoch* to support covenant nomism.

Even Sanders admits at the end of his discussion on *Ben Sirach,* "that Ben Sirach does not bring the distinction between the righteous and the wicked into connection with the election of Israel. The unre-

---

[134] Moisés Silva, "The Law and Christianity: Dunn's New Synthesis," *The Westminster Theological Journal;* 53 (1991): 348-9.

[135] D.A. Carson, "Summaries and Conclusions," in *Justification and Variegated Nomism Justification: A Fresh Appraisal of Paul and Second-Temple Judaism: The Complexities of Second Temple Judaism,* eds. D.A. Carson, Peter T. O'Brien, and Mark A. Seifrid; WUNT 140 (Tübingen/ Grand Rapids: Mohr [Siebeck]/Baker, 2001) 1:543.

pentant wicked are not explicitly said to forfeit their place among the elect, . . ."[136] And early in his discussion he says, ". . . individual soteriology (such as it is) is not discussed in terms of being 'in' or 'out' of the group of the saved on the day of the Lord."[137] So we must ask ourselves how anything in *Ben Sirach* supports his thesis of covenant nomism.

Even in the Sermon on the Mount Jesus lists the righteousness required for entrance to heaven as a righteousness greater than that required by the Pharisees (Matt 5:20). Jesus does not mention entrance by covenant. The quote from Billerbeck above was his comment on Matthew 5:20. And, apparently, Sanders spent scant time in the Tosefta because he overlooks the addition of "eternal life" in Leviticus 18:5. Nor does he pick up on the same idea in *Targum Onkelos*. For these writers, works of the Law opened the door to eternal life. It was all part of the soteriological drift fostered by the Pharisees during the Tannaitic period.

When it comes to justification, Sanders uses the same word Sanday and Headlam used to describe imputed righteousness in their classic commentary on Romans decades before Sanders came on the scene: "fiction."[138] According to Sanders:

> Luther's emphasis on fictional, imputed righteousness, though it has often been shown to be an incorrect interpretation of Paul, has been influential because it corresponds to the sense of sinfulness which many people feel, and which is part and parcel of Western concepts of personhood, with their emphasis on individualism and introspection. Luther sought and found relief from guilt. But Luther's problems were not Paul's, and we misunderstand him if we see him through Luther's eyes.[139]

---

[136] Sanders, *Paul*, 523. Kindle Edition.

[137] Ibid., 539.

[138] W. Sanday and A. C. Headlam, *Romans* (Edinburgh: T. & T. Clark, 1896), 36.

[139] E. P. Sanders, *Paul, A Very Short Introduction* (Oxford: Oxford University, 1991), 58.

Actually, Sanders' "paradox" could have been easily solved if he had thought in terms of Relationship and Fellowship. He could have described the keeping of the Law as a requirement for Fellowship rather than maintaining the Relationship. Of course, as Protestants, we would argue that the eternal Relationship with God was established in the OT by faith (just as in the NT), not by birth. But no doubt even the Gospels reveal a Pharisaic understanding of soteriology by physical birth into the covenant community (Matt 3:9; Jn 8:39). And after conceding that Gentiles could "be saved" without physical birth into the covenant community, many of the Pharisees who believed added works to their soteriology (Acts 15:5—circumcision and keeping the Law).

David Wolfe explains that good systematic theology requires four criteria to even qualify as a system.[140] He believes the adequacy, rationality, reliability, and suitability of a system of theology can be evaluated or validated on the basis of these four criteria. The failure of a system to meet these criteria indicates its weakness and the likelihood that theological reconstruction on a system-wide level is necessary or conversion to some other more suitable system is demanded for intellectual honesty. The four criteria are:

1. **Consistency**—the assertions, hypotheses, and opinions expressed by the system should be free from contradiction.

2. **Coherence**—the assertions and hypotheses should be related in a ***unified*** manner.

3. **Comprehensiveness**—the system should be applicable to <u>all</u> evidence.

4. **Congruity**—the system of assertions, hypotheses, etc. must "<u>fit</u>" all evidence. It must be accurate, adequate and precise to <u>fit</u> all data. In other words, the whole must

---

[140] David Wolfe, *Epistemology: The Justification of Belief* (Downers Grove, IL: InterVarsity Press, 1982), 50-55.

equal the sum of its parts. If one part of the whole is out of sync with the whole, then the whole must be revised to include this part without throwing the other parts out of sync. We are searching for the interpretation which best "<u>fits</u>" all the data.

Sanders' system fails on at least two of these points: consistency and comprehensiveness. He does not input all the data, and the data is contradictory (saved by grace, maintained by works).

Dunn's work also fails the comprehensiveness test. He relegates the Law to circumcision, the feast days, and the Sabbath. He calls these "the badges" of Judaism. Thus, for Dunn, the term "works of the law" does not refer to good works in general or to Jewish legalism but is limited to Jewish national identity boundaries that excluded Gentiles from salvation, i.e., circumcision, Sabbath, and dietary restrictions, which Dunn terms the "social function of the Law".[141] But the Pharisees never reduced the Law to such minimalism. Just as Galatians 5:3 and James 2:10-11 claim, the Law was viewed as a seamless garment. There was no division into three parts (moral, civil, and ceremonial). If one wants to observe circumcision, he is a debtor to keep the whole law. You cannot be a little bit pregnant.

We conclude this very brief critique of NPP with Wright's understanding of justification. For Wright, justification was not soteriological; it was ecclesiological. It was not individualistic; it was corporate. ". . . [w]hat Paul means by justification . . . is not 'how you become a Christian', so much as 'how you can tell who is a member of the covenant family.'"[142] Again, "Justification is thus the declaration of God, the just judge, that someone has had their [sic] sins forgiven and that they [sic] are a member of the covenant family, the family of

---

[141] James D. G. Dunn, *Jesus, Paul and the Law* (Louisville, KY: Westminster/ John Knox, 1990), 216-19.

[142] Wright, *Paul*, 122.

Abraham. That is what the word means in Paul's writings. It doesn't describe how people get into God's forgiven family; it declares that they are in . . . ."[143]

As such, Wright claims the Reformers were completely misled by Melanchthon's doctrine of imputed righteousness: "If we use the language of the law court, it makes no sense whatever to say that the judge imputes, imparts, bequeaths, conveys or otherwise transfers his righteousness to either the plaintiff or the defendant. Righteousness is not an object, a substance or a gas which can be passed across the courtroom."[144]

By doing away with the Reformers' understanding of forensic righteousness and justification by faith alone, the door is wide open to adulterate salvation by faith with works. Consider these statements by Wright: "Justification, at the last, will be on the basis of performance, not possession"[145]; "The Spirit is the path by which Paul traces the route from justification by faith in the present to justification, by the completed life lived, in the future"[146]; "Paul has . . . spoken in Romans 2 about the final justification of God's people based on their whole life"[147]; and, "Present justification declares, on the basis of faith, what future justification will affirm publicly (according to [Rom.] 2:14-16 and 8:9-11) on the basis of the entire life."[148]

---

[143] N. T. Wright, "The Shape of Justification," *Bible Review* 17 (April 2001): 50. See also N.T. Wright's *Justification: God's Plan & Paul's Vision* (Downers Grove, IL: IVP Academic, 2016).

[144] Wright, *Paul*, 124.

[145] N.T. Wright, *The Letter to the Romans, The New Interpreter's Bible, vol. 10* (Nashville, TN: Abingdon Press, 2002), 440.

[146] N. T. Wright, *Paul in Fresh Perspective* (Minneapolis: Fortress, 2005), 148.

[147] Ibid., 121.

[148] Wright, *Paul*, 129.

In sum, the NPP begins and ends with different presuppositions than normative evangelicalism. For example, the doctrinal basis for the Evangelical Theological Society is: "The Bible alone, and the Bible in its entirety, is the Word of God written and is therefore inerrant in the autographs."[149] Wright claims to be an evangelical but denies this very basic tenet of evangelicals. He cannot have his cake and eat it too. Sanders and Dunn do not claim to be evangelicals, but their presuppositions about Scripture are the same as Wright's. Obviously, different presuppositions will lead to different conclusions.

As far as Judaism and grace are concerned, *The Treaty of the Great King* by Meredith Kline highlights the grace of God as one of the prime motivators to obedience in Deuteronomy 6-10. Observing God's grace in His relationship with the Jews is nothing new. What is new is the contention of the NPP that the Jews thought they had to keep the Law to maintain their relationship with God. This is where grace and works cross swords. If the NPP is correct, it is just another form of legalism, the very idea Sanders rejected in the first place.

Simon Gathercole marshalled a host of Tannaitic literature to support meritorious works as the leverage to open the gates of heaven.[150] An example is *Targum Ezekiel* (which Levey dates at just after the destruction of the temple)[151] where the righteous who keep the Torah will be rewarded with eternal life (20.11, 13, 21), while the wicked are bound for hell (1:8; 26:20; 31:14 cd, 16; 32:18-32). Gathercole also cites D. R. Schwartz, who argues that the promise of life in CD 3 is eternal life: "Hier also wird ganz deutlich angenommen, daß unser Leviticus-Leben als Lohn für Einhalten der

---

[149] https://www.etsjets.org/about/accessed April 1, 2021.

[150] Simon J. Gathercole, "Torah, Life, and Salvation: Leviticus 18:5 in Early Judaism and the New Testament," in *From Prophecy to Testament*, ed. Craig A. Evans (Peabody, MA: Hendrickson Publishers, 2004): 127-45.

[151] S. H. Levey, *The Targum of Ezekiel*, The Aramaic Bible 13 (Wilmington, DE: Glazier, 1987), 4.

Torah verspricht, und hier ist weiter auch ausdrücklich gesagt, daß das Leben, das hier versprochen ist, da ewige Leben ist."[152] Smolar and Aberbach, also observe: "Eternal life in the world to come is granted to those who observe the statutes and ordinances given by God."[153] And in *Sifra Leviticus*, the Tannaim interpreted Leviticus 18:5 as the age to come.[154] Gathercole concludes his study: " . . . there is ample evidence for an understanding, both pre- and post-70 C.E., of Lev. 18:5 as talking in terms of eternal life. And this understanding was, furthermore, on the increase."[155] In other words, the soteriological drift of the Pharisees, especially when it comes to Leviticus 18:5, may have influenced Paul's own use of this passage.

Ultimately, the only way the NPP can effect its "illegitimate totality transfer"[156] of covenant nomism to all of Tannaitic Judaism is to neglect large swaths of Jewish literature and turn Judaism into a monolithic construct that does not and never has existed. By neglecting most of the NT as evidence, the NPP also overlooks at least one strand of Pharisaism claiming a works-righteousness was required to have eternal life (Matt 5:20 and Luke 18:9-14). This was not law-keeping to maintain a relationship; it was law-keeping

---

[152] D. R. Schwartz, *Leben durch Jesus versus Leben durch die Torah: Zur Religions-polemik der ersten Jahrhundert*, Franz-Delitzsch-Vorlesung 2 (Münster: Institute Judaicum Delitzschianum, 1993), 9. Here it is also clearly assumed that our Leviticus life promises as a reward for keeping the Torah, and it is also expressly stated here that the life that is promised here is eternal life [translation mine].

[153] L. Smolar and M. Aberbach, *Studies in Targum Jonathan to the Prophets*, Library of Biblical Studies (New York: Ktav,1983), 180.

[154] Gathercole, 139.

[155] Ibid., 145.

[156] Kevin Vanhoozer, "Wrighting the Wrongs of the Reformation?" in *Jesus, Paul, and the People of God: A Theological Dialogue with N. T. Wright*, eds. Nicholas Perrin and Richard B. Hays (Downers Grove: InterVarsity, 2011), 240.

to establish a relationship. But we would also contend that the soteriological teachings of the Pharisees were a corruption of the original intent of the Law. It was not for Relationship; it was for Fellowship. This is never addressed by Sanders, Dunn, and Wright since they do not believe the Gospels are authentic.

5. The Correlative View

One approach to Paul's use of Leviticus 18:5 and Deuteronomy 30:12-14 in Romans 10 is antithetical, the former pointing to works for salvation and the latter pointing to faith. Support for this approach comes from Galatians 3:11-12 where Habakkuk 2:4 and Leviticus 18:5 are quoted, with the former clearly emphasizing faith while the latter (it is proposed) teaches salvation through works of the law (at least hypothetically). Preston Sprinkle typifies this explanation when he writes:

> I will argue that Galatians exhibits an antithesis between divine and human agency; thus, "the one who does these things" cannot "live by them" because eschatological life cannot be, and has not been, given as a response to human behavior. Paul saw the Leviticus construct as a wholly inappropriate and deficient way to appropriate God's saving action because it prioritizes human deeds–something that will never be forthcoming from people who are in bondage to the present evil age. Deliverance from this evil age, with its curse (3:10), and the granting of the eschatological life and justification is solely the result of divine initiative.[157]

But some understand the quotations in both Romans 10 and Galatians 3 as correlative in the sense that both are calling for

---

[157] Preston M. Sprinkle, *Law and Life*, WUNT 241 (Tübingen: Mohr Siebeck, 2006), 152.

faith. Etienne Jodar presents this view quite well.[158] She points out numerous weaknesses in the antithetical view, not the least of which is the false promise problem in Leviticus 18:5 if indeed no one could meet the condition for the promise being fulfilled (perfect obedience to the commands). She sees a second weakness in the antithetical view being the very assumption that 18:5 calls for perfect obedience. "In fact, this verse cannot demand perfection because offering sacrifices for sin was part of 'doing' the commandments; law-keeping is not equivalent to perfection. The antithetical interpretation, however, rests on such a presupposition."[159] This author agrees with her assessment when she writes:

> According to the antithetical interpretation, the law points to Christ (as stated by Rom 10:4) in that no one can "do" the law, *so* Christ has to do it on one's behalf. That Christ is the τέλος of the law *in such an indirect way* assumes much understanding (too much?) of the Israelites that came out of Egypt. They would have understood (1) that someone else would observe the law in their place and credit his obedience to them (2) after their realizing that they could not "do" the law. In all likelihood this understanding was not reached by many because the Jews seem to have believed in the possibility of fulfilling the law. This appears to nip in the bud the assumption that the Israelites would have understood Leviticus 18:5 as unachievable and thus that Christ had to do the commandments in their place.[160]

---

[158] Etienne Jodar, "Leviticus 18:5 and the Law's Call to Faith: A Positive Reassessment of Paul's View of the Law," *Themelios* vol. 45, no. 1 (April 2020): 43-57.

[159] Ibid., 47.

[160] Ibid.

The very fact that Leviticus 18:5 contains a promise ("shall live by them") is a call to faith. It requires faith to believe God will fulfill His promise of "life" to those who keep His commandments. It is not a call to human achievement but to human dependence. They were not going to drive out the nations surrounding them; God would, if they demonstrated their faith by obedience. But what about Galatians 3:12?

Galatians 3:12

For as many as are of the works of the law are under the curse; for it is written, *"Cursed is everyone who does not continue in all things which are written in the book of the law, to do them."* [11] But that no one is justified by the law in the sight of God *is* evident, for *"the just shall live by faith."* [12] Yet the law is not of faith, but *"the man who does them shall live by them."*

ὅσοι γὰρ ἐξ ἔργων νόμου εἰσίν, ὑπὸ κατάραν εἰσίν· γέγραπται γὰρ ὅτι Ἐπικατάρατος πᾶς ὃς οὐκ ἐμμένει πᾶσιν τοῖς γεγραμμένοις ἐν τῷ βιβλίῳ τοῦ νόμου τοῦ ποιῆσαι αὐτά. ὅτι δὲ ἐν νόμῳ οὐδεὶς δικαιοῦται παρὰ τῷ θεῷ δῆλον, ὅτι Ὁ δίκαιος ἐκ πίστεως ζήσεται· ὁ δὲ νόμος οὐκ ἔστιν ἐκ πίστεως, ἀλλ᾽ Ὁ ποιήσας αὐτὰ ζήσεται ἐν αὐτοῖς.

The antithetical argument for understanding 3:11 and 3:12 appears transparent: faith (Hab 2:4) versus works of the law (Leviticus 18:5). But unraveling the argument of this text is not at all easy. In fact, Thomas Schreiner says, "This is one of the most difficult verses to interpret in the entire Pauline corpus."[161] One of the problems is imposing the negative implications of verse 10 onto Leviticus 18:5. If no one can keep all the things written in the Law and is therefore accursed, then surely those who cannot live up to the keeping of the

---

[161] Thomas R. Schreiner, *Galatians*, ZECNT (Grand Rapids: Zondervan, 2010), 210.

Law in 18:5 are accursed as well. But Jodar uses what she calls an "*alla-chi*" construction to show that, as in Romans 10, Leviticus 18:5 is a call to faith. Key to her understanding are the particles δὲ and ἀλλ' in verse 12.

Jodar does not see δὲ as a weak adversative as would be indicated by a translation of "yet." Rather she suggests Paul finished with his negativity concerning the Law and its curses after verse 10. Now with the δὲ of verse 12, he is further developing the faith he introduced with Habakkuk 2:4.[162] Even more decisive for her view is the use of ἀλλ' in verse 12. Some take the subject of the clause preceding ἀλλ' as the subject of the clause following ἀλλ'.[163] But that leaves us with the very awkward, "The law is not from faith, but the law is from the man who does them will live by them."

There is a better solution. The strong adversative is sometimes used to transpose[164] the substantives from the clauses on each side of ἀλλ'. For example, in John 15:16 Jesus says, "You did not choose me [ἀλλ'], but I chose you." This is what Jodar calls her "*alla-chi*" construction. The *chi* stands for the transposition of substantives. Other examples are found in John 10:18; Romans 11:18; 1 Corinthians 11:8, 9; 2 Corinthians 12:14; and 2 Maccabees 5:19. As it applies to Galatians 3:12 the idea would be that, "the law is not from faith, but [ἀλλ'] faith is from the law." Understood this way, the quote from Leviticus 18:5 is a call to faith just as we had in Romans 10.

Lest we forget what we are attempting to prove, let it be repeated: Paul is not contrasting a real or hypothetical works salvation with

---

[162] The conjunction δέ in the opening of verse 12 indicates a new development (Steven E. Runge, *Discourse Grammar of the Greek New Testament* [Peabody, MA: Hendrickson, 2010], 28–36).

[163] Joel Willitts, "Paul's Use of Leviticus 18:5 in Galatians 3:12," *Tyndale Bulletin* 54 (January, 2001): 118.

[164] This is where Jodar gets the *chi* of her *alla-chi* construction. The transposition of the substantives before and after ἀλλ' are a cross-over or X (*chi*).

salvation by faith when quoting Leviticus 18:5 juxtaposed with Deuteronomy 30:12-14 or Habakkuk 2:4. In this view, there is no antithesis. Rather, all three are a call to faith. In fact, this might be called a complementary-correlative view. No doubt the discussion of Paul's meaning in these passages will continue, but we have offered some plausible explanations other than "entitlement to heaven."

SUMMARY

We have attempted to establish God's dealings with Israel in terms of an eternal Relationship and temporal Fellowship. We have proposed that the eternal relationship began with the Abrahamic Covenant, while the provisions for temporal fellowship were spelled out in the Mosaic Covenant. In order to do this, we needed to excavate the differences between the Suzerainty-Vassal treaties and the Covenants of Grant. We emphasized the primary distinction as a reward for past obedience (Covenant of Grant) and motivation for future obedience (Suzerainty-Vassal). As such, the Mosaic Covenant stands as the only Suzerainty-Vassal treaty in the OT. The rest are Covenants of Grant.

This led us into the discussion of various opinions on the purpose of the Mosaic Covenant. Most of those in the Reformed camp attempt to subsume the Mosaic Covenant under the Covenant of Grace, presumed to cover the human timeline from Adam's expulsion from the garden until the eternal state. This forces most of those interpreters to find a soteriological emphasis as the primary purpose of the Mosaic Covenant. This proves to be a difficult task in that there are no conspicuous references to heaven or eternal life in the Mosaic Covenant. We marshalled evidence from Deuteronomy to show that the purpose of this covenant was to provide intimacy between God and Israel. It proves to be an OT love letter.

Nevertheless, many try to find a reference to soteriology in Leviticus 18:5, "You shall therefore keep My statutes and My judgments, which if a man does, he shall live by them: I *am* the Lord." But that led us to the discussion of Paul's use of this verse in Romans

10 and Galatians 3, where so many read these passages through the lenses of soteriology. Most of these explanations appear forced. We suggest it is easier, clearer, and unforced to simply take Leviticus 18:5 at face value (longevity in the land), especially since the injunction to keep and statutes, judgments, and ordinances of the Lord is given two other times in the chapter (vv. 26, 30) in the context of living a blessed life in the land as opposed to those who are vomited out of the land because of their abominable practices (primarily sexual).

However, any discussion of Paul must address the "New Perspective on Paul" and the covenant nomism of Sanders, Dunn, and Wright. It was suggested that their conclusions are the result of a different set of operating presuppositions than those of the Fathers of the Reformation. Given their historical-critical presuppositions, they fail to deal with gospel and Pauline evidence that does not support covenant nomism. In fact, with their exegetical lacunae and *extra textus* views on justification they open the door to a synergistic approach to heaven.

CONCLUSION

The purpose of this book has been to illustrate from New Testament passages the benefit of filtering passages of Scripture through categories of truth. Although there are many categories like justification truth versus sanctification truth, temporal judgment versus eternal judgment, the gift versus the prize, position versus condition, and more, this study primarily was a focus on the difference between our Relationship with God and our Fellowship with God. In the first part of the book, we used sermons delivered over the years to demonstrate how distinguishing between Relationship and Fellowship can shed light on certain passages. In the second part of the book, we attempted to present sufficient scholarship to undergird the exegesis behind the homiletics. In particular, we considered two covenants in the Old Testament that we believe lay the foundation for the Relationship/Fellowship truth we find in the New Testament. It was posited that the Abrahamic Covenant was a Covenant of Grant

(Reward) that Abraham earned by his faithfulness. Once the reward was given, it belonged to the recipient and his offspring in perpetuity. Ergo, an eternal Relationship was established with Abraham and his offspring through Isaac. Though individuals in the nation of Israel needed to exercise faith in God's promise of a coming Messiah in order to have eternal life, because of Abraham's faithfulness the nation of Jews, though not necessarily the majority of its individual members, will always have a Relationship with God.

However, having a Relationship with God does not guarantee Fellowship with God. Having fellowship with God means enjoying our relationship with Him. Thus, we have proposed that God drew up the Mosaic Covenant as a Suzerainty-Vassal covenant to delineate the requirements for the nation of Israel to have fellowship with Him. Whereas the Covenant of Grant was a reward for past obedience, the Suzerainty-Vassal covenant was a motivation for future obedience. We have attempted, through credible scholarship, to point out that the Law of Moses was not given to show the Way but rather the Walk; it was not an open door to eternal life in heaven, but it was a pathway to an abundant life on earth. The fact that there are types within the Law that point to the ultimate Pascal Lamb Who would take away the sins of the world neither adds nor detracts from the main point of giving the Law to Israel: Fellowship.

BIBLIOGRAPHY

BOOKS

Adams, Scott. *Win Bigly: Persuasion in a World Where Facts Don't Matter*. New York: Portfolio/Penguin, 2017.

Anderson, David R. *The King-Priest of Psalm 110 in Hebrews*. New York: Peter Lang, 2001.

_____ and Reitman, James S. *Portraits of Righteousness: Free Grace Sanctification in Romans 5–8*. Lynchburg, VA. Liberty University Press, 2013.

_____. *Free Grace Soteriology*. Houston: Grace Theology Press, 2018.

_____. *Maximum Joy*. Houston: Grace Theology Press, 2016.

_____. *Portraits of Righteousness*. Lynchburg, VA: Liberty University Press, 2013.

_____. *Position and Condition*. Houston: Grace Theology Press, 2017.

_____. *Saving the Saved*. Houston: Grace Theology Press, 2020.

Anderson, Garwood. *Paul's New Perspective: Charting a Soteriologial Journey*. Downers Grove, IL: IVP, 2016.

Avemarie, Friedrich. *Tora und Leben: Untersuchungen zur Heilsbedeutung der Tora in der frühen rabbinischen Literatur*. Tübingen: Mohr-Siebeck, 1996.

Bahnsen, Greg L. "The Theonomic Reformed Approach to Law and Gospel." In *The Law, the Gospel, and the Modern Christian: Five Views*. Grand Rapids, MI: Zondervan, 1993.

Baird, S. J. *The First Adam and the Second: The Elohim Revealed in the Creation and Redemption of Man*. Philadelphia: Lindsay and Blakiston, 1860.

Ball, John. *A Treatise of the Covenant of Grace*. London: 1645.

Baltzer, K. *Das Bundesformular*. Neukirchen: Neukirchen Verlag, 1964.

Barrett, C. K. *From First Adam to Last: A Study in Pauline Theology*. New York: Charles Scribner & Sons, 1962.

Bateman, Herbert, ed. *Three Central Issues in Contemporary Dispensationalism*. Grand Rapids, MI: Kregel Academic & Professional, 1999.

Bavinck, Herman. *Reformed Dogmatics*. Ed. John Bolt, translated by John Vriend. 2:570. Grand Rapids: Baker, 2008.

Beale, G. K., and D. A. Carson, eds. *Commentary on the New Testament Use of the Old Testament*. Grand Rapids: Nottingham, England: Baker Academic ; Apollos, 2007.

Berkhof, Louis. *Systematic Theology*. Grand Rapids: Eerdmans, 1939.

Bird, Michael F., *Saving Righteousness of God: Studies on Paul, Justification and the New Perspective*. Eugene: Wipf & Stock, 2007.

Blaising, Craig A., and Darrell L. Bock. *Progressive Dispensationalism*. Wheaton, IL: BridgePoint, 1993.

_____, eds. *Dispensationalism, Israel and the Church*. TN: Zondervan Academic, 1992.

Bock, Darrell L., Walter C. Kaiser, and Craig A. Blaising, eds. *Dispensationalism, Israel and the Church: The Search for Definition*. Grand Rapids: Zondervan Pub. House, 1992.

Bock, D. L. "A Theology of Luke-Acts." In *A Biblical Theology of the New Testament*, eds. R. B. Zuck and D. L. Bock. Chicago: Moody Press, 1994.

Bonhoeffer, Dietrich. *The Cost of Discipleship*. New York: Macmillan Publishing Co., 1976.

Brown, C., ed. *The New International Dictionary of New Testament Theology*. Grand Rapids: Zondervan Publishing House, 1975; Exeter: Pasternoster Press, 1975. S.v. "Death," by W. Schmithals; and "Life," by H.-G. Link.

Buford, Bob. *Half Time*. Grand Rapids: Zondervan, 2004.

Burgess, Anthony. *Vindiciae Legis: or A Vindication of the Moral Law and the Covenants*. London: n.a., 1647.

Calderstone, P. J. *Dynastic Oracle and Suzerainty Treaty: II Samuel 7, 8-16*. Loyola House of Studies, 1966.

Calvin, John. Calvin's comment on Galatians 3:17, cited by I. John Hesselink, "Calvin's Concept and Use of the Law." Ph.D. diss.; Basel, 1961. VI, 5.

Carson, D. A. *Exegetical Fallacies*. 2d ed. Grand Rapids: Baker Books, 1996.

_____. *Justification and Variegated Nomism A Fresh Appraisal of Paul and Second-Temple Judaism: The Complexities of Second Temple Judaism*. Eds. D.A. Carson, Peter T. O'Brien, and Mark A. Seifrid; WUNT 140. Tübingen/Grand Rapids: Mohr [Siebeck]/ Baker, 2001.

_____. *Justification and Variegated Nomism A Fresh Appraisal of Paul and Second-Temple Judaism: The Paradoxes of Paul*. Eds. D.A. Carson, Peter T. O'Brien, and Mark A. Seifrid. Ada, MI: Baker Academic, 2004.

Chamberlain, W. D. *The Meaning of Repentance*. Grand Rapids: Wm. B. Eerdmans Publishing Co., 1943.

Chamblin, Knox. "The Law of Moses and the Law of Christ," in *Continuity and Discontinuity*, ed. John S. Feinberg. Wheaton, IL: Crossway Books, 1988.

Chapman, Gary. *The Five Love Languages*. Chicago: Northfield Publishing, 1992.

Charlesworth, James H., ed. *The Old Testament Pseudepigrapha*. 1st ed. Garden City, N.Y: Doubleday, 1983.

_____, ed. *The Old Testament Pseudepigrapha*. 1st ed. Garden City, N.Y: Doubleday, 1983.

Clements, R. E. *Abraham and David*. Naperville, IL.: Alec R. Allenson, Inc., 1967.

Colson, Chuck. *Loving God*. New York: Harper Collins Publishers, 1983.

Cooper, Jordan. *The Righteousness of One: An Evaluation of Early Patristic Soteriology in Light of the New Perspective on Paul*. Eugene: Wipf & Stock, 2013.

Craigie, P. C. *The Book of Deuteronomy*. The New International Commentary on the Old Testament. Grand Rapids: Wm. B. Eerdmans Publishing Co., 1976.

Davies, W. D. *Paul and Rabbinic Judaism: Some Rabbinic Elements in Pauline Theology*, 4th ed. Philadelphia: Fortress, [1948] 1980.

Demarest, B. *The Cross and Salvation*. Wheaton: Crossway Books, 1997.

Dillow, Joseph. *Reign of the Servant Kings*. Hayesville, NC: Schoettle, 2002.

Driver, S. R. *A Critical and Exegetical Commentary on Deuteronomy*. Edinburgh: T. & T. Clark, 1895.

Dunn, James D. G. *The Theology of Paul the Apostle*. Grand Rapids and Cambridge: Eerdmans, 1998.

_____. *The New Perspective on Paul*. rev. ed. Grand Rapids: Eerdmans, 2007.

Eaton, Michael A. *No Condemnation: A New Theology of Assurance.* Downers Grove, IL: InterVarsity Press, 1997.

Eichrodt, W. *Theology of the Old Testament.* 2 volumes. The Old Testament Library. Translated by J. A. Baker. Philadelphia: The Westminster Press, 1961.

Elwell, W., ed. *Evangelical Dictionary of Theology.* Grand Rapids: Baker Book House, 1984. S.v. "Federal Theology," by G. N. M. Collins and "Imputation," by R. K. Johnston.

Estelle, Bryan D., J. V. Fesko, and David VanDrunen, eds. *The Law Is Not of Faith: Essays on Works and Grace in the Mosaic Covenant.* Phillipsburg, NJ: P & R Pub, 2009.

_____. "Leviticus 18:5 and Deuteronomy 30:1-14 in Biblical Theological Development." In *The Law is not of Faith.* Eds. Bryan D. Estelle, J. V. Fesko, and David VanDrunen. Phillipsburg, NJ: P&R Publishing Company, 2009.

Evans, Craig A., ed. *From Prophecy to Testament: The Function of the Old Testament in the New.* Peabody, MA: Hendrickson Publishers, 2004.

Fairbairn, Patrick. *An Exposition of Ezekiel.* Evansville, IN: Sovereign Grace, 1960.

Farris, T. V. *Mighty to Save: A Study in Old Testament Soteriology.* Nashville, TN: Broadman Press, 1993.

Feinberg, J. S. "Salvation in the Old Testament." In *Tradition and Testament: Essays in Honor of Charles Lee Feinberg,* 39-77. Eds. J. S. Feinberg and P. D. Feinberg. Chicago: Moody Press, 1981.

Fensham, F. C. "Father and Son as Terminology for Treaty and Covenant." In *Near Eastern Studies in Honor of W. F. Albright,* 121-35. Ed K. Goedicke. Baltimore: Johns Hopkins Press, 1971.

Ferry, Brenton C. "Works in the Mosaic Covenant." In *The Law is not of Faith.* Eds. Bryan D. Estelle, J. V. Fesko, and David VanDrunen. Phillipsburg, NJ: P&R Publishing Company, 2009.

Flavius, Josephus. *War Against the Jews*. Book VI, Chapter 9, Section 3, www.bible.ca/pre-flavius-josephus-70AD-Mt24-fulfilled htm. Accessed January 10, 2018.

Frankena, R. "The Vassal-Treaties of Esarhaddon and the Dating of Deuteronomy." In *Oudtestamentische Studien*. Edited by P. A. H. De Boer. Leiden: E. J. Brill, 1965.

Gathercole, Simon J. *Where is Boasting? Early Jewish Soteriology and Paul's Response in Romans 1–5*. Grand Rapids: Eerdmans, 2002.

_____. "Torah, Life, and Salvation: Leviticus 18:5 in Early Judaism and the New Testament." In *From Prophecy to Testament*, ed. Craig A. Evans. Peabody, MA: Hendrickson Publishers, 2004.

Gentry, Peter John and Wellum, Stephen J. *God's Kingdom through God's Covenants*. Wheaton, IL: Crossway, 2015.

_____. *Kingdom through Covenant*. Wheaton, IL: Crossway, 2018.

Güterbock, H. G. *Siegel aus Bogasköy*. Berlin: Im Selbstverlage des Herausgebers, 1940.

Hahn, Scott. *Kinship by Covenant: A Canonical Approach to the Fulfillment of God's Saving Promises*. The Anchor Yale Bible Reference Library. New Haven: Yale University Press, 2009.

Hammurabi. *The Code of Hammurabi*. Claude Hermann Walter Johns, trans. Cheapest Books, 2019.

Harrison, R. K., and Avraham Gileadi, eds. *Israel's Apostasy and Restoration: Essays in Honor of Roland K. Harrison*. Grand Rapids: Baker Book House, 1988.

Hillers, D. R. *Treaty Curses and the Old Testament Prophets*. Biblica at Orientalia 16. Rome: Pontifical Biblical Institute, 1964.

Hirsch, E.D. *Validity in Interpretation*. New Haven: Yale University Press, 1967.

Hodges, Z. C. *Absolutely Free!* Grand Rapids: Zondervan Publishing House, 1989.

Hoffner, H. A., Jr. "Propaganda and Political Justification in Hittite Historiography." In *Unity and Diversity*, 49-64. Edited by Hans Goedicke and J. J. M. Roberts. Baltimore and London: The Johns Hopkins University Press, 1975.

Horton, Michael Scott, *Christ* the *Lord, The Reformation and Lordship Salvation*. Eugene, OR: Wipf & Stock, 2008.

Horton, Michael Scott. *Covenant and Salvation: Union with Christ*. 1st ed. Louisville: Westminster John Knox Press, 2007.

Hughes, P. E. *The True Image: The Origin and Destiny of Man in Christ*. Grand Rapids: William B. Eerdmans, 1989.

Husbands, Mark and Daniel J. Treier, eds. *Justification: What's at Stake in the Current Debates*. Downers Grove, IL: IVP Academic, 2004.

Jewett, Robert. *Romans: A Commentary (Hermeneia: A Critical & Historical Commentary on the Bible)*. Minneapolis, MN: Fortress Press, 2006.

Johnson, S. Lewis, Jr. "Romans 5:12—An Exercise in Exegesis and Theology." In *New Dimensions in New Testament Study*, ed. R. N. Longenecker and M. C. Tenney. Grand Rapids: Zondervan Publishing House, 1974.

_____ and John S. Feinberg, eds. *Continuity and Discontinuity: Perspectives on the Relationship between the Old and New Testaments: Essays in Honor of S. Lewis Johnson, Jr.* Westchester, IL: Crossway Books, 1988.

Kaiser, Walter C., Jr. *Toward an Old Testament Theology*. Grand Rapids: Zondervan Publishing Company, 1978.

_____. "The Law as God's Gracious Guidance for the Promotion of Holiness." In *The Law, the Gospel, and the Modern Christian: Five Views*. Grand Rapids, MI: Zondervan, 1993.

_____. "Response to Willem A. Vangemeren." In *The Law, the Gospel, and the Modern Christian: Five Views*. Grand Rapids, MI: Zondervan, 1993.

Keil, C. F. and Delitzsch, F. *The Books of Samuel*, 2 volumes. Translated by J. Martin, Commentary on the Old Testament, 10 volumes. N.p.; reprint, Grand Rapids: Eerdmans Publishing Company, 1982.

Kim, Seeyon. *Paul and the New Perspective: Second Thoughts on the Origin of Paul's Gospel*. Grand Rapids, MI: Eerdmans Publishing, 2001.

King, L. W., ed. *Babylonian Boundary-Stones*. British Museum Dept. of Egyptian and Assyrian Antiquities, 1912.

Kitchen, K. A. *Ancient Orient and Old Testament*. Downers Grove: Inter-Varsity Press, 1966.

Kline, Meredith G. *By Oath Consigned: A Reinterpretation of the Covenant Signs of Circumcision and Baptism*. Grand Rapids: Eerdmans, 1968.

_____. *The Structure of Biblical Authority*. Revised ed., Grand Rapids: Wm. B. Eerdmans Publishing Co., 1975.

_____. *Treaty of the Great King*. Grand Rapids: Wm. B. Eerdmans Publishing Co., 1963.

_____. *Kingdom Prologue*. Eugene, OR: Wipf & Stock, 2006.

_____. *Genesis: A New Commentary*. Peabody, MA: Hendrickson Publishers Marketing, 2016.

Korosec, V. *Hethitische Staatsverträge: Ein Beitrag zu ihrer juristischen Wertung*. Leipzigerrechts wissenschaftliche Studien, 60. Leipzig: Verlag von Theodreicher, 1931.

Lightfoot, John. *The Whole Works of the Rev. John Lightfoot*, vol. 4. London: n.a., 1822.

Luther, M. *What Luther Says*. St. Louis: Concordia, 1959.

MacArthur, J. F. *The Gospel According to Jesus*. Grand Rapids: Academie Books, 1988.

Manning, Brennan. *The Ragamuffin Gospel*. Colorado Springs, CO: Multnomah Books, 2005.

Matthews, Kenneth A. *The New American Commentary, Genesis 11:27-50:26*, 1b. Nashville: Broadman & Holman, 2005.

McCarthy, D. J. *Old Testament Covenant: A Survey of Current Opinions*. Richmond, VA: John Knox Press, 1972.

_____. *Treaty and Covenant: A Study in Form in the Ancient Oriental Documents and in the Old Testament*. Analecta Biblica, 21. Rome: Pontifical Biblical Institute, 1963.

McKenzie, Robert. *Identifying the Seed: An Examination and Evaluation of the Differences between Dispensational and Covenant Theology*. N.p., 2018.

McMillan, S. I. *None of These Diseases*. Old Tappan, NJ: Fleming H. Revell Company, 1984.

Merkle, Benjamin L. *Discontinuity to Continuity: A Survey of Dispensational and Covenantal Theologies*. Bellingham: Lexham Press, 2020.

Michael, Scott Horton. *Christ the Lord, The Reformation and Lordship Salvation*. 1992. Reprint, Eugene, OR: Wipf & Stock, 2008.

Montefiore, C. G. *Judaism and St. Paul: Two Essays*. New York: Dutton, 1915.

Moo, Douglas. "Response to Willem A. Vangemeren." In *The Law, the Gospel, and the Modern Christian: Five Views*. Grand Rapids, MI: Zondervan, 1993.

Moore, George Foot. *Judaism in the First Centuries of the Christian Era, The Age of Tannaim*, 3 vols. Cambridge: Harvard University Press, 1927.

Murray, John. *The Covenant of Grace*. London: Tyndale, 1954.

Neusner, Jacob. *A Rabbi Talks with Jesus*. Rev. ed. Montreal; Ithaca: McGill-Queen's University Press, 2000.

Noth, M. "God, King, and Nation in the Old Testament." In *The Laws in the Pentateuch and Other Studies*, 145-78. Translated by D. R. Ap-Thomas. Edinburgh and London: Oliver and Boyd, Ltd., 1966.

Nygren, Anders. *Commentary on Romans*. Minneapolis, MN: Augsburg Fortress Pub, 1978.

Owen, John. *The Works of John Owen*, 16 vols., vol. 3: *A Discourse concerning the Holy Spirit*. 1677; reprint, Edinburgh: Banner of Truth Trust, 1965.

Pentecost, J. D. *Things to Come*. Grand Rapids, MI: Zondervan Publishing House, 1969.

Perkins, William. *The Works of that Famous and Worthy Minister of Christ in the University of Cambridge, Mr. William Perkins*, 3 vols., vol. 3. Cambridge: n. p., 1608–09.

Peterson, Jim. *Living Proof*. Colorado Springs: NavPress, 1989.

Piper, John. *Desiring God*. Sisters, OR: Multnomah Publishers, 2003.

Postgate, J. N. *Neo-Assyrian Royal Grants and Decrees*. Rome: Pontifical Biblical Institute, 1969.

_____. *The Future of Justification: A Response to N. T. Wright*. Wheaton, IL: Crossway, 2007.

Price, R. *Secrets of the Dead Sea Scrolls*. Eugene, OR: Harvest House Publishers, 1996.

Pritchard, J. B., ed. *Ancient Near Eastern Texts relating to the Old Testament*. 3d ed., with supplement. Princeton University press, 1969.

Quek, S.-H. "Adam and Christ According to Paul." In *Pauline Studies.*, ed. D. A. Hagner and M. J. Harris, 67-79. Exeter: The Paternoster Press, 1980; Grand Rapids: William B. Eerdmans, 1980.

Quell, G. "kuvrio", The Old Testament Name for God." In *Theological Dictionary of the New Testament*, 1984, edition.

Reisinger, John G. *Continuity and Discontinuity*. Frederick, MD: New Covenant Media, 2011.

Runge, Steven E. *Discourse Grammar of the Greek New Testament*. Peabody, MA: Hendrickson, 2010.

Sanday, W. and Headlam, A. C. *Romans*. Edinburgh: T. & T. Clark, 1896.

Sanders, E. P. *Paul and Palestinian Judaism*. Philadelphia: Fortress Press, 1977.

_____. *Paul, A Very Short Introduction*. Oxford: Oxford University, 1991.

_____. *The Historical Figure of Jesus*. London: Penguin, 1993.

Saucy, Robert. *The Case for Progressive Dispensationalism*. TN: Zondervan Academic, 2010.

Schaff, P. *History of the Christian Church*. 5th ed. Vol. 2, *Ante-Nicene Christianity*. N.p.: Charles Scribner's Sons, 1910; reprint, Grand Rapids: Wm. B. Eerdmans Publishing Co., 1967.

Schreiner, Thomas R. *The Law and Its Fulfillment: A Pauline Theology of Law*. Grand Rapids: Baker Books, 1993.

_____. *Galatians*, ZECNT. Grand Rapids: Zondervan, 2010.

Schwartz, D. R. *Leben durch Jesus versus Leben durch die Torah: Zur Religions-polemik der ersten Jahrhundert*, Franz-Delitzsch-Vorlesung 2. Münster: Institute Judaicum Delitzschianum, 1993.

Schweitzer, Albert. *Von Reimarus zu Wrede: Eine Geschichte der Leben-Jesu-Forschung*. Tübingen: Mohr/Siebeck, 1906.

Scofield, C. I. *The Scofield Reference* Bible. New York: Oxford University Press, 1917.

Scroggs, R. *The Last Adam: A Study in Pauline Anthropology*. Philadelphia: Fortress Press, 1966.

Seamands, David. *Healing for Damaged Emotions*. Wheaton, IL: Victor Books, 1981.

Shank, R. *Elect in the Son*. Springfield, MO: Westcott Publishers, 1970.

_____. *Life in the Son*. Springfield, MO: Westcott Publishers, 1961.

Shishko, William. In Andrew Elam, Robert Van Kooten, and Randall Bergquist. *Merit and Moses: A Critique of the Klinean Doctrine of Republication*. Eugene, OR: Wipf & Stock, Kindle Edition, 2014.

Sprinkle, Preston M. *Law and Life: The Interpretation of Leviticus 18:5 in Early Judaism and in Paul*. Wissenschaftliche Untersuchungen Zum Neuen Testament. 2. Reihe 241. Tübingen: Mohr Siebeck, 2008.

_____. *Paul and Judaism Revisited: A Study of Divine and Human Agency in Salvation*. Downers Grove, IL: IVP Academic Press, 2013.

Sproul, R. C. *Willing to Believe*. Grand Rapids: Baker, 1997.

Spurgeon, C. H. *Spurgeon's Expository Encyclopedia*. Vol. 7. Grand Rapids: Baker, 1978.

Steinmetzer, F. X. *Die babylonischen Kudurru (Grenzsteine) als Urkudnenform*. Paderborn: Verlag von Ferdinand Schöningh, 1922.

Strack, Herman L. and Billerbeck, Paul. *Kommentar zum Neuen Testament aus Talmud und Midrasch*, Erster Band Das Evangelium nach Matthäus. München: C. H. Beck'sche Verlagsbuchhandlung, 1924.

Strickland, Wayne G. "Inauguration of the Law of Christ with the Gospel." In *The Law, the Gospel, and the Modern Christian: Five Views*. Grand Rapids: Zondervan, 1993.

Thompson, J. A. *Deuteronomy: An Introduction and Commentary*. Tyndale Old Testament Commentaries. Inter-Varsity Press, 1974.

_____. *The Ancient Near Eastern Treaties and the Old Testament*. London: The Tyndale Press, 1964.

Tozer, A. W. *I Call It Heresy!* Harrisburg, PA: Christian Publications, 1974.

Turretin, Francis. *Institutes of Elenctic Theology*, ed. James T. Dennison Jr., translated by George Musgrave Giger, 2:712. Phillipsburg, NJ: P&R, 1994.

VanGemeren, Willem, ed. *The Law, the Gospel, and the Modern Christian: Five Views*. Grand Rapids: Zondervan, 1993.

Vanhoozer, Kevin. "Wrighting the Wrongs of the Reformation?" In *Jesus, Paul, and the People of God: A Theological Dialogue with N. T. Wright*. Eds. Nicholas Perrin and Richard B. Hays. Downers Grove: InterVarsity, 2011.

VanLandingham, Chris. *Judgment & Justification in Early Judaism and the Apostle Paul*. Peabody, MA: Hendrickson Publishers, 2006.

Waltke, Bruce K. "The Phenomenon of Conditionality within Unconditional Covenants," in *Israel's Apostasy and Restoration*, ed. Avraham Gileadi. Grand Rapids: Baker Book House, 1988.

_____ and Cathi J. Fredricks. *Genesis: A Commentary*. Grand Rapids: Zondervan, 2001.

_____ and Charles Yu. *An Old Testament Theology: An Exegetical, Canonical, and Thematic Approach*. 1st ed. Grand Rapids: Zondervan, 2007.

Weinfeld, Moshe, ed. *Deuteronomy 1-11: A New Translation with Introduction and Commentary*. 1st ed. The Anchor Bible, v. 5. New York: Doubleday, 1991.

_____. *Deuteronomy and the Deuteronomic School*. Winona Lake, IN: Eisenbrauns, 1992.

Wellum, Stephen J. and Parker, Brent E., eds. *Progressive Covenantalism*. Nashville, TN: B & H Academic, 2016.

Westerholm, Stephen. *Perspectives Old and New on Paul: The "Lutheran" Paul and His Critics*. Grand Rapids: Eerdmans, 2003.

Willis, Wesley R., John R. Master, and Charles Caldwell Ryrie, eds. *Issues in Dispensationalism*. Chicago: Moody Press, 1994.

Wilson, Kenneth M. *Augustine's Conversion from Traditional Free Choice to "Non-Free Free Will": A Comprehensive Methodology*. Studien und Texte zu Antike und Christentum = Studies and Texts in Antiquity and Christianity 111. Tübingen: Mohr Siebeck, 2018.

Winship, Michael P. *Making Heretics: Militant Protestanism and Free Grace in Massachusetts 1636-1641.* New Jersey: Princeton University Press, 2002.

Wiseman, D. J. *The Alalakh Tablets.* London: The British Institute of Archaeology at Ankara, 1953.

Wolfe, David. *Epistemology: The Justification of Belief.* Downers Grove, IL: InterVarsity Press, 1982.

Wooden, John. *They Call Me Coach.* Waco, TX. Word Books, 1973.

Woolf, B. L. *Reformation Writings of Martin Luther.* London: Lutterworth Press, 1952.

Wright, G. E. "The Lawsuit of God: A Form-Critical Study of Deuteronomy 32." In *Israel's Prophetic Heritage.* Edited by B. W. Anderson and W. Harrelson. New York: Harper and Row Publishing Co., 1962.

Wright, N. T. *Jesus and the Victory of God.* Minneapolis: Fortress, 1996.

_____. *Justification: God's Plan & Paul's Vision.* Downers Grove, IL: IVP Academic, 2016.

_____. *What Saint Paul Really Said.* Grand Rapids: Eerdmans, 1997.

_____. *The Letter to the Romans, The New Interpreter's Bible, vol. 10.* Nashville, TN: Abingdon Press, 2002.

_____. *The Resurrection of the Son of God.* Minneapolis: Fortress, 2003.

_____. *Paul in Fresh Perspective.* Minneapolis: Fortress, 2005.

Yinger, Kent L. *The New Perspective on Paul: An Introduction.* Eugene: Cascade, 2011.

Periodicals

Allis, O. T. "Thy Throne, O God, is for Ever and Ever." *Princeton Theological Review* 21 (1923): 237-39.

Arnold, G. Philip. "Pauline Perspectives: A Summary and Critique on the New Perspective on Paul." *Wisconsin Lutheran Quarterly* 2/3 (September, 2015):184-94.

Barrosse, T. "Death and Sin in Saint Paul's Epistle to the Romans." *Catholic Biblical Quarterly* 15 (1953): 438-59.

Ben-Barak, Z. "Meribaal and the System of Land Grants in Ancient Israel," *Biblica* 62 (January 1981): 73-91.

Best, E. "Dead in Trespasses and Sins (Eph. 2.1)." *Journal for the Study of the New Testament* 13 (1981): 9-25.

Bird, Michael F. "What is there between Minneapolis and St. Andrews? A Third Way in the Piper-Wright Debate." *Journal of the Evangelical Society* 54 (2011): 299-309.

Black, C. C. II. "Pauline Perspectives on Death in Romans 5-8." *Journal of Biblical Literature* 103 (1984): 413-33.

Braswell, J. P. "The Blessing of Abraham versus the Curse of the Law: Another Look at Gal 3:10-13." *Westminster Theological Journal* 53 (1991): 73-91.

Campbell, Douglas. "An Apocalyptic Rereading of 'Justification' in Paul." *Expository Times* 123 (2012): 182-93.

Clines, D. J. A. "The Psalms and the King." *Theological Student's Fellowship Bulletin* 71 (Spring 1975): 1-6.

Combrink, H. J. B. "Some Thoughts on the Old Testament Citations in the Epistle to the Hebrews." *Neotestamentica* 5 (1971): 22-36.

Cooke, G. "The Israelite King as Son of God." *Zeitschrift für die alttestamentiche Wissenschaft* 73 (161): 202-25.

Danker, F. W. "Romans 5:12: Sin Under Law." *New Testament Studies* 14 (1968): 424-39.

Dorsey, D. A. "The Law of Moses and the Christian: A Compromise." *Journal of the Evangelical Theological Society* 34 (September 1991): 321-34.

Dunn, James D. G. "A New Perspective on the New Perspective." *Early Christianity* 4 (2013): 157-82.

Farnell, F. D. "The New Perspective on Paul: Its Basic Tenets, History, and Presuppositions." *The Masters Seminary Journal*16/2 (Fall, 2005): 189-243.

Fensham, F. C. "Common Trends in Curses of the Near Eastern Treaties and Kudurru Inscriptions compared with Maledictions of Amos and Isaiah." *Zeitshcrift für die alttestamentliche Wissenschaft* 75 (1963): 155-75.

_____. "Maledictions and Benediction in Ancient Near Eastern Vassal-Treaties and the Old Testament." *Zeitschrift für die alttestamentliche Wissenschaft* 74 (1962): 1-9.

Gerstenberger, E. "Covenant and Commandment." *Journal of Biblical Literature* 84 (1965): 33-51.

Gordis, R. "The 'Begotten' Messiah in the Qumran Scrolls." *Vetus Testamentum* 7 (1957): 191-94.

Harner, P. B. "Exodus, Sinai, and Hittite Prologues." *Journal of Biblical Literature* 85 (1966): 233-36.

Hassler, Andrew. "Ethnocentric Legalism and the Justification of the Individual: Rethinking Some New Perspective Assumptions." *Journal of the Evangelical Theological Society* 54 (2011): 311-27.

Heen, Erik M. "A Lutheran Response to the New Perspective on Paul." *Lutheran Quarterly* 24 (2010): 263-91.

Hill, A. E. "The Ebal Ceremony as Hebrew Land Grant?" *Journal of the Evangelical Theological Society* 31 (December 1988): 399-406.

Hooker, M. D. "Adam in Romans 1." *New Testament Studies* 6 (1960): 297-306.

Bibliography

Huffmon, H. B. "The Treaty Background of Hebrew YADA'." *Bulletin of the American Schools of Oriental Research* 181 (1966): 31-37.

Jodar, Etienne. "Leviticus 18:5 and the Law's Call to Faith: A Positive Reassessment of Paul's View of the Law," *Themelios* vol. 45, no. 1 (April, 2020): 43-57.

Jones, B. W. "Acts 13:33-37: A Pesher on II Samuel 7." *Journal of Biblical Literature* 87 (Spring 1987): 321-27.

Kaiser, W. C., Jr. "The Old Promise and the New Covenant: Jeremiah 31:31-34." *Journal of the Evangelical Theological Society* 15 (1972): 11-23.

_____. "Leviticus :18:5 and Paul: Do This and You Shall Live (Eternally?)." *Journal of the Evangelical Theological Society*, 14 (1971): 22.

Katz, P. "The Quotations from Deuteronomy in Hebrews." *Zeitschrift für die neutestamentliche Wissenschaft* 49 (1958): 213-23.

Kaufman, S. A. "The Structure of the Deuteronomic Law." *Maarav* 1/2 (1978-79): 105-58.

Korosec, V. "The Warfare of the Hittites—From the Legal Point of View." *Iraq* 25 (1963): 159-66.

Loewenstamm, S. E. "The Divine Grants of Land to the Patriarchs." *Journal of the American Oriental Society* 91.4 (1971): 509-10.

Macleod, Donald. "The New Perspective: Paul, Luther and Judaism." *Scottish Bulletin of Evangelical Theology* 22 (2004): 4-31.

McCarthy, D. J. "Covenant in the Old Testament: Present State of Inquiry." *Catholic Biblical Quarterly* 27 (1965): 217-41.

_____. "Notes on the Love of God in Deutronomy and the Father-Son Relationship Between Yahweh and Israel." *Catholic Biblical Quarterly* 27 (1965): 144-47.

_____. "Three Covenants in Genesis." *Catholic Biblical Quarterly* 26 (1964): 179-89.

Mendenhall, G. E. "Ancient Oriental and Biblical Law." *Biblical Archaeologist* 17 (May 1954): 50-76.

_____. "Covenant Forms in Israelite Tradition." *Biblical Archaeologist* 17 (September 1954): 50-76.

Milne, D. J. W. "Genesis 3 in the Letter to the Romans." *Reformed Theological Review* 39 (1980): 10-18.

Muilenburg, J. "The Form and Structure of the Covenantal Formulations." Essays In Honor of Miller Burrows, reprinted from *Vetus Testamentum* 13 (1963): 380-89.

Pentecost, J. Dwight. "The Purpose of the Law," *Bibliotheca Sacra* vol. 128 (Dallas: July/September, 1971): 227-44.

Silva, Moisés. "The Law and Christianity: Dunn's New Synthesis," *Westminster Theological Journal* 53 (1991): 348-9.

Thompson, J. A. "Covenant Patterns in the Ancient Near East and Their Significance for Biblical Studies." *Reformed Theological Review* 18.3 (October 1959): 65-75.

_____. "The Significance of the Near Eastern Treaty Pattern." *Tyndale House Bulletin* (1963): 1-6.

Tucker, G. M. "Covenant Forms and Contract Forms." *Vetus Testamentum* 15 (1965): 487-503.

Waldschmidt, Daniel W. "The Hermeneutics of the New Perspective on Paul." Wisconsin Lutheran Seminary Symposium (September 20, 2016).

Weaver, D. "The Exegesis of Romans 5:12 among the Greek Fathers and Its Implication for the Doctrine of Original Sin: The 5th-12th Centuries (Part 2)." *St. Vladimir's Theological Quarterly* 29 (1985): 133-59.

_____. "The Exegesis of Romans 5:12 among the Greek Fathers and Its Implication for the Doctrine of Original Sin: The 5th-12th Centuries (Part 3)." *St. Vladimir's Theological Quarterly* 29 (1985): 231-57.

Wedderburn, A. J. M. "The Theological Structure of Romans 5:12." *New Testament Studies* 19 (1973): 332-54.

Weinfeld, M. "Berit-Covenant vs. Obligation." *Biblica* 56 (1975): 120-28.

————. "Covenant Terminology in the Ancient Near East and Its Influence on the West." *Journal of the American Oriental Society* 93 (1973): 190-99.

————. "Deuteronomy—The Present State of Inquiry." *Journal of Biblical Literature* 86 (1967): 249-62.

————. "The Covenant of Grant in the Old Testament and the Ancient Near East." *Journal of the American Oriental Society* 90 (1970): 184-203.

Willitts, Joel. "Paul's Use of Leviticus 18:5 in Galatians 3:12," *Tyndale Bulletin* 54 (January, 2001): 118.

Wiseman, D. J. "Abban and Alalah." *Journal of Cuneiform Studies* 12 (1958): 124-29.

————. "The Vassal-Treaties of Esarhaddon." *Iraq* 20 (1958): 1-99 + 53 (plates).

Wright, N. T. "The Shape of Justification," *Bible Review* 17 (April 2001): 50.

Yadin, Y. "A Midrash on 2 Sam. vii and Ps. 1-11 (4QFlorilegium)." *Israel Exploration Journal* 9 (1959): 95-98.

Zahl, Paul F. M. "Mistakes of the New Perspective on Paul." *Themelios* 27 (2001): 5-11.

Unpublished Materials

Derosse, Anthony Bernard. "A Critical Assessment of the New Perspectives on Paul." Shepherds Theological Seminary. December 2, 2015.

King, L. W., ed. *Babylonian Boundary-Stones. British Museum Dept. of Egyptian and Assyrian Antiquities*, 1912.

Merrill, E. H., interview by author, March 15, 1994. Dallas Theological Seminary, Dallas.

Paynter, Stephen E. "The New Perspective on Paul: A Reformed Assessment." Trinity College, Bristol. June 21, 2012.

Rieser, John-Mark. "Justification and the New Perspective on Paul." Phoenix Seminary. August 6, 2012.

Shank, R., interview by author, April 7, 1976. Conroe, Texas.

Weinfeld, M., interview by author, February 24, 1998. Hebrew University, Jerusalem.

Wendland, P. O. "A Lutheran Look at the New Perspective." May 10, 2015. Academia.

Wilkin, R. N. "Repentance as a Condition for Salvation in the New Testament." Th.D. diss., Dallas Theological Seminary, 1985.

Available Titles from Grace Theology Press

Bewitched
The Rise of Neo-Galatianism

By Dr. Dave Anderson

**Companions
With Christ**
How to Walk with Jesus

By Jeremy Vance

**God's Grace for
Daughters of Eve**
Lovers, Mothers and Others

By Sandra Abbott

Final Destiny
The Future Reign of the
Servant Kings

By Dr. Jody Dillow

Maximum Joy
First John—Relationship or
Fellowship?

By Dr. Dave Anderson

Going for the Gold
Bible Study Edition

By Dr. Joe Wall

Triumph Through Trials
The Epistle of James

By Dr. Dave Anderson

Free Grace Soteriology
Third Edition

By Dr. Dave Anderson

gracetheology.org

CPSIA information can be obtained
at www.ICGtesting.com
Printed in the USA
LVHW081638260322
714492LV00017B/1129